Television Drama in Contemporary China

Due to high audience numbers and the significant influence upon the opinions and values of viewers, the political leadership in China attributes great importance to the impact of television dramas. Many successful TV serials have served as useful conduits to disseminate official rhetoric and mainstream ideology, and they also offer a rich area of research by providing insight into the changing Chinese political, social and cultural context.

This book examines a group of recently released TV drama serials in mainland China which focus upon, and to various degrees represent, topical political, social and cultural phenomena. Some of the selected TV serials reflect the present ideological proclivities of the Chinese government, whilst others mirror social and cultural occurrences or provide coded and thought-provoking messages on China's socio-economic and political reality. Through in-depth textual analysis of the plots, scenes and characters of these selected TV serials, the book provides timely interpretations of contemporary Chinese society, its political inclinations, social fashions and cultural tendencies. The book also demonstrates how popular media narratives of TV drama serials engage with sensitive civic issues and cultural phenomena of modern-day China, which in turn encourages a broader social imagination and potential for change.

Advancing our understanding of contemporary China, this book will appeal to students and scholars of contemporary Chinese culture, society and politics, as well as those with research interests in television studies more generally.

Shenshen Cai is a Lecturer in Chinese Studies at Swinburne University of Technology. She is the author of *State Propaganda in China's Entertainment Industry* (Routledge 2016), and she has recently published articles in *Social Semiotics* (2015), *Asian Studies Review* (2016), and *Visual Anthropology* (2016).

Routledge Contemporary China Series

For a full list of titles in this series, please visit www.routledge.com

151 **China's Energy Security**
A multidimensional perspective
Edited by Giulia Romano and Jean-François Di Meglio

152 **Chinese Muslims and the Global Ummah**
Islamic revival and ethnic identity among the Hui of Qinghai Province
Alexander Blair Stewart

153 **State Propaganda in China's Entertainment Industry**
Shenshen Cai

154 **Assessing the Balance of Power in Central-Local Relations in China**
Edited by John Donaldson

155 **Television Regulation and Media Policy in China**
Yik Chan Chin

156 **Space, Politics, and Cultural Representation in Modern China**
Cartographies of revolution
Enhua Zhang

157 **The Occupy Movement in Hong Kong**
Sustaining decentralised protest
Yongshun Cai

158 **The Chinese Family Today**
Edited by Xu Anqi, John DeFrain, and Liu Wenrong

159 **Television Drama in Contemporary China**
Political, social and cultural phenomena
Shenshen Cai

Television Drama in Contemporary China

Political, social and cultural phenomena

Shenshen Cai

LONDON AND NEW YORK

First published 2017
by Routledge
2 Park Square, Milton Park, Abingdon, Oxon OX14 4RN

and by Routledge
711 Third Avenue, New York, NY 10017

First issued in paperback 2018

Routledge is an imprint of the Taylor & Francis Group, an informa business

© 2017 Shenshen Cai

The right of Shenshen Cai to be identified as author of this work has been asserted in accordance with sections 77 and 78 of the Copyright, Designs and Patents Act 1988.

All rights reserved. No part of this book may be reprinted or reproduced or utilised in any form or by any electronic, mechanical, or other means, now known or hereafter invented, including photocopying and recording, or in any information storage or retrieval system, without permission in writing from the publishers.

Trademark notice: Product or corporate names may be trademarks or registered trademarks, and are used only for identification and explanation without intent to infringe.

British Library Cataloguing in Publication Data
A catalogue record for this book is available from the British Library

Library of Congress Cataloging-in-Publication Data
Names: Cai, Shenshen, editor.
Title: Television drama in contemporary China : political, social and cultural phenomena / [edited by] Shenshen Cai.
Description: New York : Routledge, 2017. | Series: Routledge contemporary China series | Includes bibliographical references and index.
Identifiers: LCCN 2016020593 | ISBN 9781138645783 (hardback) | ISBN 9781315627939 (ebook)
Subjects: LCSH: Television series—China. | Television broadcasting—Social aspects—China. | Television broadcasting—Political aspects—China. | Television plays—Social aspects—China. | Television plays—Political aspects—China.
Classification: LCC PN1992.3.C6 T45 2017 | DDC 791.450951—dc23
LC record available at https://lccn.loc.gov/2016020593

ISBN 13: 978-1-138-33954-5 (pbk)
ISBN 13: 978-1-138-64578-3 (hbk)

Typeset in Times New Roman
by Apex CoVantage, LLC

Contents

	Acknowledgments	vii
	Introduction	1
1	*Empresses in the Palace*: historical drama and its reflections on the political and workplace culture in contemporary China	20
2	*Angel Heart*: harmonizing contemporary Chinese society through exemplary model doctors	40
3	A trans-media reading of a white-collar workplace bestseller and its TV and film adaptations: *A Story of Lala's Promotion* and *Go Lala Go*	58
4	*Honey Bee Man*: divorced women and an elaboration of the contemporary Chinese female	77
5	*See without Looking*: from vulnerable people to competent and respectful citizens	97
6	*Parents of the Single Child*: China's one-child policy and its social repercussions	116
	Conclusion	133
	Index	137

Acknowledgments

I would like to express my sincere gratitude to Dr William Lakos (Bill) for his ongoing support and advice during the writing process of this book. Bill was so patient and devoted in helping me in polishing and fine-tuning my arguments and writing. Without his careful and time-consuming editing on the drafts, this book would not have become what it is now.

Also, I would like to thank the Asian Studies editors at Routledge, Stephanie Rogers and Rebecca Lawrence, and the copy editors for their kind support during the reviewing and production process of the book. Finally, and most importantly, I want to thank my family for accompanying me during the writing process of the manuscript.

The author thanks UTSePress (Sydney) for permission to reprint portions of her article, "A Cultural Reading of a White-Collar Workplace Bestseller and its Filmic Adaptation: A Story of Lala's Promotion and Go Lala Go!," which was originally published on *PORTAL Journal of Multidisciplinary International Studies*, vol 11, no 1, 2014. doi:10.5130/portal.v11i1.3251.

Introduction

As the unmatched popular media entertainment genre of the 1990s, Chinese TV drama confronts "encroachment" from both inside and outside the TV industry in the recent decades. The steady growth of commercial blockbusters and films made by established Chinese moviemakers and celebrities turned film directors (a new force within the film industry),[1] alongside the maturing and growing group of "culture" shows, which include variety shows, reality shows, talk shows and dating shows, has evolved today's China's entertainment industry into a more competitive and multifarious entity.[2]

Emerging at the beginning of socialist China and undergoing a "silent" era during the heyday of Maoist revolutions when the revolutionary model operas and films were the only available entertainments for the Chinese masses, TV drama reemerged in the mainland region as a dominant form of recreational media. It gained momentum at the beginning of the 1990s with the appearance of a group of groundbreaking TV drama serials, such as *Yearning* (*Kewang*, 1990) and *A Native of Beijing in New York* (*Beijingren zai niuyue*, 1994). Different from previously made propaganda-oriented TV drama works, which were expected to "assist the Party-state's project of socialist modernity and political mobilization" (Sun & Gorfinkel 2015: 33), these TV drama hits shifted their focus from revolutionary and collective causes, and social and economic makeovers, to the domestic encounters and personal life journeys of ordinary Chinese people. Some scholars (Lull 1991; Keane 2001 cited in Bai & Song 2015: 6) further noted that these dramas mapped out a comparatively unrestricted space where new concepts and images disseminated and became resources with which Chinese audiences might conceive a diverse world and forge novel self-identities. Despite their "privatizing" and "liberal" proclivity, these TV serials still gained approval from government officials for their exemplification of "socialist ethics and morals" (Zhu, Keane & Bai 2008: 6), and a new type of socialist neoliberal subjectivity which emphasized self-governance and self-renovation.

Since the Opening Up reforms initiated by Deng Xiaoping and his followers, there has been an accelerating trend of commercialization within the Chinese TV drama industry, as private capital has become the main investor in TV drama production and advertising has turned itself into the dominant generator of the annual revenues for TV stations (Zhu, Keane & Bai 2008: 10; Berry 2009:

2 *Introduction*

73–75; Shanghai TV Festival 2004: 20, 25 cited in Kong 2014: 34; Bai & Song 2015: 3; Ng 2015: 90).[3] From the late 1990s to the end of the first decade of the 2000s, TV drama, and the related industry, has seen extreme growth (Shanghai TV Festival 2004: 79 cited in Kong 2014: 34). However, this deepening commercialization within the landscape of TV drama manufacturing did not provide the market with the monopolizing power to creatively steer the TV show, as this privilege remained with the state, which has never withdrawn from its role as the rule maker and regulator within the TV drama industry. However, rather than forming an adversarial relationship, the state and the marketplace colluded, or to borrow Yin Hong's words (cited in Zhong 2010: 163), they became "accomplices" (*gongmou*), although tensions remained between the two forces,[4] in their "cooperated" effort of creating TV narratives. For example, state discourse has adapted to the market system, and TV broadcasting in China has witnessed an apparent shift "from a stern-faced political propaganda machine running in a monopolistically structured and highly hierarchic system for decades to become more market-oriented and audience-friendly" (Cooper-Chen 2010: 88). While contradictions still remain between the entertainment industry and the state propaganda discourse, the state confirms the conventional role played by market-driven popular culture (in which TV drama occupies one of the dominant positions) in social conciliation. In withstanding the Party's ongoing political domination, the state assents to and values the regime-sustaining role of private media and cultural entrepreneurs (Zhao 2008).

Under an evolved situation where the established official supervision and intervention, an increasing market presence and a maturing audience preference and influences play vital roles in TV drama making simultaneously, the Chinese TV drama industry has gradually come of age with stable growth in production outputs and subgenres. The thriving TV drama market of contemporary China (since the 1990s) is loaded with divergent goals, including reflecting social vicissitudes and transformations; echoing intellectual movements and government propaganda; mirroring and retrieving deteriorating family values and social morality; and cultivating a matured TV audience with critical thinking habits. It is a diverse range of TV drama subgenres, including historical/costume/dynasty drama, crime drama, suspense and espionage drama, revolutionary nostalgic drama, white-collar workplace drama, unban romance drama, idol drama, ordinary folks drama and dramas that focus on the life of disadvantaged social groups such as migrant workers, laid-off workers and disabled groups.

In the following discussion, I will briefly outline the three features of contemporary Chinese TV drama, which I have labeled as: "TV drama informed by intellectual thinking and government propaganda"; "TV drama mirroring social change and social reality"; and "TV drama as a cultural public sphere." These three observations of contemporary Chinese TV drama creation have so far attracted the most attention from media and cultural studies scholars from the Western world, and a mounting number of research articles and books have been penned on these topics, as they provide "close-ups" of contemporary Chinese society and those changes, interests, concerns and problems embedded in it. These themes also juxtapose different ideological positions and perspectives, ideas and competing values that mirror social tension and conflicts (Zhong 2010: 162). In summary, examining these TV discourses, which serve as a conduit in the grid of power interactions, provides insights into understanding the "tension-fraught and paradox-permeated conditions of Chinese post-socialism" (Bai & Song 2015: 1).

TV drama informed by intellectual thinking and government propaganda

TV has acquired an essential role in the lives of almost all Chinese people, as it physically reaches 96.23 percent of the country's entire population of 1.3 billion (Cooper-Chen 2010: 83). China has currently the largest number of TV sets and the largest number of people watching TV in the world (Zhang 2009: 172). TV drama is currently the second most watched TV genre (Qian 2015: 159), and it is "a dominant form of storytelling in contemporary China" (Zhong 2010: 163). Virtually all TV stations in China, from CCTV (China Central Television) and local stations to provincial satellite TV networks, allocate one primetime slot in the evening to TV dramas, plus two slots in the morning and afternoon. According to data collected by CMS media research, TV drama's share of the broadcasting market is estimated at 24 to 30 percent from 2007 to 2010, and its reception rate was 32 to 38 percent, with each drama serial being broadcast an average of five times (Li 2011 cited in Kong 2014: 34). According to the 2011 statistics, in the case of provincial satellite channels, ten of thirty of them scheduled seven to ten hours of TV dramas in their daily program line-ups (Lu 2011 cited in Bai & Song 2015: 5). In regard to the viewing habits of Chinese TV audiences, a report on Beijing residents suggests that the majority of people watch TV with their families and that TV is able to enhance family bonding and improve domestic relationship (Zhang 2009: 171), which lays the foundation for social harmony. Based on TV's popularity and utility in attracting and uniting Chinese viewers, the political leadership attributes an extremely high score of impact to TV in general and to TV dramas in particular (Schneider 2012: 180). The government "senses the potential of television to consolidate its control on a national scale by reaching out to its people in the most remote areas of its territory and connecting citizens across the country" (Sun & Gorfinkel 2015: 22). The prime goals that the Chinese Communist Party (CCP) places on TV is to serve as an ideological and cultural tool and act as part of the ideological state device, according to which "television needs to support the CCP's number one political agenda, maintaining social stability, and it must contribute to the CCP's cultural agenda – i.e., stabilizing and re-energizing the dominant moral order" (Bai 2015: 80).

During the sweeping commercialization trend within China's media sphere in general and within the domain of TV drama since the later half of the 1990s and onwards, there has existed more cooperation and complicity than frictions and clashes between the state and the market, and according to some scholars, such as Chris Berry (2009: 73), the state and the market "complement rather than contradict each other" and "exercise hegemony through their new alliance." Another

4   *Introduction*

scholar, Ng (2015: 90), suggests that "the Chinese state-market complex has become yet another monolithic and totalizing institution of power."

The compromise and cooperation between financial capital and official policies means that TV productions in contemporary China are "politically mainstream, market-oriented, and conducive to the security and stability of society" (Qian 2015: 185). In his investigation into the process of how Chinese TV dramatic works arrive at their "overarching political discourses of the Chinese nation," Schneider (2012: 213) remarks that the Chinese leadership still plays an active role through continuingly exerting control over the content and production system of TV drama in order to guarantee the political domination of the government and the Party. Government heads and publicity executives, together with official media channels, issue speeches that intend to steer the direction of TV drama creation (Zhao 2008). Viewed from another perspective, within the domain of TV production, although the Party-state apparatus has stopped setting the agenda for programming, it remains to pilot in a reactive way, proposing modifications or blocking programs (Berry 2009: 73–75), as TV, which enjoys the largest audience reach, is most firmly controlled in China (Zhao 2008: 42). As a result, any TV programming, including non-political and entertainment-oriented programs, may face criticism by the State Administration for Radio, Film and Television (SARFT) for "going against state policies and 'socialist morality'" (Kong & Hawes 2015: 36). Through these combined methods, the state unleashes its "cultural governance" (Schneider 2012) via TV serials, which continue to be one of the most popular TV formats in China (Zhu 2008b; Schneider 2012). In the recent decades, TV drama's role in reflecting and promoting the Party's rule and policy, building social reconciliation and stability and recuperating the established moral order has been proved effective.

Dynasty dramas that promote the ideal of a strong central government and benevolent leadership accommodate the new-authoritarian, neo-conservative, and New Left political thought in China (Zhu 2008a; Schneider 2012). Schneider's (2012: 206) analysis of the historical epic TV serial *The Great Han Emperor Wu* (*Hanwudadi*, 2005) points out that the harmonious relationship between a fatherly, thoughtful and humane ruler and his devoted and sensible people is repetitively foregrounded throughout the show text. The narrative arc of the drama successfully adopts the orthodox view of the paternalistic ruler and weaves it into the Maoist precept of service to the people (Schneider 2012: 206). Likewise, Zhu (2008a) argues that in the TV drama serial *Yongzheng Dynasty* (*Yongzheng wangchao*, 1999), the portrayal of Emperor Yongzheng of the Qing Dynasty is informed by the political views of the neo-conservative and New Left intellectual schools in terms of painting the monarch as an exemplary ruler who cracked down on corruption, put the welfare of the nation and his subjects ahead of personal political gain and reputation and resumed economic equality. The Hong Kong journalist Yan Hua from the *Asia Times* claims that these historical costume dramas that screen "relentless, though smoothly presented, propaganda" are designed to sanction the rule of the CCP over China (cited in Schneider 2012: 2).

Introduction 5

Similarly, the anti-corruption TV drama subgenre is successfully appropriated by the official propaganda apparatus and the private TV producers to retrieve the waning reputation of the CCP government among the Chinese people. By employing the image of "clean officials" (*qingguan*) who are upright and impartial, who care for the destitute and who pit themselves against mighty criminals to preserve the interests of common people, these dramas send a message that society is ameliorated and fairness is restored (Bai 2008: 49). In so doing, the anti-corruption drama fashions an imagined "moral community" where "moral consensus" is shared by the viewers. Being heroes of this hypothetical "moral community," "clean officials . . . mediate and reduce the gap between the propaganda and the popular" and "blend the Party's need for good publicity with a powerful popular belief in and desire for the redemptive power and heavenly justice embodied by clean officials" (Bai 2008: 57). Furthermore, the "clean official" cultural icon, acting as representative of the Party-state, helps "anchor the Party in the role of moral leadership and create a sense of moral unity between the Party and the people," which provides "the moral basis for the Party leadership of the community" (Bai 2008: 57).

Another typical TV drama subgenre that highlights the "correctness" of the Communist cause and the noble quality and virtues of the CCP members is the revolutionary spy-themed TV serial subgenre. The emergence of the revolutionary spy-themed TV serials is largely due to a compromise or "collaboration" between the commercial market and the state (Hao 2008: 302), as it finds ways to merge the goal between the commercial pursuits and the state via re-igniting feelings of collectivism and honorable principles. This may be viewed as the commercial market "cashing in" on the "mainstream" discourse by repackaging the Red classics (*hongsejingdian*) and by utilizing its official canonical status while at the same time remaking it in a fashion that caters to the demands of the marketplace (Qian 2008; Liu 2010). Following the overall commercializing trend of the revolutionary-themed cultural products, through the suspense, mystery and fantasy associated with spying, and by allowing the audience to "participate" in the skills and knowledge of undercover operations, the popularity of the spy-themed TV serial set in the revolutionary eras is assured. By portraying the CCP spies as unbeatable, suave, and charismatic, as Chinese "James Bonds," the show moves the audience into a dominant reading situation where they are intrigued and identify with the spy icon dedicated to the CCP cause.

Apart from these "mainstream" TV drama subgenres, dramas that focus on the life of disadvantaged social groups such as migrant and laid-off workers have also been enlisted to reflect state policy and rhetoric. In Sun's (2008) analysis of the domestic helper characters in *Professor Tian and His Twenty-eight Maids* (*Tian jiaoshou jiade ershiba ge baomu*, 2001), she argues that those once "despised," "uncivilized," "uneducated" and "marginalized" maids and their transformations have been used as a simile by the show's narrative to illustrate a competent and modern subjectivity which serves as a "useful" citizen icon for the modern Chinese state. Sun notes that the story of one of the leading protagonists in the show, a middle-aged laid-off female worker, has been successfully turned into "a

6 *Introduction*

new-liberalist fairy tale about self-transformation and entrepreneurship" (Kong 2014: 55) and provides a role model for laid-off female workers. In contemporary China, TV propaganda mainly offers "guidance" (*daoxiang*) for good behavior, thus the government and the media workers alike "regard television drama as a medium that supplies viewers with role models" (Schneider 2012: 194). There is a long-standing Confucian tradition that intensely stresses upright role models as prototypes for appropriate behavior (Schneider 2012: 222), and in this drama examined by Sun, those self-reliant and self-esteemed migrant workers and laid-off workers are created as "role models" for the viewers to identify with and respect.

TV drama mirroring social reality and social changes

Since the reform era of the 1980s, TV has proven to be China's fastest growing and most advanced medium. It has witnessed and reflected the country's political, economic and social changes (Hong 1998: 47), and as the strongest force within the TV industry, contemporary Chinese TV drama serves as a conduit for the new state and market alliance during its nascence, where it is gradually forming a more accommodative bond between the two factions. It also serves as a prism through which the ever-changing, more individualistic and practical social reality of current China is exposed. Through a close reading of the life encounters, workplace struggles, family relationships and domestic concerns of ordinary Chinese people, TV drama texts retain their appeal to the general audience and strike a chord with their own living experiences and emotive requirements, as they deliver comfort and a feeling of social adherence (Kong 2008: 80, 83) and provide an outlet for their stress and anxiety. With its main focus on the life of urbanites, the increased competition in the career field, fading family values, worsening human relationships in the broader social context and a rising consumerism, TV drama, "because of its fictional character and its more popular social basis, has been able to address popular sensibilities and social conflicts in unique ways" (Zhao 2008: 206–207). The solid growth in the creation and consumption of TV drama has a weighty impact on the molding of the social imagination and on interpreting the social change in contemporary China (Zhu, Keane & Bai 2008; Zhu 2008b; Zhong 2010; Kong 2014: 34). By reproducing social occurrences and conversions and by reflecting on their meaning, TV drama works have "exerted a complex and profound influence on the ethos, value formation, and cultural trends [of society]" (Yin 2002 cited in Zhong 2010: 9) and have been functioning "as a cultural site where contemporary social-economic issues are addressed and different cultural legacies and ideological views transmitted and contested" (Zhong 2010: 12).

A number of youth TV dramas, including director Zhao Baogang's "Youth Trilogy", which comprises *Struggle* (*Fendou*, 2007), *My Youthfulness* (*Wode qingchun shuizuozhu*, 2009) and *Beijing Youth* (*Beijing qingnian*, 2012),[5] and a most recent release of this subgenre, *Swan Dive for Love* (*Bei shang guang bu xiangxin yanlei*, 2015), all portray the career struggles, friendship, love affection, life pursuits and dreams of a group of post-1980s Chinese youths. These young people confront a changed and harsher living environment, where there is escalating competition in the career sphere and unclear and varying concepts regarding individuality, marriage and family relationships.

In a similar vein, a TV drama subgenre focuses on white-collar, female office workers in joint ventures or foreign corporations such as *Go Lala Go!* (*Du Lala shengzhiji*, 2010), which paints the life stories of China's emerging middle-class and their career trajectories, living styles, cultural aesthetics and the cosmopolitan spectacle of first-tier Chinese cities including Beijing, Shanghai and Guangzhou. The workplace experiences and achievements of these white-collar professional workers, and the corresponding financial autonomy and public recognition they gain, mark a novel and enviable social subject which personifies self-struggle, self-sustenance and self-regard. The young, middle-class social group's diligence and tenaciousness serves as a metaphor for the widespread neoliberalism sentiment and fashion which has been fostered among the Chinese people since the outset of the reform periods and has been gaining momentum since the reforms have deepened.

Besides its focus on the workplace, contemporary Chinese TV drama maintains its strength in depicting the domestic lives of ordinary households, as it holds a mirror at a micro level, on the gigantic socio-economic transformations of China. Chinese TV drama also provides glimpses into the downwardly mobile social cohorts, such as laid-off workers from the previously state-run work units and poverty-stricken city dwellers. Popular "ordinary folk" dramas, produced during the 2000s, such as *Garrulous Zhang Damin's Happy Life* (*Pinzui Zhang Damin de xingfu shenghuo*, 2000), paint the grim daily life situations of destitute urban social groups which have been sidelined and victimized by rapid economic expansion. By providing close-up representation of the domestic arena and its waning family ethics and human relationships, a utilitarian society is displayed, and the egocentric values harbored by many in today's China are exposed in the show. Based on the show's plots, the Confucian cultural relics that foreground filial piety and mutual support within a family boundary have slowly been eroded by more selfish principles embraced by many contemporary Chinese people. Through illustrating in detail the day-to-day life experiences of poverty-stricken families, although in a "tragicomic" manner (Kong 2008: 81), *Garrulous Zhang Damin's Happy Life* appeals to the audiences' emotions. Following Schneider's (2012: 201) argument, and based on his understanding of a high-ranking CCTV official's words, the TV show must "allow viewers to identify with the loss and suffering of the characters, and thereby give them the opportunity to grow emotionally through a cathartic experience." This view demonstrates "a therapeutic function" of TV dramas and other media outlets, where the drama acts as a psychological painkiller in its efforts to appease the agitated and dejected mood of the economically and socially underprivileged social cohorts.

Though *Garrulous Zhang Damin's Happy Life* offers a more traditional and conservative moral outlook in resolving family conflicts in which harmony and stability prevail (Kong 2008: 83), from another perspective its storyline reflects on the harsh social reality and could be read as being full of "bitter emotion" which could lead to animosity and social disruption. These "side effects" of the show may be the reason that the more recently aired TV serials with domestic

8 *Introduction*

staples as their main theme, such as *Beautiful Daughter-in-Law* (*Xifu de meihao shidai*, 2009) and *Life in Two Cities* (*Shuangcheng shenghuo*, 2011), have moved their attention from the gloomy living conditions of impoverished households to the more promising life standards of prosperous families, and in a light and comic mode. As a result, the updated version of "ordinary folk" dramas fulfills its social function as pure recreational programming that fills up the leisure time of the viewers rather than as inspiring social commentary that has the potential to cultivate within viewers a critical thinking habit.

Another popular subgenre that keeps the creation of contemporary Chinese TV drama in check with the overall makeover and progression of the society are the life stories of urban women. Rather than being viewed and used as symbols of political and social achievements in the pre-socialist and early socialist periods, contemporary TV drama narratives about women approach the subject from a more gender-oriented perspective and reflect their life journey with a more subtle perception. Via the cultural and media platform provided by TV, contemporary Chinese women's individual life matters (especially those gender-specific ones), relationship and marriage issues, social identity and role and ensuing emotional concerns (all of which are impacted by intense socio-economic dynamics) are highlighted and explored. More recently, the accelerating economic conversion and the resultant cumulative social variations it has aroused have caused apparent social impasses and ethical dilemmas for contemporary Chinese women, which in turn have garnered immense attention from TV producers. As females compose the bulk of Chinese TV drama spectators, the ambiguities and hardships facing women are more likely to lift audience ratings.

In addition to the above-mentioned TV drama serials that are set in contemporary China, historical TV shows shed light on the social veracity and vicissitudes of today's China. Besides their "conformist" role in the spreading of official discourse, Chinese dynasty dramas produced in the mainland region pursue confrontational political and cultural subjects pertinent to present Chinese society (Zhu 2009: 226). As Yin (2002 cited in Zhao 2008: 206–207) observes:

> [W]hile television dramas about imperial dynasties tend to cultivate a profoundly antidemocratic political culture via the glorification of autocratic power and the naturalization of traditional values of patriarchy, submission, and social hierarchy, their narratives often smuggle in contemporary political and social critiques – for example, by presenting upright imperial officials to attack contemporary widespread corruption and express popular desires for social justice and a clean and responsible government.

Apart from involving itself in the attack on corruption, a major negative social reality of today's China, the historical TV plays set in imperial time, such as *Empresses in the Palace* (*Zhenhuanzhuan*, 2011, see Chapter 1), and the espionage-themed shows set during the Chinese War of Resistance to Japan and the subsequent civil war periods, such as *Undercover* (*Qianfu* 2009), cleverly interweave the ubiquitous "unspoken rules" (*qianguize*) of China's government and business circles into its plots and engage the audience in an innovative and intriguing manner. These popular and entertainment-oriented TV drama serials' exposition of sensitive social topics, although in a "coded" manner, has been proved to be effective and impressive.

TV drama as nurturer of a "cultural public sphere"

Contemporary Chinese TV drama not only performs a "conformist" role to spread the official rhetoric, and an "objective" role to mirror the social changes and evolution, it also plays a "critical" and "subversive" role in terms of nurturing a virtual cultural public sphere. In Kong's (2014: 240–242) analysis of the 2009 espionage-themed TV drama hit *Undercover* (*Qianfu*), she insightfully investigates how a virtual community of active online fan club followers of the drama form an "affective engagement" with the show via social networking media devices. Moreover, Kong notes that through the dynamic exchanges of ideas within the online communal fandom, "intellectual interaction and emotional nurture can occur" between netizen viewers. Based on Kong's observation, this cybernetic fandom maps out a new pattern of social bonding and cultural consumption by China's young generations. It also creates vital ethnographic sites for the analysis of popular culture and civic discourse in new and evolving forms of cultural public spheres in modern-day China. Using *Undercover* as a representative example, Kong examines how through the virtual community/cultural public sphere created by the show, fans relate the plots and lines of the show to the deteriorating social reality of China today. Through "alternative reading" and sharing of their esthetic viewing experiences of the drama, the fans and critics find a way to openly discuss the much-suppressed subjects of social inequity, corrupt bureaucracy, perverted public morality and eventually the meaning or meaninglessness of revolution (Kong 2014: 261). Through Chinese viewers' "meaningful encounters with texts" (Jenkins 2006: 140 cited in Kong 2014: 261), as demonstrated in their substitute interpretations of the plots, characters and lines of *Undercover*, they circumvent mainstream ideas and "appropriate" and "hijack" the primary text to implant ancillary ideas into its orthodox paradigm, which turns "fan talk into a public forum" and transforms TV drama into the "most productive sites of discourse" in modern-day China (Kong 2014: 261–262). By turning out fresh or "hidden/unorthodox" meanings of the original media texts, the fans turn their discussions about the TV shows into political and social commentary. Alternatively, the power of TV rests partly in the personal appraisals, elucidations and uses of program content that are produced by viewers, and in the modes that those audience-initiated actions involve and transform socio-political and cultural realities (Lull 1991: 154). Moreover, instead of articulating direct critique of government, the netizen audience issues popular media reviews and deliberations, which are politically safer yet no less poignant in their reproduction of general dissatisfaction (Kong 2014: 315).

10 *Introduction*

Similarly, in Zhu's (2008b: 42) discussion about the popular 2003 histori-cal epic drama *Marching towards the Republic* (*Zouxiang gonghe*, 2003), she remarks that the show offered radical reinterpretations of the struggle with Chi-na's political direction in the late Qing Dynasty and early Republican eras, which provoked discussion of a political overhaul among contemporary intellectuals and viewers. Zhu (2008b: 55–56) cites a Chinese scholar's arguments which state that the comparison between China's post-Mao transformation and the reform in the late Qing Dynasty as reflected in the show is salient. Sun Yat-sen's 1905 argument about curbing corruption in China at the time was that states without exhaustive political refurbishment, even with the introduction of Western mod-ern technology, would simply breed corruption, and this way of thinking "hits home with the contemporary political and economic situation in China." Based on Zhu's (2008b: 62) observation, politically charged dynasty dramas that have been informed by and vigorously engaged in the relevant intellectual debates of the time, which in the case of *Marching towards the Republic* is the assessment of political reform and a possible form of democracy at the outset of the 2000s, have "served to transform intellectual and elite policy debates into public forums." Here, the show's reach to a gigantic audience and its function as a "public forum" might provide reasoning for the government's hardline policy towards it, which prohibited its reruns and blocked the sale of broadcasting rights to provincial TV stations (Zhu 2008b: 55).

Ho's (2015) study about another recent TV drama hit, *Narrow Dwelling* (*Woju*, 2009), which analogously attests the show's utility as a workable virtual public sphere that foregrounds the unaffordable housing prices in contemporary China and the rampant government and business corruption, generated strong emotional responses off screen. According to Kong (2014: 36), TV drama often becomes a benchmark and elicits public opinion and social reactions. The collusion between businessmen and Party officials (which is revealed clearly in the narratives of *Narrow Dwelling*) is the predominant cause of soaring and unreasonable real estate prices, which turns the Chinese commoners into pitiful mortgage slaves. Based on Ho's (2015: 110) opinions, viewers quickly decrypt the show's criti-cism of housing prices and corruption, and they come to understand that the show's narrative seizes and imitates their wrath, agony, distress and helpless-ness of being unable to afford a home of their own. These kind of individual encounters and setbacks, which might be categorized as a "pedestrian form of suffering" (Ang 1985: 78 cited in Kong 2014:141), create an emotional hatred and social critique (Kong 2014:141). *Narrow Dwelling*'s candid depiction of the harsh reality in present-day Chinese society engendered extensive discussion in both traditional mass media outlets and on the Internet (Ng 2015: 87). The heated debates incited by the show and in cultural public spheres have attracted the attention of the government propaganda officials, who took prompt action to curb further sentimental vexation of the viewing public (Ho 2015). In other words, the strong audience reactions to the show pushed SARFT to intervene and "restrict" certain themes and topics which it considers as catalysts of social unrest (Kong 2014: 315).

The above discussion provides evidence of a progressive trend that is growing among Chinese popular culture consumers as "they aspire to cultural power, pursue cultural democracy, and practice forms of political expression in the cultural sphere" (Kong 2014: 284). TV not only offers family entertainment or a means to get away from reality, but it is also a rich supply for the manufacture of an alternate reality and a new political consciousness (Lull 1991: 77). The clarification on contemporary Chinese TV drama's role as a "public forum" and "subversive conduit" proves that it should not be regarded as simply a recreational device or a pseudo propaganda tool. Rather, watching TV drama permits viewers to partake in the formation of China's social and political veracity, which is a position that innately doubts the habitual argument of an inert audience who are "passive, easily distracted, uneducated, and uncivilized" held by Chinese elites and certain conservative CCP censors (Zhao 1998: 24; Schneider 2012: 207). Some scholars argue that post-socialist China is assumed to be an enhanced Communist polity fortified by a repressive media propaganda system (Ng 2015: 90), and this in turn is indicative of a passive audience. In other words, instead of encouraging a media ecology where dissimilar discourse is contested, and of fostering discussions about media content by viewers, the cultural control practices in China incline to suppress debate and possibly discipline audiences to remain uncritical (Schneider 2012: 222). Further, the Chinese elites see the general public as "muddleheaded and short-sighted" (Zhao 1998: 24) and assist the propaganda institution's manipulation and victimization of Chinese audiences. As a result, in the case of TV drama production, many Chinese TV directors believe that TV drama content should convey paternalistic messages and should deliver these messages in paternalistic ways, as the Chinese audience would not understand the message in any other mode (Schneider 2012: 207). However, this customary view that sees Chinese audiences as cultural dopes, and popular culture exclusively as a site for ideological domination (Kong 2014: 50), has been challenged by many media and cultural studies scholars, especially by those based in the Western world.

Chinese media scholars generally believe that TV has a solid faculty to mold the minds of viewers, in either a positive or a negative way (Schneider 2012: 132); however, Western academics argue that Chinese TV viewers will not construe messages as they are intended to be understood (Lull 1991: 1), and they actually actively engage with TV content instead of passively consuming it (Kramer 2006 cited in Schneider 2012: 132), through intelligently and customarily reading between the lines and discerning hidden meanings in order to "reinterpret" the dramas as expressions of their own individual experiences (Kong 2014: 118). From a broader socio-political perspective, some Western scholars, such as Lull (1991: 219), argue that Chinese TV drama creation stirs up public dialogue, social interaction and political discussion among the audiences, which confirm individual viewers' political sentimentalities and socially endorse their opinions via the formation of constituencies of resistance. Lull further points out that because of its extensive presence, appeal, and social function, TV as a medium serves as a unique and irreplaceable "ideological agenda" which is sometimes in line with the objectives of its regulators, sometimes not (Lull 1991: 219). Lull's remarks

12   *Introduction*

coincide with the argument that the Chinese TV drama discourse and the Chinese audience alike are capable of performing critically and "rebelliously," particularly when they yield more exposés and critiques of social injustice (Zhang 2009: 174). With the advent of the Internet and other social networking media channels, contemporary Chinese TV drama watchers not only act energetically and imaginatively in unraveling and occasionally reinventing the meanings of media accounts, but also they sometimes become the motivating strength for shaping a virtual public communicative domain where civic matters and interests are uttered and discussed via exchanging their aesthetic understandings (Kong 2014: 57).

This cultural public sphere generated by consuming TV drama and by offering "alternative" and sometimes "subversive" reading to its content from the Chinese viewers/netizens provides a conduit in which a "cultural storm" (Lull 1991: 220) could take place. This "cultural storm" enables netizens to challenge totalitarian rule in China, which is different from a simply cry for alteration in the political system or an eager reaction to a wavering economy (Lull 1991: 220). The social potential and civic functions of this aesthetic public sphere have yet to be fully realized and are persistently threatened to be mitigated or usurped by numerous political and commercial interests (Hu 2012 cited in Kong 2014: 319), and the communications and debates it spawns may not essentially result in noticeable political or social movements and changes. Yet, the arrival of this aesthetic public sphere in the popular media scene does stipulate convincing verification for the immense progress in public democratic communication in China and will definitely contribute to the cultivation of a cultural citizenship mindset which lays the foundation for the shaping of a genuine democratic culture in China's future (Kong 2014: 319).

Building on this established research on contemporary Chinese TV drama series, my book will focus on a group of recently released and well-liked TV serials in mainland China which are, to various degrees, informed by government policies, mirror social and cultural occurrences or provide coded and thought-provoking messages on China's socio-economic and political reality that prompt "substitute" and "nonconforming" readings to the mainstream discourse. Through in-depth textual analysis of the plots, scenes and characters of these selected TV serials, the book provides timely, sharp and invigorating interpretations and understanding of contemporary Chinese society, its political inclinations, social fashions and cultural tendencies. The book also demonstrates how popular media narratives of TV drama serials engage with topical, controversial and sensitive civic issues and cultural phenomena of modern-day China and reflects them in a poignant, intriguing and motivating manner, which fashions a broad and influential social imagination and catapults potential social variations and conversions. Following this Introduction, the body of the book is divided into six chapters.

Chapter 1 examines the TV drama serial *Empresses in the Palace* (*Zhenhuanzhuan*, 2011), which was an instant sensation in mainland China upon its release in 2011. It is different from previously made dynasty dramas of the 1990s and 2000s, where the detailed representation of the infighting at court and the political tactics and purges employed by the emperors and their ministers generated most of the interest among the viewers. The continual exposition about the darker side of Chinese government and bureaucracy in these dynasty dramas, even fixing their portrayal on remote historical events and figures, has a potential to render a negative impact on the contemporary Chinese audience, therefore the descriptive concentration of dynasty dramas has shifted from court infighting among the government officials to power struggles between the concubines of the Emperor in the imperial harem: thus the *Empresses in the Palace*. However, a close reading of the plots and characters of *Empresses in the Palace* shows that this drama not only superficially distances itself from the male-dominated court brawls and persecutions, but it also creates a coded reading about the current Chinese political sphere and the ferocious power struggles among different political cliques within it. This correlation of the historical drama and the present real-life dramas of the Chinese political and workplace cultures in terms of the desperate pursuit of power, factional infighting and the unscrupulous and vicious means used to achieve one's own goals, mirrors the socio-political reality of China and strikes a chord of familiarity with the audience.

Thus, *Empresses in the Palace* cannot be simply read as a domestic drama depicting the life and conflicts within the imperial harem; it should instead be taken seriously as a highly politically veiled dynasty drama text which indicates a new fashion in the development of the historically themed TV shows in contemporary China. In doing so, the show engages skillfully and cleverly with official propaganda rhetoric in terms of creating an iron-fisted, determined, astute and resourceful leader who has the confidence to achieve the seemingly unachievable and eventually to restore justice to the entire society.

Chapter 2 analyzes *Angel Heart* (*Xinshu*, 2012), one of the major medical dramas produced in mainland China recently. The show's storyline is centered on clashes between health care providers and patients, occurrences that are usual incidents in nowadays China. By designing characters who are model doctors and nurses, *Angel Heart* endeavors to moderate the adverse sentiments between medical workers and patients. Unlike the dishonest, conceited and corrupt persona of doctors held by many Chinese people, the doctor characters in *Angel Heart* have a spirit of altruism, collectivism, heroism and sacrifice. Established as exemplary citizens of today's China, these doctors devote themselves unstintingly and nobly to their careers and their patients. In this way, *Angel Heart* fulfills its social function in placating the contradictory needs and views between these two interreliant and antagonistic groups in particular, and in harmonizing the entire Chinese society in general by analogy. Echoing the government's call to its people to build a harmonious and egalitarian society (which indicates an obvious left turn in politics), *Angel Heart* enlists the relationship between medical workers and patients as a simile to illustrate the strained social bond between China's "haves" and "have-nots." In its efforts to alleviate the dwindling enmity between these two cohorts and the widening gap between their incomes and social status, the show plays a mediator role between the government and its citizens. The fundamental ambition of *Angel Heart* is to persuade the audience to believe that that the CCP government is dependable and aims to provide reliable social welfare for its

14   Introduction

people. Through creating new models and finding novel ways to spread the ideological message of official discourse, *Angel Heart* sets the standard to follow for similarly themed "pseudo-main melody" TV drama serials.

Chapter 3 focuses on Li Ke's novel *A Story of Lala's Promotion* (*Du Lala shengzhiji*, 2007) and its TV drama and film adaptations *Go Lala Go!* (*Du Lala shengzhiji*, 2010). In 2007, Li's novel became a bestseller among Chinese white-collar workers in joint ventures and foreign-owned (Western) corporations. The success of *A Story of Lala's Promotion* and its TV serial and film renditions is not accidental. The theme of the Du Lala phenomenon that is reflected in these literary and visual narratives – the life and career struggles of professional middle-class staff employed by joint ventures and foreign-invested enterprises – has recently become a trendy subject in Chinese popular culture. The novel account revolves around office politics, Western company culture, the white-collar lifestyle, middle-class aesthetics, and the "strong woman" phenomenon. In order to untangle the implanted cultural codes of this book, this chapter undertakes a textual scrutiny of the plots and scenes of *A Story of Lala's Promotion* and its TV serial and film versions. This trans-media study (from fiction to TV drama and film) examines three interrelated themes in the novel, the film and the TV serial. First, fixing on the impact of Western corporate culture on Chinese white-collar workers, this chapter sheds light on the overall economic and cultural trend towards assimilation and globalization, where Western economic and cultural paradigms have gained the upper hand. The chapter also examines how, on the platform offered by foreign enterprises and with the influence and guidance of Western corporate culture, educated and assiduous young Chinese women aspire, struggle and realize their dreams in the workplace. Second, adopting a feminist standpoint, the examination addresses the state of modern-day Chinese professional women represented by the ardently discussed social sensation of "strong women," and how they epitomize female independence and individualism. Third, through an exploration of the film and TV adaptations and an emphasis on white-collar females' lifestyle and consumption patterns, this chapter underlines the present-day Chinese quest of a middle-class identity and aesthetic that emulates the overpowering consumerism of post-socialist China.

Chapter 4 investigates *See without Looking* (*Tuina*, 2013), a pioneering TV drama serial which zooms in on the lives of people with disabilities and explores their vulnerability within Chinese society. As a cutting-edge and favorably commended televised story about disabled groups, *See without Looking* foregrounds the daily work and romances of a cluster of blind masseurs. This chapter probes how this group of blind masseurs have been calculatedly presented by the mainstream discourse as "useful" and "respectful" citizens because of their strong work ethic and their upbeat outlook, which empowers them to be self-supporting in the aggressive and realistic present Chinese society. By its meticulous and deliberate rendering of this group of self-sustaining blind masseurs who have high personal qualities, positive attitudes and outstanding massage skills, some of whom are well-off small-time entrepreneurs and high-income specialists, the show's narrative typifies the government-driven neoliberal ethos of contemporary China, which encourages a resilient, persistent and competitive citizenry. Furthermore, by probing into the characters and plots of *See without Looking*, this chapter expounds how those established social mores, family values and notion of love bonds, which are generally diminishing in modern-day China, are preserved and performed by this group of blind masseurs. In addition, this chapter examines a notable feature of the show as it foregrounds the love and sexual encounters of people with a disability, and enlists body politics in an attempt to gather more attention to the needs and rights of this disadvantaged social group.

Chapter 5 examines *Honey Bee Man* (*Woai nanguimi*, 2014), a televised romantic comedy about the post-divorce life of contemporary Chinese women, particularly those who were born in the 1960s, 1970s and 1980s, and some of their important challenges and confrontations. With a focus on the post-divorce lives of three generations of contemporary Chinese women, *Honey Bee Man* maps out a fresh and discursive gendered space which gives light to the considerable economic renovations that have impacted on the lives of ordinary Chinese people, and particularly on Chinese women. This chapter probes the changing perceptions about what is required to be a qualified and desirable woman in the briskly growing socio-economic powerhouse that is present-day China. It discusses varying and nuanced relationships and marital forms and status and discloses the utility and value of China's divorced women in accordance with the state's propaganda rhetoric, as it bids to stimulate what it defines as competent, considerate and buoyant citizenry. Concurrently, by constructing an "idealized woman image," "a good national female subject" and a "preferred femininity" via the TV screen, the state discourse sketches what counts as a suitable, virtuous and wanted Chinese woman. In doing so, state propaganda promotes a particular "model" of divorced women (such as the Huiyun character in the show) as even-tempered, caring and strong females who do not complain about their fate but instead strive to become even more tender, virtuous and kind after their marriage breakups, while it remolds those "unqualified/ incompetent wives" (such as the Ye Shan and Fang Yiyi characters in the show) into a submissive and traditional Chinese good wife–wise mother figure and rewards her with a happy "second spring." Further, by producing "mismatched" couples, which are politically useful, the show helps to relieve the sour taste of social disparity and wealth discrimination that is the upshot of a resurfacing class demarcation and social discord generated by the ongoing economic transformations.

Chapter 6 scrutinizes *Parents of the Single Child* (*Dushengzinu de popomama*, 2013), a family-based drama that engages with a number of topical social concerns about people from the one-child generations. By representing domestic and workplace-related conflicts of the only-child generations, the show forefronts the intrinsic bonds imposed upon these single-child generations in particular and upon the entire Chinese society in general; a child and society damaged and disturbed by the demographic policies of previous national governments. However, by divulging only some detrimental social outcomes of the one-child policy, the

16   *Introduction*

show limits the topics and nullifies some of the debates and concerns about the deleterious repercussions of the CCP administration's birth control policy. In other words, the drama takes a superficial approach towards the more distressing social harms, such as the sex ratio imbalance and the "shidu" (loss of an only child) family issues, which might trigger wider public disgruntlement and even social unrest. In this way, the show's narratives keep a reasonable distance from those sensitive topics and side effects of the one-child policy. It also shields the government from public interrogation and censure and obscures the possible intent of the state, which is to keep these distressing social repercussions associated with the one-child policy within the category of individual difficulties rather than social quandaries. The traumas and misfortunes manufactured by the birth control policies testify again to the concessions and sacrifices made by Chinese individuals for the collective causes and state undertakings imposed by the CCP government.

Notes

1   For example, Guo Jingming (b. 1983) is a celebrity writer-turned-director whose *Tiny Times* (*Xiaoshidai*) film series (*Tiny Times 1*, 2013; *Tiny Times 2*, 2013 and *Tiny Times 3*, 2014) made 1.292 billion RMB box office income and made Guo an important person in the Chinese film industry. Guo was awarded the "best new director" prize at the 16th session of the Shanghai International Film Festival. Han Han (b. 1982), another famous Chinese post-1980s writer-turned-director, was successful in the extremely competitive film marketplace with his debut auteur film *The Continent* (*Houhuiwuqi*, 2014). The film grossed over 600 million RMB at the box office and won acclaim from both film industry professionals and ordinary viewers.

2   According to Bai and Song (2015: 5), in 2005, the astonishing recognition and commercial achievement of Hunan TV's *Super Girl*, which is a singing competition reality show fashioned on *American Idol*, became a sensation and triggered a new wave of reality TV. Ever since *Super Girl* was cancelled in 2007 by the State Administration of Radio, Film and Television (SARFT), reality TV as an adaptable and miscellaneous meta-genre has continued, giving rise to several waves of dating shows, workplace-themed talent shows and singing contest shows. In recent times, reality TV has become almost as popular as drama in TV entertainment.

3   Television drama contributes 70 percent of the total advertising income of television stations, with the most lucrative primetime television drama generating an advertising revenue that is ten times the show's purchasing cost (China TV Drama Market Report, 2003–2004 cited in Zhao 2008: 202–203). Advertisers feed the media with their livelihood (Zhao 2008). In 2009, the total advertising revenue from Chinese television reached 675.82 billion yuan, which is more than the amount (19.3 billion yuan) that is generated from the Internet (Kong & Hawes 2015: 34).

4   One of the tensions is shown when TV texts are frequently used as a simile for the uncertainties between a relic of socialist rhetoric and culture and a neoliberal market schema. According to Kong and Hawes (2015: 35–36), the ambiguous identity of Chinese TV stations is another dilemma created by the state and market "combination," as they are simultaneously "part commercial businesses and part public enterprises," which take root in the larger paradoxes of "socialism with Chinese characteristics." Therefore, the current situation finds all mainland TV stations under continuing control and management by the state apparatus that supervises their content and means that they can never be operated effectively as entirely commercial concerns.

5   Zhao Baogang is famous for his successful directing of popular writer Hai Yan's crime dramas, which according to Zhu, Keane and Bai (2008) "blended detective elements with sentimental love stories in order to attract more female and young viewers," such as *A Romantic Story* (*Yichang fenghua xueyue de shi*, 1997), *I Will Never Close My Eyes* (*Yongbu mingmu*, 2000) and *How Can I Save You, My Love* (*Na shenme zhengjiu ni, wode airen*, 2003).

References

Ang, Ien. 1985. *Watching Dallas: Soap Opera and the Melodramatic Imagination*. New York: Methuen & Co.

Bai, Ruoyun. 2008. "'Clean Officials,' Emotional Moral Community, and Anti-Corruption Television Dramas," in *TV Drama in China*, Ying Zhu, Michael Keane, and Ruoyun Bai (eds.). Hong Kong: Hong Kong University Press, pp. 47–60.

Bai, Ruoyun. 2015. "'Clean Up the Screen,' Regulating Television Entertainment in the 2000s," in *Chinese Television in the Twenty-First Century: Entertaining the Nation*, Ruoyun Bai and Geng Song (eds.). London and New York: Routledge, pp. 69–86.

Bai, Ruoyun and Song, Geng. 2015. "Introduction," in *Chinese Television in the Twenty-First Century: Entertaining the Nation*, Ruoyun Bai and Geng Song (eds.). London and New York: Routledge, pp. 1–14.

Berry, Chris. 2009. "Shanghai Television's Documentary Channel: Chinese Television as Public Space," in *TV China: A Reader on New Media*, Ying Zhu and Chris Berry (eds.). Bloomington: Indiana University Press, pp. 71–89.

Cooper-Chen, Anne. 2010. "Television Entertainment," in *New Media for a New China*, James F. Scotton and William A. Hachten (eds.). Malden, MA: Wiley-Blackwell, pp. 83–97.

Hao, Jian. 2008. *Chinese TV Drama: Cultural and Genre Studies*. Beijing: China Film Press.

Ho Wing Shan. 2015. *Screening Post-1989 China: Critical Analysis of Chinese Film and Television*. New York: Palgrave Macmillan.

Hong, Junhao. 1998. *The Internationalization of Television in China: The Evolution of Ideology, Society, and Media since the Reform*. Westport, CT: Praeger.

Hu, Yong. 2012. "Cong yaque wusheng dao zhongsheng xuanhua" [From Total Silence to Utter Cacophony], viewed on 21 March 2016, available at http: //blog.caijing.com.cn/expert_article-151265–35720.shtml.

Jenkins, Henry. 2006. *Fans, Bloggers, and Gamers: Exploring Participatory Culture*. New York: New York University Press.

Keane, Michael. 2001. "By the Way, FUCK YOU!: Feng Xiaogang's Disturbing Television Dramas." *Continuum* 15 (1): 57–66.

Kong, Shuyu. 2008. "Family Matters: Reconstructing the Family on the Chinese Television Screen," in *TV Drama in China*, Ying Zhu, Michael Keane, and Ruoyun Bai (eds.), Hong Kong: Hong Kong University Press, pp. 75–88.

Kong, Shuyu. 2014. *Popular Media, Social Emotion and Public Discourse in Contemporary China*. Hoboken, NJ: Taylor and Francis.

Kong, Shuyu and Hawes, Colin S. 2015. "The New Family Mediator: TV Mediation Programs in China's 'Harmonious Society,'" in *Chinese Television in the Twenty-First Century: Entertaining the Nation*, Ruoyun Bai and Geng Song (eds.). London and New York: Routledge, pp. 33–50.

Kramer, Stefan. 2006. *Das Chinesische Fernsehpublikum: Zur Rezeption und Reproduktion eines neuen Mediums* [The Chinese Television Audience: Concerning the Reception and Reproduction of a New Medium]. Bielefeld: Transcript Verlag.

18 Introduction

Li, Hongling. 2011. "2010 nian dianshiju bochu yu shoushi huigu" [Survey Analysis of the Broadcasting and Ratings of Television Dramas of 2010], *Shoushiyuekan* (Ratings Monthly), No. 3, viewed on 13 May 2012, available at www.csm.com.cn/index.php/knowledge/showArticle/kaid/387.

Liu, Kang. 2010. "Reinventing the Red Classics in the Age of Globalization." *Neohelicon* 37: 329–347.

Lu, Haiyuan. 2011. "Xianyu Jiaju Weishi Jingzheng, Jiemu Bianpai Duoyuan Tuxian" [The Entertainment Rule Intensifies Competition among Provincial Satellite TVs, Resulting in Diversified Programming]. *Guanggao Daguan* [Advertising Panorama] 12: 26–27.

Lull, James. 1991. *China Turned On: Television, Reform and Resistance*. London: Routledge.

Ng, How Wee. 2015. "Rethinking Censorship in China: The Case of Snail House," in *Chinese Television in the Twenty-First Century: Entertaining the Nation*, Ruoyun Bai and Geng Song (eds.). London and New York: Routledge, pp. 87–103.

Qian, Gong. 2008. "A Trip Down Memory Lane: Remaking and Rereading the Red Classics," in *TV Drama in China*, Ying Zhu, Michael Keane and Ruoyun Bai (eds.). Hong Kong: Hong Kong University Press, pp. 157–172.

Qian, Gong. 2015. "Remolding Heroes: The Erasure of Class Discourse in the Red Classics Television Drama Adaptations," in *Chinese Television in the Twenty-First Century: Entertaining the Nation*, Ruoyun Bai and Geng Song (eds.). London and New York: Routledge, pp. 158–174.

Qian, Kun. 2015. "*Tianxia* Revisited: Family and Empire on the Television Screen," in *Chinese Television in the Twenty-First Century: Entertaining the Nation*, Ruoyun Bai and Geng Song (eds.). London and New York: Routledge, pp. 175–191.

Schneider, Florian. 2012. *Visual Political Communication in Popular Chinese Television Series*. Leiden and Boston: Brill.

Shanghai TV Festival. 2004. CV/SC- SOFRES Media, *Zhongguo dianshiju shichang baogao* [China TV Drama Market Report, 2003–2004]. Beijing: Huaxia chubanshi.

Sun, Wanning. 2008. "Maids in the Televisual City: Competing Tales of Post-Socialist Modernity," in *TV Drama in China*, Ying Zhu, Michael Keane, and Ruoyun Bai (eds.). Hong Kong: Hong Kong University Press, pp. 89–102.

Sun, Wanning and Gorfinkel, Lauren. 2015. "Television, Scale and Place-Identity in the PRC: Provincial, National and Global Influences from 1958 to 2013," in *Television History in Asia: Issues and Contexts*, Jinna Tay and Graeme Turner (eds.). London and New York: Routledge, pp. 19–37.

Undercover (Qianfu). (2009) Directed by Jiang Wei and Fu Wei. Beijing: Dongyang Qingyu Television Culture Co., Ltd., first aired on Jilin satellite TV.

Yin, Hong. 2001. "Chongtu Yu Gongmou – Lun Zhongguo Dianshiju De Wenhua Celue" [Conflicts and Collaborations: On the Cultural Strategies of Chinese Television Drama]. *Wenyiyanjiu* [Literary and Arts Research] 6: 8–15.

Yin, Hong. 2002. "Meaning, Production, Consumption: The History and Reality of Television Drama in China," in *Media in China: Consumption, Content, Crisis*, Stephanie K. Donald, Michael Keane, and Yin Hong (eds.). London: Routledge and Curzon, pp. 28–39.

Zhang, Tongdao. 2009. "Chinese Television Audience Research," in *TV China: A Reader on New Media*, Ying Zhu and Chris Berry (eds.). Bloomington: Indiana University Press, pp. 168–180.

Zhao, Yuezhi. 1998. *Media, Market, and Democracy in China: Between the Party Line and the Bottom Line*. Urbana and Chicago: University of Illinois Press.

Zhao, Yuezhi. 2008. *Communication in China: Political Economy, Power and Conflict.* Lanham, MD: Rowman & Littlefield Publishers.

Zhong, Xueping. 2010. *Mainstream Culture Refocused: Television Drama, Society, and the Production of Meaning in Reform-era China.* Honolulu: University of Hawaii Press.

Zhu, Ying. 2008a. "Yongzheng Dynasty and Totalitarian Nostalgia," in *TV Drama in China*, Ying Zhu, Michael Keane, and Ruoyun Bai (eds.). Hong Kong: Hong Kong University Press, pp. 21–32.

Zhu, Ying. 2008b. *Television in Post-reform China: Serial Dramas, Confucian Leadership and the Global Television Market.* London and New York: Routledge.

Zhu, Ying. 2009. "Transnational Circulation of Chinese-Language Television Dramas," in *TV China: A Reader on New Media*, Ying Zhu and Chris Berry (eds.). Bloomington: Indiana University Press, pp. 221–241.

Zhu, Ying, Keane, Michael and Bai, Ruoyun. 2008. "Introduction," in *TV Drama in China*, Ying Zhu, Michael Keane, and Ruoyun Bai (eds.). Hong Kong: Hong Kong University Press, pp. 1–19.

1 *Empresses in the Palace*

Historical drama and its reflections on the political and workplace culture in contemporary China

Introduction

The TV drama *Empresses in the Palace* (*Zhenhuanzhuan*, 2011) became an immediate hit in mainland China upon its debut in 2011. Different from many of the previously made historical dramas of the 1990s and 2000s in the mainland region, which highlight court infighting, struggles for power and corruption by ministers in the male-dominated official circle, *Empresses in the Palace* (hereafter *Empresses*) focuses on the struggle for favor among the many concubines in the imperial harem. This chapter discusses the factional rivalry and wrangling among the concubines in their attempts to gain favor with the Emperor. This "favor" or recognition by the Emperor would sustain their own status, glory and wealth in the imperial palace, as well as that of their family members. The correlation of the historical drama with contemporary Chinese political and workplace cultures in terms of the desperate pursuit of power, factional squabbling and the unscrupulous and vicious means used to achieve one's own goals that are revealed in the following analyses strikes a chord of familiarity with the TV audience.

Empresses in the Palace

Empresses is a seventy-six-episode TV drama serial that was produced by the Beijing TV Art Center between 2010 and 2011. It first aired on local satellite TV stations in mainland China in 2012, and due to its popularity it was purchased and shown by the local TV channels of Taiwan, Hong Kong and later Japan and other Asian countries. In March 2015, the American version of *Empresses*[1] was released on Netflix, a global provider of on-demand streaming movies and TV series, and it ranked third in its audience ratings (*Baidu Encyclopedia* 2015). To date, *Empresses* is the first and only mainland-produced TV serial that is aired on Netflix, the biggest pay-per-view video website in the world, which only broadcasts the most popular movies and TV shows. Within the following half month after its release on Netflix, *Empresses* scored 3.8 out of the highest 5 marks on Netflix, which almost approached the record 3.9 mark set by Ang Lee's groundbreaking film *Crouching Tiger Hidden Dragon* (*Wohucanglong*, 2000). The storyline of *Empresses* tells about the life journey of Zhen Huan, the daughter of a

Empresses in the Palace   21

high-ranking government official of the Qing Dynasty under the rule of Emperor Yongzheng (1678–1735). Zhen Huan, at the age of sixteen, participates in the selections for imperial concubine, which are held once every three years during the rule of Qing Dynasty. If selected, she would be conferred with honorable entitlements and become an imperial concubine in the palace. Plus, if Zhen Huan wins the Emperor's favor, or if she gives birth to a son, she could be promoted quickly, and if her son becomes the successor, she could become Empress Dowager after her son ascends the throne.

Zhen Huan is chosen by the Emperor and becomes one of his concubines, although at the time this was against her wishes. As an imperial concubine in feudal China, women like Zhen Huan had to be favored by the Emperor in order to secure their status and a wealthy life in the imperial harem. In addition, the fate of their family and the promotion of the male family members as officials depended on this status. According to traditional Chinese culture, whether a woman could produce a male offspring for the family line was the pivotal factor in deciding her position and destiny in her husband's family, and the imperial concubines were no exception. Concubines, therefore, put a lot of effort into attracting the Emperor, encouraging him to spend more nights in their bed in order to give themselves a better chance of becoming pregnant with the Emperor's child. Zhen Huan is not only young and pretty, but also intelligent and knowledgeable and she soon stands out amongst the other concubines and wins ongoing favor from the Emperor. At first she is a low-level concubine who is innocent and kind-hearted, but over time she changes and after several decades of living in the imperial harem and of being locked in constant strife with other concubines, she has been turned into a tactful and "cruel" woman who is adept at intrigue, infighting and power struggles in the imperial harem when she finally becomes the most honorable Empress Dowager. Zhen Huan is the nominal mother of Crown Prince Qianlong, who eventually ascends the throne after Yongzheng's death.

Emperor Yongzheng has more than a dozen concubines and they are granted hierarchical titles from the highest to the lowest ranks. These titles include the Queen Empress (*huanghou*, the highest title for imperial concubines in the Qing Dynasty), Imperial Noble Empress (*huangguifei*), Noble Empress (*guifei*), Empress (*fei*), Dame (*pin*), Noble Lady (*guiren*), Attendant (*daying*) and Respondent (*changzai*, the lowest title), and all of these imperial women compete to have children (preferably sons) with the Emperor. For those who are not successful in giving the emperor a male heir, they find different ways to compensate in order to secure favor from the Emperor and their status in the imperial harem. For example, Empresses Jing and Duan adopt babies from other concubines who have either passed away or lost favor with the Emperor; Dame Shen risks becoming pregnant by an imperial doctor; Noble Empress Hua and Empress An put poison or harmful medicine in other pregnant concubines' food in order to induce abortions; Noble Empress Hua also tries to kill other pregnant concubines; and even the Queen Empress kills her biological sister's (one of Yongzheng's favorite concubines) unborn baby.

22 Empresses in the Palace

Because of their desperate and fierce competition to win the favor of the Emperor, the relationships among the concubines are complicated and often very hateful. Similar to the minister's political strife, the concubines of the Emperor fight a largely unseen war in the imperial seraglio. These mentally fatiguing battles lead to drastic decisions, often with dire consequences. For example, Zhen Huan's first fetus is aborted due to her persecution by Noble Empress Hua; and Zhen Huan's childhood best friend, Dame Shen, almost drowns after she is pushed into a pool in the imperial garden by Noble Empress Hua's servant due to Noble Empress Hua's jealousy. Furthermore, because of the coldness of the Emperor, and the conspiracies of other concubines, Zhen Huan is expelled from the imperial palace after she gives birth to a princess. As a result, Zhen Huan lives in a remote temple where she must endure bullying from some of the nuns who run the temple. Her father is also implicated by her loss of favor with the Emperor and his own favor with the Emperor and thus his influence and standing within the official circle at court is jeopardized.

However, during her time outside the imperial palace, Zhen Huan finds her soulmate, Emperor Yongzheng's younger half-brother, Prince Guo. Believing that Prince Guo died on the frontline during war, and in order to save her dying father who has been framed by corrupt officials, Zhen Huan, who becomes pregnant with Prince Guo's child, decides to return to the imperial palace upon the pardon and amnesty of Emperor Yongzheng. Prince Guo survives the cruel battle; however, he is finally killed by Emperor Yongzheng when he finds out about the adultery between Zhen Huan and his brother, thus pushing Zhen Huan to take fierce revenge. Since her return to the imperial palace, Zhen Huan is no longer a naïve and simple girl but a woman who is very adept at scheming and acting entirely strategically. In doing so, she hides her capabilities, but cleverly uses flattery, cheating, mischief-making, circumvention and backstabbing, in order to put her rivals into weak and vulnerable positions. Finally, Zhen Huan defeats all her adversaries, including Emperor Yongzheng, and takes revenge for the death of her lover, her friends and her servants. After Emperor Yongzheng's death, Zhen Huan becomes one of the most honored and powerful people in the imperial palace; second only to Emperor Qianlong.

Through an in-depth textual analysis of the plot design and character building of *Empresses*, this chapter examines the practical significance of the drama when it is correlated alongside the socio-political reality of present-day China. *Empresses* reflects much of the current political, social and cultural dynamics and associated problems of China today, especially its allusion to the complex and officially unseen corruption within the political arena. The factional power struggles, backbiting and ethically challenging strategies displayed in *Empresses* mirror the flagging modern-day political and workplace ecology and moral standards. In doing so, *Empresses* skillfully and effectively weaves its plotlines and characters into the political struggles and social malaises of today's China, and thus fulfills the civil function of cultural works, which is to provide timely public commentary and engagement with major civic issues. Moreover, by creating a strong, determined and iron-fisted concubine figure, Zhen Huan, the show indirectly endorses

Empresses in the Palace   23

the arguably positive image of the current Chinese president Xi Jinping, which is in line with the state propaganda discourse.

Empresses engages with government policy and propaganda

Since the middle of the 1990s, historical or dynasty TV serials have been a success in the mainland TV drama market and have created the phenomenon of "empire fever" (Qian 2015: 175). Employing an "orthodox" interpretation of history, dynasty TV dramas eulogize benevolent and responsible rulers such as the great Han Emperor Wu in *The Emperor of the Han Dynasty* (*Hanwudadi*, 2005), Emperors Yongzheng and Kangxi of the Qing Dynasty in *Yongzheng Dynasty* (*Yongzheng wangchao*, 1997) and *Kangxi Dynasty* (*Kangxi wangchao*, 2001). This "emperor fever" such as exhibited in *The Emperor of the Han Dynasty* is a domestic product of "the confluence of intellectual discourses and government policies in conjunction with public appeal" (Qian 2015 cited in Bai & Song 2015: 12). These shows provide a much-needed assertion of faith in the government and the state leaders and "a rejuvenation of imperial thinking that inspires and justifies contemporary policy" (Qian 2015: 188).

Popular dynasty dramas of the 1990s and 2000s, *Yongzheng Dynasty* and *Kangxi Dynasty*, were "informed by the major political and intellectual debates of the time" and were generally "aligned with the intellectual Left, in all its variations" (Zhu 2008: 22). These variations would include neo-authoritarianism, neo-conservatism and the New Left schools, which agree that contemporary China is best served by an authoritarian government and a strong leadership. In the case of Chinese historical drama production, it is clear that it is not the state that embraced the intellectual Leftist vision and superimposed it on the manufacture of TV dramas; instead, TV dramas arise from vigorous dialogues between political and economic influences and the convergence of intellectual ideas of China's future, which is projected onto China's imperial times (Qian 2015: 186). From another perspective, this "self-imposed" political conformity demonstrated in the dynasty shows is a result of the "soft" censorship applied by the government, such as the incentives it provides for the production of "ideologically obedient" content rather than one that is "politically unconventional and challenging" (Schneider 2012: 157).

There is an array of factors that creators and producers must take into consideration when making a TV drama in contemporary China, and this includes current conventions, the popularity of a genre and political concerns and commercial deliberations. It is this intricate, interactive and interdependent relationship among these various considerations that eventually turns a TV serial into reality (Schneider 2012). Amongst these influences, political suitability and conformity are certainly critical in the concern of the TV producers. Although previous dynasty dramas provide anecdotes of the past that allude to the present and would feature broadminded leaders and ethical officials, they also shed light on the ferocious political infighting and maneuvers between upright bureaucrats and those corrupt ones that may voice hidden criticism of the political reality of current

24 Empresses in the Palace

China, which is a very sensitive topic for the Chinese government (Schneider 2012: 175). This coincidental and unintended correlation between ancient history and present political occurrences contributes both to the appeal of the dynasty dramas and to their potentially problematic situation of being regarded by the state's propaganda institutions as highlighting negative elements of the society and misguiding public opinions. Thus, over the past decade, a de-politicizing trend has been noticed in the production of dynasty dramas.[2]

Empresses follows this de-politicizing path in terms of distancing its plotlines and character design from court intrigues and political power struggles. Dynasty dramas such as *Empresses*, which have shifted their focus from the intrigues in the political arena to the intrigues in the domestic field, demarcate themselves intentionally from the previously manufactured historical TV serials which foregrounded power struggles among male officials in the political field. The plots of *Empresses* revolve around the Emperor and his concubines, with the Emperor always at the center of power and dominance over all his women. Instead of attending to national events and coordinating the relationships among ministers and government officials, the authoritarian Emperor is the final arbiter of who wins and who loses a particular round of infighting within the imperial harem. In addition, rather than establishing an image of a clean, respectable and hardworking Emperor, *Empresses* endeavors to create for the Emperor or the most honorable concubine such as Zhen Huan the persona of a clear-minded yet iron-fisted judge with veracity over the matters of the imperial seraglio. Although *Empresses* has reoriented the narrative emphasis from politics to domestic matters, it is still noticeable that it differs from those purely entertainment-driven historical idol dramas and time-travel costume dramas, as it could be read as a coded political tale, and its self-imposed political concerns demonstrate its ideological imperative. As Chinese audiences have become accustomed to read between the lines of media and cultural texts, *Empresses* shows its potential to be read as a veiled political narrative which engages in a subtle manner with the official Party line and propaganda. Instead of directly portraying the struggles and conspiracies in the political domain, the show reveals the equally brutal infighting in the domestic arena within the imperial harem and thus cleverly mirrors the political reality of contemporary China.

In the case of Zhen Huan, absolute power and overall control of the imperial seraglio is what she needs to restore justice for herself and all the people who have been wrongly persecuted or killed, including her family members, lover, friends and servants. Thus, the second half of the show, which begins from her return to the imperial palace, is predominantly concerned with her journey to secure exclusive power, and her maturation process as she becomes a strong and decisive ruler within the imperial harem. Here, the grip of power befits the pivotal point in Zhen Huan's voyage of retaliation. From the quasi-power that is the favor of the Emperor to the real power that enables her to take control of her own fate, Zhen Huan achieves what she wants – justice and virtue. Here, the imperial harem that is permeated with unscrupulous infighting among the Emperor's concubines serves as a metaphor for the corrupt officialdom and a political environment riddled with frantic power struggles that have become a vicious circle and are considered by many Chinese people as beyond any cure. However, as the end of the show approaches, the imperial seraglio under the rule of Zhen Huan (a person who believes in justice, although she was not above using covert strategies to destroy her enemies) returns to being a place that is once again ethical and peaceful. Justice is ultimately restored in the imperial harem by a capable, iron-handed and strong leader who has control over all of the concubines.

In order to realize her goals, Zhen Huan waits until her status and influence in the imperial harem grows and consolidates, and only then does she begin to find opportunities to defeat all her rivals. Zhen Huan has many rivals and some of them are still very powerful, such as the Queen Empress and Noble Empress Hua. However, due to her intelligence, determination and courage, Zhen Huan overthrows her enemies one by one and eventually reinstates righteousness in the seraglio. Here, Zhen Huan's struggle to reestablish justice in the imperial harem could be read as a coded political message that hints at the current Chinese Communist Party (CCP) leadership's competency to rebuild impartiality into China's official circle. It is a message which is embedded delicately and adroitly in the storyline of the show and is conveyed to the viewers in an elusive mode. Particularly, Zhen Huan's ruthless eradication of the evil concubines tacitly endorses the iron-handed crackdown on both the high- and low-ranking corrupt officials launched by the former Hu Jintao administration, and which is being continued by the current Chinese president Xi Jinping and his colleague Wang Qishan, the Secretary of the Central Commission of Discipline Inspection, who has emerged as the public face of Xi Jinping's anti-corruption campaign.

The situation faced by Zhen Huan in the imperial seraglio is similar to the political circumstances confronting Xi Jinping in that Xi's allies were not strong enough in the years when he was still a designated successor of Hu Jintao, thus he had to wait patiently until the opportunity arose for him to gain the highest and most powerful position within the Party. Only then, and with the help of close colleagues, did he have the ability to remove those high-ranking corrupt state leaders in government administration, the military and public security services. Soon after becoming the new General Secretary of the CCP in 2012, Xi Jinping, with the help of Wang Qishan, removed the following officials: Xu Caihou and Guo Boxiong (the former Vice-Chairmen of the Central Military Commission, which is the country's top military council); Zhou Yongkang (a retired senior leader of the CCP, a former member of the 17th Politburo Standing Committee and former Secretary of the Central Political and Legislative Affairs Committee); and Ling Jihua (one of the principal political advisers to Hu Jintao, and the former Director of the General Office of the CPC Central Committee). These high-grade corrupt officials and ex-officials were the so-called big tigers (the most powerful of the corrupt officials) in Chinese politics, and their defeat by Xi and his colleagues is generously acclaimed and admired by most Chinese people. The competence, fortitude and valor of the Xi Jinping administration in its quest to eliminate official corruption has attracted great attention from the rest of the world and offered hope

26 Empresses in the Palace

and reassurance for the Chinese people that their government institution may now begin to be less corrupt and become fairer and more capable.

Arguably, official corruption is the root of many of China's internal problems, and as the classic lines from the popular mainstream blockbuster *Founding of a Republic (Jianguodaye*, 2009)[3] remind us: if we combat corruption, the CCP will go bankrupt, but if we do not combat corruption, the Chinese nation will collapse. It seems that Xi Jinping and Wang Qishan have taken a huge risk in their joint action against corrupt officials. Some political commentators describe their current anti-corruption campaign as unrestrained gambling (Wenxuecity 2015a). After dealing with Xu Caihou and Guo Boxiong (who had been promoted by Jiang Zemin during his term of office and who had been used by Jiang after he stepped down to control the forces of Hu Jintao), Zeng Qinghong is widely believed to be the next big tiger in the sights of Xi Jinping and Wang Qishan. Zeng Qinghong was a top-ranked member of the Politburo Standing Committee and the Vice-President of the People's Republic of China between 2003 and 2007. Zeng was a close ally of the then General Secretary Jiang Zemin and was seen as a power broker in the Party. Reports about the political life-and-death struggles between Xi Jinping, Wang Qishan and Zeng Qinghong are extensively circulated on Internet blogs and news pages both inside and outside of China (*French Radio International* 2015). These political power struggles that are presently taking place within China's ruling hierarchy are just as dramatic and entertaining as the plots and scenes of *Empresses*. Zhen Huan's determination to conquer all her rivals, no matter how powerful they are, and to restore justice in the imperial harem brings to mind Xi Jinping's endeavors to exterminate corruption within the Chinese government and society and to regain legitimacy for the CCP with the Chinese people. The similarity between Zhen Huan and Xi Jinping lies in their determination to achieve the unachievable and to act as saviors who bring justice and salvation for the victimized group. Another similarity between Zhen Huan and Xi Jinping is their personalities, as both are adept at biding their time and are good strategic thinkers in that they can hide the strength of their positions, waiting for the right time to launch an attack on their adversaries.

A present-day political reading of *Empresses* will show that it is a veiled yet politically informative text, as the power struggles and infighting among the imperial concubines mirrors the political contests within the current Chinese official circle. Most interestingly, the lead character in *Empresses*, Zhen Huan, has many similarities with Xi Jinping other than those mentioned above, such as their strong and determined way of doing things and their unswerving disposition and resolution to root out the forces of evil. In this way, *Empresses* echoes the official rhetoric that promotes a strong, confident and unyielding leader, and one who is the ideal of the Chinese people. Therefore, the creation of the Zhen Huan character in *Empresses* and the emergence of Xi Jinping as a capable and strong leader cater to the expectation of the contemporary Chinese audience. Here, I agree with the views of both Zhao (1998: 24) and Schneider (2012: 207) that the Chinese general public is not "muddle-headed and short-sighted." I postulate that the common

Chinese TV viewer is capable and shrewd enough to detect the hidden political messages embedded in a non-political TV show like *Empresses*.

Factional struggles on and off the screen

Differences and discord are permanent traits of officialdom and have been from ancient times. From ancient times to the CCP's socialist regime, forming factions is a distinguishing characteristic of Chinese high officialdom. The most famous modern example is the Gang of Four and their political ambitions leading to the attempted appropriation of the Party and the government.[4] Over the past couple of decades, factional politics has increased and the factions have become stronger. According to Zheng (2014: 119), Bo Xilai (former Member of the Political Bureau of the CPC Central Committee and former Minister of Commerce), Zhou Yongkang, Ling Jihua and Xu Caihou are believed to have formed a faction within the higher echelons of Chinese bureaucracy; however, they have since been removed by the Xi Jinping administration. It is also believed that there is a type of "princeling" faction within the current Chinese political arena, which is formed by the offspring of the older generation of high-ranking CCP officials, such as Zeng Qinghong and Xi Jinping. Among the twenty-five members of the 17th session of the Politburo, there are five "princelings": Xi Jinping, Wang Qishan, Liu Yandong, Yu Zhengsheng and Bo Xilai (Ai 2011: 279). Moreover, a "princeling" clique within the contemporary Chinese military circle comprising descendants of high-ranking CCP officers from the Mao era is also the subject of speculation by political observers (Meng 2010). Furthermore, there are some accounts of a so-called "grandsons of the Emperor bloc", comprising the grandsons and granddaughters of the top-ranking officials from Mao's time (*New Century Magazine* 2013). In addition, it is believed there is a faction formed by the officials who have served important positions in the Chinese Communist League such as the former CCP General Secretary Hu Jintao and the current premier Li Keqiang. There is also an oil faction made up of those who control the big state-run oil enterprises, which was headed by Zhou Yongkang (Wang 2014: 235). There is similarly a Shanghai faction and a Beijing faction, whose members came from government positions based in Shanghai (such as Jiang Zemin, the former Shanghai Municipal Mayor, and Chen Liangyu, the former Shanghai Municipal Mayor who was removed from his post and sentenced for diverting public funds for personal use) and Beijing (such as Chen Xitong, the former Beijing Municipal Mayor who has been sentenced and put into jail for his dereliction of duty and taking bribes from the foreign guests).

There is some debate about whether or not the downfall of Chen Xitong, the former mayor of Beijing, was due to the victory of Jiang Zemin's Shanghai faction over the Beijing faction. Moreover, it is not certain whether or not the removal of the previous Shanghai mayor, Chen Liangyu, was the result of a factional struggle between the political powers-that-be of Shanghai and the Communist League (*New Historical Record Magazine* 2012). Furthermore, the choice of Xi Jinping as the successor of Hu Jintao is the result of a power tussle between different

28 Empresses in the Palace

factions of the party. Xiang (2011: 45) argues that the head of China's "princeling" faction, Zeng Qinghong, used his finely honed political strategy and tactics to help Xi Jinping to ascend the chair, in a triumph by the "princeling" faction, which was under siege from both the Shanghai faction led by Jiang Zemin and the Communist League faction led by Hu Jintao. Bo (2014: 283) remarks that after Xi Jinping assumed the reins of power, he began to rein in the remnants of power held by Jiang Zemin's Shanghai faction within the Politburo. Similarly, the Communist League faction, led by the former president Hu Jintao, was entirely sidelined by the standing committee during the 18th national congress (EOFRM 2012: 56–57). Also, Xi Jinping promoted generals from his own faction in order to consolidate his control over the military forces and the People's Liberation Army (Bo 2014: 52).

This factional wrangling within the top echelon of Chinese politics has been a constant source of conjecture and rumor with the general public. Some political pundits believe that Xi Jinping's iron-fisted crackdown on the new Gang of Four did not arise from his goal of eradicating corruption from within government, but was instead a wish to expel and purge the political adversaries from other factions and to reshuffle and consolidate his own power base. Likewise, it is the strong view of many political commentators that Bo Xilai's conspiracy with Zhou Yongkang and Xu Caihou to threaten the power of Xi Jinping serves as the underlying reason for Xi's expulsion of him and his accomplices (Wang 2014: 235; Tiezzi 2015).[5]

Factional struggles are another similarity between the real occurrences within present-day China's officialdom and the plots in *Empresses*. The machinations in the imperial harem create a scenario where factional power brawls mirror the real-life political contests of contemporary China. In *Empresses*, the concubines of Emperor Yongzheng gravitated to their own factions in order to defend and to strengthen their own status and power. Zhen Huan forms a faction with Dame Shen, a close childhood friend of hers, and a person who is seen as being gentle, intelligent and generally aloof from politics and material pursuits. Zhen Huan's faction also includes Attendant An (the later Empress An), who is from a low-ranking official's family in a remote town in the south of China, and due to this low ranking, An is despised by other concubines and seldom gains attention and favor from Emperor Yongzheng. Noble Empress Hua is arrogant and willful, and she is allowed to be due mainly to the esteem attached to her older brother Nian Gengyao, a much admired statesman and general of the Yongzheng dynasty who assisted Yongzheng to put down many serious military rebellions. Hua is a conniving and extremely merciless woman who hungers to replace the Queen Empress and to this end kills anybody she deems as a barrier to her ambitions. Hua gathers around her a group of comparably vicious concubines and they are manipulated by her to persecute other concubines. However, the most devious and hypocritical woman in *Empresses* is the Queen Empress, who kills her own sister in order to take her position. The Queen Empress pretends to be agreeable and generous to all the concubines of the Emperor, as she is theoretically the head of the imperial seraglio, but, she manipulates her factional members to frame and trap the more favored concubines of the Emperor, such as Zhen Huan, out of fear that the young and beautiful concubines will replace her in the imperial harem.

The central plot of *Empresses* focuses on the strategic moves and the ramifications of actions by these three main factional groups. Whenever one of the group members monopolizes the attentions of the Emperor, she tries her best to defame and bully the concubines of other factions. At the same time, she guides and aids her group members to gain favor with the Emperor (which mostly happens within Zhen Huan's faction). Here, the storyline of *Empresses* has much in common with the shady nature of the current Chinese political powerbrokers. According to Zhang (2013: 310), within contemporary Chinese officialdom, 60 percent of cadre promotions rely on connections and nepotism. In the show, if a concubine receives favor from the Emperor, her factional and family members and servants gain political or material rewards. However, if a concubine falls out of favor or offends the Emperor and is given the royal "cold shoulder," the members of her faction, her family and her servants would certainly be implicated as well. This nepotism, and the priority given to connections between factional members, mirrors the reality within China's official circle at all levels. For instance, the loss of favor by Dame Shen and Zhen Huan's attempts to persuade the Emperor to pardon Shen almost lead to her own downfall. In another instance, Attendant An betrays Zhen Huan and Dame Shen and defects to the Queen Empress's faction as she believes that to be aligned with the head of the imperial seraglio would enhance her own status among the concubines, and the Queen Empress would speak well of her in front of the Emperor, which will ultimately bring to her the Emperor's attention and favor. In this sense, the concubines in each faction are bound together for good or ill. When members of her faction conspire to frame Zhen Huan for a crime, it is revealed that the Queen Empress is the mastermind so she also loses favor with the Emperor. Similarly, when Zhen Huan and her team start to take their revenge, they set traps for the members of the factions controlled by the Queen Empress and the Noble Empress Hua which will eventually implicate the two factional heads in actions against the Emperor.

There is also internal fighting within different factions. When the Queen Empress finds out that Empress Qi wants her own son to become crown prince, she expels her from the faction. In so doing, she convinces Empress Qi to poison a favored concubine of the Emperor and when the matter is eventually brought to light, the Queen Empress coaxes Empress Qi to commit suicide so as not to impede her son's future. In another instance of inner factional infighting, the Queen Empress gives Dame Qi, one of her faction co-conspirators, a musk necklace which is meant to prevent her from getting pregnant with the Emperor. Dame Qi also hates Dame An (Attendant An after being promoted), as she is a rival for the attention and favor of the Emperor, and so she gives Dame An a potion which leads to her losing her voice, as Dame An has a beautiful voice and her singing is the Emperor's delight. Consequently, Dame An loses not only her voice but also favor with the Emperor.

30 Empresses in the Palace

These ruthless and aggressive inner- and interfactional struggles amongst the concubines in *Empresses* remind the contemporary Chinese TV audience of the intrigues and corruption and nepotism within contemporary China. The politics of personal relations and connections that is paraded via factional brawls in *Empresses* reveals a time-honored but ugly trait of Chinese socio-political ecology, which not only fashions China's officialdom at all levels but also unleashes its impact on workplaces throughout Chinese society. The narratives and messages conveyed by a TV show set in an ancient imperial seraglio cause the contemporary Chinese viewer to reflect on the politics and social reality of modern-day China. The show's plots are familiar in essence for contemporary Chinese audiences as they may identify what they perceive as similarities with their own knowledge and experiences of graft and corruption in their own surroundings. Unfortunately for the average Chinese people, the reality is that they must still work within the present socio-cultural milieu and join the "likely to be successful" faction in their workplaces in order to be promoted quickly and gain favor from their supervisors and leaders.

Deceit and cruelty as tactics of survival

In *Empresses*, ethics is not a salient feature of the show and there are no clear boundaries between positive and negative traits of character. Those of seemingly good character could be as venomous and scheming as those considered as being the bad guys, and they are often more strategic and calculating when they ensnare their adversaries. During her early days in the imperial palace, Zhen Huan is an innocent and generous young woman without any strategies. However, the bitter and harsh experiences she and the other concubines have to endure lead her to become an "immoral," brutal and deceitful woman in order to achieve her ultimate and "moral" goals (which is to take revenge for her friends, lover and servants and to restore justice in the imperial harem). For example, Noble Empress Hua cruelly gives a newly selected concubine of the Emperor an exceedingly brutal physical punishment which leads to the concubine becoming paralyzed. When Dame Shen is considered by the Emperor to be an appropriate person to assist the Queen Empress with the management of domestic affairs at the imperial harem, Noble Empress Hua is filled with jealousy and tries to remove her. She instructs her servants to push Dame Shen into a pond in the imperial garden but Shen luckily survives the murder attempt, which drives Noble Empress Hua to construct another rancorous plan. She bribes an imperial doctor who falsely diagnoses that Dame Shen is pregnant, the news of which causes the Emperor to be extremely happy. However, when the non-pregnancy is revealed, the Emperor loses trust in Dame Shen and she is exiled to live in the "cold palace" where "not-favored" concubines gather to spend the rest of their lives. However, Noble Empress Hua is still not satisfied that Dame Shen's exile and loss of favor will neutralize her threat, so she decides to kill her. In so doing, she connives to get Dame Shen to drink from the same teacup previously used by a eunuch who died from a transferable disease. Dame Shen does in fact catch the disease, but she is fortunate and does not die from it.

In another scene, a concubine who has lost popularity with the Emperor and who envies Zhen Huan's exclusive favor from Yongzheng, poisons Zhen Huan in an attempt to turn her into an imbecile. Likewise, after Dame An betrays Zhen Huan and joins the Queen Empress' faction, she provides Zhen Huan with a medicinal paste, supposedly to remove her scar, but in which she puts musk, a traditional Chinese herbal, that causes Zhen Huan's abortion. Further, the Queen Empress manipulates Zhen Huan to wear the old clothes of her dead sister, who was the favorite concubine of Yongzheng, which then leads the Emperor to penalize Zhen Huan for her disrespect of the deceased concubine. In another sequence, in order to set a trap for Zhen Huan, Noble Empress Hua poisons one of the daughters of the Emperor and blames it on Zhen Huan. Also, in order to cause her to abort, Noble Empress Hua punishes Zhen Huan by making her kneel down under the midday sun for several hours when she is about to give birth. After Zhen Huan loses her unborn baby, she finally sees through the life-and-death nature of the fights between the concubines and is determined to take revenge and destroy her rivals one by one. Relying on her intelligence and careful planning, Zhen Huan assists Yongzheng to eradicate the Nian family, who have been resting on their laurels and are contemptuous of others. Moreover, Zhen Huan coerces and bribes Dame Cao, who is a member of the faction led by Noble Empress Hua, to expose Hua's many crimes that have been perpetrated on other concubines, and when this occurs it removes any sympathetic feelings towards her by the Emperor. Hua loses favor completely, her titles are removed, and she is banished to the "cold palace" where she takes her own life.

Zhen Huan gradually realizes that the imperial harem is as complicated and dangerous a place as the imperial court, and if she does not take the initiative to oust her enemies, she and her faction members will be persecuted and destroyed. She uses her guile to foment dissent among her rivals. Making use of the conflicts of interests among them, Zhen Huan successfully sets them at loggerheads and waits patiently as her enemies fight it out, and then finally catches them all. In her desperate struggle with her enemies, Zhen Huan acts more strategic and sadistic than her opponents. In one conflict with Dame An, Zhen Huan bribes Dame An's imperial maids and eunuchs to burn a kind of incense which is really an aphrodisiac that stimulates sexual passion, and then leads to violent sex between the pregnant Dame An and the Emperor: Dame An's unborn baby dies, the Emperor is disappointed, and Dame An loses favor. In her conflict with Noble Empress Hua, Zhen Huan does not hesitate to set fire in her own palace and burn herself in order to frame Noble Empress Hua. In her final contest with the Queen Empress, Zhen Huan sacrifices her unborn child in order to blame the Queen Empress for killing her baby. In her ultimate and deadly revenge on Emperor Yongzheng, when he is lying on his death-bed, Zhen Huan tells him the truth that her lover, Prince Guo, is the biological father of her son and daughter and that her objective in living with Yongzheng was only to take revenge. These revelations quicken the death of the Emperor.

In both of Schneider's (2012) and Kong's (2014) studies on contemporary Chinese TV drama series, they adopt a detailed visual discourse analysis,

32 Empresses in the Palace

including visual clues, signs and tactics which assist the viewers to understand how coated visual and acoustic symbols transmit emotional meaning and how TV dramas engage and enchant viewers. These two scholars' arguments are useful in understanding the character building in the case of *Empresses*, in particular the Zhen Huan role. In its depiction of Zhen Huan's conversion from an innocent and kind-hearted young girl to a calculated and cruel head concubine in the imperial seraglio, the show counts on visual ruses that stimulate the audience's sympathetic mood. Through the camera's repetitive close-up shots, Zhen Huan's stony face cannot hide her disappointment in the Emperor; the suffering from bullying by other empresses; the unbearable pain of losing her child, lover, best friends and servants; and her determination to seek revenge. The audience empathizes with Zhen Huan and understands the need and reasons behind her brutal and revengeful actions. In two particular close-up shots of Zhen Huan, one when she announces the death of her lover, Prince Guo, who died from drinking the poisonous wine bestowed by the Emperor, and the other when she declares the ultimate death of the Emperor, the camera reveals tears overflowing from Zhen Huan's dull and death-like eyes and rolling down her ghastly pale face, indicating her accumulated grievances. Zhen Huan's hatred is finally released, thereby eliciting an emotional appeal to the audiences. Another reaction shot of Zhen Huan is included in a group of short extracts from the show that are played accompanying the theme song at the beginning of each episode. Wearing the clothes of an Empress Dowager, who is the most powerful and honorable woman in the imperial harem, Zhen Huan's facial expression does not show a trace of pleasure, but instead is full of abhorrence and ferociousness. The implication is that the unspeakable, inhuman and heartrending traumas she experienced in the imperial seraglio have transformed her from a naïve and happy girl to a sophisticated, tactful and merciless middle-aged royal concubine.

The underhanded and ruthless life-and-death struggles between Zhen Huan and her rivals and the tragedy-turned-victory life trajectory of Zhen Huan not only generated exceptionally high audience ratings for the TV show but also engendered concern and invited critique from media officials. In September 2013, the *People's Daily* (mouthpiece of the CCP), published an article accusing *Empresses* of promoting incorrect views on life by suggesting that a good person is always defeated by a bad person, and only if the good person becomes the "bad" person (by adopting the bad person's tricks and despicable means or becoming even more sneaky and devious than the bad person) will the "good" person finally win (Tao 2013). These observations about *Empresses* are similar to what Bai (2015: 76) has argued about the anti-corruption TV dramas that "underwent a major transformation under commercial pressures from anti-corruption melodramas to cynical tales." Bai also points out that in cynical tales "the cunning and the manipulative are rewarded, and the dumb and the honest only have themselves to blame for their bad luck," and "the 'all-powerful evil force' indicates a moral order upside down, in which there is not a single hero who can represent the unyielding moral force."

Empresses in the Palace   33

In China, propaganda officials use the commentaries in newspaper editorials and the reviews of intellectuals published in the print media, in particular the state media outlets, to assess whether a program is perceived as socially and politically suitable (Schneider 2012: 149). When assessed, *Empresses* is considered unsatisfactory in that it disseminates negative worldviews rather than positive ones that would help to promote people's mental health and the development of the entire society and to correctly guide public opinion, which is the key criterion used in China to gauge a cultural and media work's appropriateness for broadcast (Brady 2008: 68; Schneider 2012: 181). The *People's Daily* article discussed above also points out that the most necessary standards for judging historical cultural work is not that it has truthfully restored the historical facts and figures, but whether it has established a correct world outlook for the audience to follow. Likewise, these criteria apply to other media and cultural texts that are released in the mainland region. Schneider (2012: 187) observes that based on the rationale that the CCP censors deploy, the Taiwanese TV drama *Meteor Garden* (*Liuxing Huayuan*, 2002) propagates consumption and hedonism among teenage viewers and causes them to neglect their schooling. The show, therefore, was eventually banned from being broadcast on the mainland. Similarly, the plot and character design of *Empresses* foreground the inevitability of illegal tussles and the desperate pursuit of one's goals (Tao 2013) and allude to the savage competition within Chinese officialdom and workplaces. The harmful worldviews conveyed by *Empresses* may thus lead to the adoption of improper ideas about values and strategies for life by the audience, as the astute contemporary audience may simply correlate the ancient stories and situation with the present-day circumstances and reality. Therefore, the viewers may absorb practical tips and tactics from the characters of *Empresses* regarding how to succeed in their personal struggles with other people, especially in the workplace. In other words, they may learn how to manipulate other people and even abuse or persecute them when it is required to serve one's ultimate purpose. Thus *Empresses* was officially criticized – however, it was not banned.

Unlike its Korean counterpart, *Jewel in the Palace* (*Dachangjin*, 2003), which depicts the career, life trajectory and accomplishments of a diligent and intelligent woman in the Korean imperial palace, *Empresses* demonstrates the unethical strategies used to gain success in a Chinese political and social backdrop. The plots and characters of *Empresses* mirror some characteristics of present Chinese society, where some people are so desperate for their own advantage and goals that they disregard the ethical constraints and the negative social effects caused by their actions. *Empresses* thus reveals the callous nature of present-day Chinese society and unfortunately represents much of Chinese society and its people, in particular many of those working in government and business who will use whatever method or manner they can to obtain power and wealth.

Imperial concubines vs contemporary females

When the ancient and contemporary situations of Chinese women are contrasted and compared, *Empresses* provides a unique feminist perspective. In *Empresses*

34 Empresses in the Palace

the Emperor's many concubines compete ferociously for his favor. The likes and dislikes of the concubines by the Emperor become the lifeblood of their own survival, as well as that of their families; they are totally dependent on a man's favors and decisions. In contemporary China the custom where some women rely on men for living and material enjoyment has been revived. It is oft reported that wealthy married businessmen and government officials continue to employ "concubines."[6] Many CCP officials continue to this day to be involved in the trade of power and sex. The women involved are usually promoted following their affairs with the leaders in their organizations or with other powerful high-ranking government officials. It is also widely known that the number of women volunteering their services in exchange for work advancements and other prospects is increasing. Some of these women hold the view that in a male-dominated society a clever woman has to make use of the value that men place on feminine attributes (Jeffreys 2006: 173).

Compared with those previously produced dynasty dramas in which the Emperors are always busy with the affairs of state, in *Empresses*, Emperor Yongzheng is rarely seen engaging in state affairs – instead, he is seen flirting and playing with his concubines most of the time. All the concubines in the show are played by beautiful actresses, which almost gives it a beauty contest feel. The concubines utilize their beauty and sexuality to attract and compete for the Emperor's attention and favor, thus downgrading females as only male playthings. This strikes a familiar chord with some of the contemporary Chinese "gold-diggers" who believe that womanly charms can secure them material enjoyments and comfortable lifestyles. In *Empresses*, most of the concubines are women who savor seduction and unscrupulously pursue their goals. This disparaging portrayal of female figures inserts a feminist perspective into the reading of the show. These charming, seductive and pragmatic concubines in *Empresses* shed light on contemporary "gold-diggers," especially on those who serve as concubines to government officials and the business elites. As noted by scholars, the "incorruptible" male government officials are inevitably corrupted when they encounter sex-related bribery (Zhao 2001 cited in Jeffreys 2006: 174). This view confirms the old-fashioned and disparaging belief that female sexuality is destructive.

In the case of Zhou Yongkang, it is widely reported that he has numerous concubines, some of whom are famous hosts of the China Central Television Station (CCTV) (IFENG.com 2015). In recent years, it has been revealed that many well-known Chinese TV presenters and entertainers are, or were, concubines or mistresses of high-ranking corrupt officials. There is even a joke going around that the CCTV has become the imperial harem of *Zhongnanhai*, the central headquarters for the CCP and the State Council of the PRC.[7]

There are also recent news reports about female city mayors and Party chiefs who got their jobs by sexually bribing their male leaders (Wenxuecity 2015b). This kind of corrupt action by Chinese female officials indicates that the current Chinese political arena is still dominated by a male chauvinism which obstructs women's career pathways.

Women's subordination and subjugation to the male-dominated political field rejects a culture of female and male equality, which designates a negative turn in the development of Chinese women and their career struggles and social status. Although the concubine culture of present-day China does not parallel the life-and-death struggles among the imperial concubines depicted in *Empresses*, it demonstrates a regression in terms of establishing a society where men and women benefit from equivalent developmental prospects. In *Empresses*, female characters are created to be aggressive, fierce and deceitful, and when correlated with today's situation, this portrayal taints and damages the image of women and places them in an inferior and secondary human group. In summary, the female characters in *Empresses* shed a negative light on females and cater to male chauvinism.

Conclusion

Since the middle of the 1990s, dynasty dramas have been televisual cultural hits in China. A series of dynasty drama serials focusing on the depiction of the historical achievements of the Qing Dynasty emperors such as Kangxi, Yongzheng and Qianlong enjoy unparalleled popularity. The detailed representation of the infighting at court and the political tactics and purges employed by the emperors and their ministers generates lots of interest among the viewers. Many viewers discern a pedagogical message with practical hints and tips which emanate from the palace wrangling of early times but which are still highly adaptable to the modern Chinese officialdom and workplace. Thus, these "user guides to official circles and career fields," dressed as dynasty dramas, attract a considerable male audience, especially middle-aged males who were previously disinterested in this type of entertainment. However, the continual exposition of the darker side of Chinese bureaucracy in these dynasty dramas, even fixing their portrayal on the remote historical events and figures, has a potential to render a negative impact on the contemporary Chinese audience. Thus, together with the overriding de-politicization trend within the entertainment circle of contemporary China, the descriptive concentration of dynasty dramas has shifted from court brawls among the government officials to power struggles among the concubines of the Emperor's imperial harem, or to the presentation of romantic, poignant and emotional love stories of princes and princesses.

In *Empresses*, the shift of focus from the political realm to the power tussles in the domestic field in the imperial harem is a de-politicizing path undertaken by the dynasty dramas in an overt attempt to reduce its relevance to the socio-political reality of present-day China. However, a close reading of the plots and characters of *Empresses* undertaken here has shown that this drama only superficially distances itself from those political themes and power intrigues, and it creates a coded reading about the current Chinese political sphere and the struggles taking place within it. In doing so, the show implies the intense and violent power wrangles among different political factions and hints at those underhanded tactics and sly and rancorous means employed by politicians and government officials, which strikes a familiar chord with the Chinese audience regarding similar maneuvers and hidden rules they encounter and endure on a daily basis at work. *Empresses* also engages with official propaganda in terms of creating the image of

36 Empresses in the Palace

a determined, astute and resourceful leader who has the confidence to achieve the seemingly unachievable, and eventually to restore justice to the entire society. In this way, *Empresses* uses Zhen Huan's successful eradication of her adversaries in the imperial seraglio to suggest a link to, and a likeness of, President Xi Jinping's committed and adventurous crackdown on the enormous and obstinate corrupt forces within the CCP officialdom. Apart from these, *Empresses* sheds light on the life situation and career obstacles faced by contemporary Chinese women, which I argue is retrogressing, even in comparison with the Mao era of radical socialist revolution. In short, *Empresses* cannot be simply read as a "domestic" drama depicting the life of and conflicts between the Emperor's concubines within the imperial harem; it should instead be taken seriously as a highly politically coded dynasty drama text which indicates a new fashion in the development of the historically themed TV shows in contemporary China.

Notes

1 The American version of *Empresses* is an abridged version of the original TV drama, which compressed the original TV serial into six 90-minute episodes.
2 The depiction of the negative facets of officialdom and the continual exposition of the questionable and underhanded maneuvering within it has invited criticism from the official censor. In response to the scrutiny and judgments of the censor, the current trend in historical dramas has shifted from concentrating on the struggles at the top strata of power to the presentation of romantic and poignant love stories, such as found in the 2002 TV drama hit *Princess Huanzhu* (*Huanzhugege*). In 2011, historical TV dramas such as *Palace* (*Gong*) and *Startling Step-by-Step* (*Bubujingxin*) made a ground-breaking appearance, obtaining extensive applause and achieving high audience ratings. The travelling–back-in-time fantasies, as a TV drama subgenre, feature distinctive scenarios which relate to going back to more romantic or nostalgic times and revolve around emotional love stories rather than intriguing and cruel political brawls.
3 Released to coincide with the sixtieth anniversary of the founding of the People's Republic of China, *Founding of a Republic* (dir Han & Huang 2009) was a huge box-office success and cultural hit in mainland China in 2009. In contrast to previous official propaganda films, from both the socialist and post-socialist periods, which were both times of immense transformation in Chinese society, *Founding* has a more commercial flavor, as demonstrated by its more nuanced approaches to the CCP's policies and ideology.
4 This is the most widely held view of the Cultural Revolution in China; however, it is not the only understanding. Much of the historical scholarship on this period has been aimed at providing different interpretations of the intentions of the "Gang of Four."
5 The removal and punishment of Zhou Yongkang and Xu Caihou was partly because of their close association with Bo Xilai, a recently sentenced "princeling" who has been involved in the murder of a British businessman in China. On the surface, Bo's dismissal was the upshot of his clash with one of his underlings, Wang Lijun (the former deputy mayor of Chongqing). Wang felt his safety was threatened by Bo Xilai, so he fled to the American embassy in Chongqing, Sichuan province, to seek political asylum, which eventually led to his confession that he worked with Bo and his wife in the murder of the British businessman and other illegal practices. However, many political commentators argue that Bo's obsession of becoming the supreme leader of China, and his conspiracy with Zhou Yongkang and Xu Caihou to usurp power from Xi Jinping, was the decisive reason for Xi's eradication of them. Bo had many political successes

in his quest to climb the political ladder. He adopted Mao's egalitarian road and revived the revolutionary traditions and passions of the Mao era in Chongqing. The Chongqing Model of Socialism was promoted by Bo during his rule in Chongqing as an attempt to reestablish the revolutionary customs popularized in Mao's China, such as singing the classic Red songs and cracking down on rich business entrepreneurs. Bo's Chongqing Model differs in essence from the political concept that is upheld by the Communist League faction, which arguably supports the rule of law and the establishment of a civil society, and was tried in Guangdong province and led by Wang Yang, a member of the Communist League faction (EOFRM 2011: 263–265).

6 Although those powerful men's mistresses in present-day China are subject to many constraints and pressures that did not exist in premodern China, they still share many characteristics with ancient concubines, such as their reliance on their youthfulness and beauty to gain men's favor and therefore to gain wealth and status. However, this parallel between premodern and contemporary China regarding the concubine/mistress phenomenon to some extent risks oversimplifying the complexities of modernity, and therefore should be understood in this context.

7 The term *Zhongnanhai* is closely related with the central government and senior CCP executives. It is often used as a metonym for the Chinese leadership at large in the same sense that the term "White House" often refers to the president of the United States and his associates.

References

Ai, Jiabing. 2011. *Guanerdai* [Second Official Generation]. New York: Mirror Books.

Baidu Encyclopedia. 2015. "American Version of *Empresses* Arrives on the TV Show Channel Netflix," available at: http://baike.baidu.com/subview/979532/13590687.htm (accessed 25 March 2015).

Bai, Ruoyun. 2015. "'Clean Up the Screen:' Regulating Television Entertainment in the 2000s," in *Chinese Television in the Twenty-First Century: Entertaining the Nation*, Ruoyun Bai and Geng Song (eds.). London and New York: Routledge, pp. 69–86.

Bai, Ruoyun and Song, Geng. 2015. "Introduction," in *Chinese Television in the Twenty-first Century: Entertaining the Nation*, Ruoyun Bai and Geng Song (eds.). London and New York: Routledge, pp. 1–14.

Bo, Gong. 2014. *Xi Li Quandou Dajiemi* [Exposing the Secrets of the Power Struggles between Xi Jinping and Li Keqiang]. Hong Kong: Ludi Publishing House.

Brady, Anne-Marie. 2008. *Marketing Dictatorship – Propaganda and Thought Work in Contemporary China*. Lanham and Plymouth: Rowman & Littlefield.

EOFRM [Editorial Office of the Foreign Reference Magazine]. 2011. *Caozong Shibada* [Manipulating the 18th National Congress of Chinese Communist Party]. New York: Foreign Reference Magazine Press.

EOFRM. [Editorial Office of the Foreign Reference Magazine]. 2012. *Shibada de Mimi* [Secrets of the 18th National Congress of the Chinese Communist Party]. New York: Foreign Reference Magazine Press.

French Radio International. 2015. "Xi Jinping Warns the Leader of the Princelings Faction – Zeng Qinghong," broadcast 8 February, available at: http://cn.rfi.fr/中国/20150208-习近平警告朋党之王曾庆红/.

Han, Sanping and Huang, Jianxin. 2009. *Jianguodaye* [Founding of a Republic]. Beijing: China Film Group Corporation.

IFENG.com. 2014. "Ye Yingchun he Shen Bing juanru Zhou Yongkang an, zhengjieshou diaocha" [Ye Yingchun and Shen Bing Are Involved in the Zhou Yongkang Case and

38 Empresses in the Palace

Both of Them Are Being Investigated], posted 7 August, available at: http://news.ifeng.com/a/20140807/41487861_0.shtml (accessed 25 March 2015).

Jeffreys, Elaine. 2006. "Debating the Legal Regulation of Sex-Related Bribery and Corruption in the People's Republic of China," in *Sex and Sexuality in China*, Elaine Jeffreys (ed.). New York: Routledge, pp. 159–178.

Kong, Shuyu. 2014. *Popular Media, Social Emotion and Public Discourse in Contemporary China*. Hoboken, NJ: Taylor and Francis.

Lu, H. Sheldon. 2007. *Chinese Modernity and Global Biopolitics: Studies in Literature and Visual Culture*. Honolulu: University of Hawaii Press.

Meng, Ping. 2010. *Junzhong Taizidang* [The "Princeling" Faction in the Army]. Hong Kong: Xiafeier International Publishing House.

New Century Magazine. 2013. *Zhonggong Taisundang* [The "Grandsons of the Emperor" Faction of the Chinese Communist Party]. Hong Kong and Taiwan: Editorial Office of the New Century Magazine Press.

New Historical Record Magazine. 2012. *Zhengzhiju Cansha: Cong Yang Baibing dao Bo Xilai* [Slaughter in the Politburo: From Yang Baibing to Bo Xilai]. New York: Haye Publishing House.

Qian, Kun. 2015. "Tianxia Revisited: Family and Empire on the Television Screen," in *Chinese Television in the Twenty-First Century Entertaining the Nation*, Ruoyun Bai and Geng Song (eds.). London and New York: Routledge, pp. 175–191.

Schneider, Florian. 2012. *Visual Political Communication in Popular Chinese TV Series*. Leiden and Boston: Brill.

Tao, Dongfeng. 2013. "Renmin ribao kanwen duibi Zhenhuanzhuan, dachangjin jiazhiguan" [A Comparison between the Values of *Empresses in the Palace* and *Jewel in the Palace*]. *People's Daily Online*, 19 September, available at: http://culture.people.com.cn/GB/n/2013/0919/c1013-22969994.html (accessed 25 March 2015).

Tiezzi, Shannon. 2015. "Zhou Yongkang's Greatest Crime." *The Diplomat Magazine*, 21 April, reposted on Wenxuecity 28 April 2015, available at: www.wenxuecity.com/news/2015/04/28/4225327.html (accessed 29 April 2015).

Wang, Chunshan. 2014. *Zhou Yongkang Jituan* [The Zhou Yongkang Group]. Hong Kong: Hong Kong University of Finance and Economics.

Wenxuecity. 2015a. "Zalan zhongguo guanchang, Xi Jinping zai jinxing yichang maoxian-haodu" [Smashing Chinese Officialdom, Xi Jinping Is Taking a Big Risk], reposted 13 March 2015, available at: www.wenxuecity.com/news/2015/03/13/4102936.html (accessed 20 March 2015).

Wenxuecity. 2015b. "Yu Zhou Yongkang Liu Han youran, Sichuan meinu shuji bei pibu" [A Beautiful Party Chief of Sichuan Province Was Arrested for Her Relationship with Zhou Yongkang and Liu Han], reposted 28 April 2015, available at: www.wenxuecity.com/news/2015/04/28/4225361.html (accessed 28 April 2015).

Xiang, Jiangyu. 2011. *Xi Jinping Bandi* [The Key Cadres of the Xi Jinping Administration]. New York: Mirror Books.

Zhang, Youping. 2013. *Zhongguo Zhengzhi Dazhan* [Big Fights within China's Political Circle]. New York: Haye Publishing House.

Zhao, Chengliang. 2001. "Tanguan nanguo nurenguan" [Corrupt Officials Find It Difficult to Go Past Women]. *Fazhan daobao*, 23 January.

Zhao, Yuezhi. 1998. *Media, Market, and Democracy in China: Between the Party Line and the Bottom Line*. Urbana and Chicago: University of Illinois Press.

Zheng, Changliu. 2014. *Xi Wang Shoushi Jiang Hu Jiubu* [Xi Jinping and Wang Qishan Crackdown on the Former Underlings of Jiang Zemin and Hu Jintao]. New York: Haye Publishing House.

Zhenhuanzhuang [*Empresses in the Palace*]. 2011. TV serial, Beijing TV Art Center, Beijing, broadcast on Anhui and Dongfang satellite TV in 2012.

Zhu, Ying. 2008. *TV in Post-Reform China: Serial Dramas, Confucian Leadership and the Global TV Market*. London and New York: Routledge.

2 *Angel Heart*

Harmonizing contemporary
Chinese society through
exemplary model doctors

Introduction

Angel Heart (*Xinshu*, 2012), the popular TV serial under examination in this chapter, is one of the major medical dramas produced in mainland China. The show's narrative focuses on hospital life and the disputes between health providers and patients, events that are common occurrences in contemporary China. By creating characters that are exemplary doctors, *Angel Heart* attempts to assuage the antithetical sentiments between medical staff and patients. In line with the government's endorsement to build a harmonious and an egalitarian society (which indicates an observable left turn in politics), *Angel Heart* uses the relationship between doctors and patients as a metaphor to mirror the overall social relationship between China's "haves" and "have-nots." In its efforts to mitigate the deteriorating antagonism between these two groups caused by the expanding gap between their incomes and social status, the show acts as a mediator between the government and its citizens. The principal goal of *Angel Heart* is to provide the Chinese people with the understanding that the government aims to provide reliable social welfare. Apart from the public focus on conflicts between health providers and patients, the show also extends its purview to other social debates and concerns. In doing so, *Angel Heart* turns the hospital's micro society into a metaphor for the macro society of today's China.

Angel Heart made its debut in 2012 and is a thirty-six-episode TV drama serial adapted from the Singapore-based, Chinese female writer Liuliu's novel of the same title. Liuliu's books are about the lives of ordinary urban Chinese people and are famous for their irony and their outspoken and insightful depictions of sensitive social and cultural topics which are intertwined with romantic relations. A number of Liuliu's books have been adapted into TV drama serials and they are all popular and engage with topical social issues. Her 2005 novel *Double Sided Adhesive Tape* (*Shuangmianjiao*), which was adapted into a same-titled TV show in 2007, is regarded as a classic textbook of marriage and was the catalyst for intense discussion on family ethics on the Internet. The show highlights the complicated and troublesome in-law relationships in a single-child family. *Narrow*

Dwelling (*Woju* 2009) is another TV play that has been adapted from Liuliu's 2007 book with the same title, which candidly demonstrates the "house slave" social stigma confronting many contemporary young Chinese working couples and reflects the moral deterioration of society in regard to "the second wife phenomenon" as it relates specifically to government officials.

The storyline of *Angel Heart* revolves largely around hospital life and specifically around the worsening relations between patients and medical workers. Rather than a one-sided exposition of the negative emotions of the patients, the show also paints the misunderstood, frustrated and "wronged" doctors as it reveals their stressful, busy and overly burdened daily jobs. Besides its particular concentration on hospital life, *Angel Heart* also deals with the concerns and worries of the Chinese people as it engages with topical social problems such as the left-over women social stigma, unwritten workplace rules and the practical, materialistic and hedonist values of young Chinese women. These topics respond to official discourse that requires the on-screen presentation to be "close to the people," or, in other words, to reflect the daily social encounters and economic experiences of viewers (Schneider 2012: 196).

In present-day China, for many less privileged Chinese people, inadequate and overly expensive medical services have become one of their biggest anxieties, and many patients sometimes use their entire savings on medical expenses. Unreasonably high healthcare expenses are one of the key sources of the recurrent disputes between hospitals and patients. In recent years, more patients have resorted to violence as they become frustrated and disillusioned with the medical services they are receiving and the excessive medication fees incurred. According to a CCTV (China Central Television) news report, a joint statement on hospital security came only after nearly 20,000 medical disputes had occurred between hospitals and patients. This accumulated antagonism between health providers and patients has emerged and gradually intensified since the Opening Up reforms during which the state-run work units and enterprises became insolvent or were privatized. Due to this overall trend of reform and commercialization, the healthcare system, which was originally an undertaking meant to be of benefit to the public, has inevitably been affected and has slowly been transformed into a profit-seeking entity. As a result, direct financial input from the government into hospitals has been reducing as marketization has been steadily implemented. This inclusive marketization, together with the top-down state-led healthcare reform that was initiated in 1985 (and has so far proved unsuccessful), has led to the situation where government grants to hospitals have dropped to a historically low level and constitutes only 10 percent of the overall operating expenses of the hospitals. Obviously, less input from the government impels the hospitals to generate their own income to cover the remaining 90 percent of operational costs and further to make profit in order to survive in the competitive marketplace. This need for increased income then leads to the need to increase medical expenses, which then leads to the escalation of conflicts between hospitals and patients (*Vision China Times* 2015). Public medical care services in China's cities cover part of the medication and pharmacy cost; however, the patients

42 Angel Heart

are still required to pay a significant "gap" amount on self-funded treatments and medicines, which serve as an important source to engender more income for the hospital. The cost of these self-funded medical services is very flexible and depends on the doctors' plan for medical treatment and prescription medicines. Therefore, in order to create more income for hospitals and for themselves ('grey income'), doctors employ different tactics to increase the medical expenses of the patients, a practice which is indicative of widely circulating hidden rules in the medical domain.

For example, many doctors have close connections with medical representatives or pharmaceutical companies and accept commissions from them in exchange for recommending and prescribing their products (usually self-funded medicines) for the patients, normally at extra expense to the patients (*Xinhua Net* 2005). According to one salesman from a pharmaceutical company, in order to get a hospital to purchase their products, they have to build up connections, and actually bribe various staff members in the hospital, including those who sit atop managerial ladders, such as the directors of the hospital and heads of different hospital departments, as well as other employees such as pharmacists, accountants, statisticians and doctors. Finally, this gift money paid by the pharmaceutical company will be amortized into the costs of the drugs and the price increases will be passed on by the firm to the patients (*Vision China Times* 2015). Apart from taking gift money from the pharmaceutical companies, many doctors, surgeons and anaesthetists require gift money from patients for surgical operations, especially the larger operations such as cancer treatment and heart and brain procedures (*People's Daily Online* 2014). Moreover, some high-status doctors only attend or do operations for patients with whom they have various "connections." So, in order to receive better medical treatment, patients often have to find any relatives or friends who work in the hospital and use them as their "connection." This type of corruption has become so common that patients often see it as a "normal" practice, for which they have no other choices and so must accept and endure what they can afford.

Further, in order to make sufficient profit to cover its increasing costs due to government funding cutbacks, doctors' workloads have increased sharply. Normally, each doctor has to attend an average of more than 100 patients on a daily basis. This requirement is upheld more particularly in the big hospitals in the first-tier cities such as Beijing and Shanghai, where many patients travel from second-tier and third-tier cities, as they believe that it is there that they will find the best doctors and medical equipment. In the case of doctors, they are under great stress to cope with the excess workload assigned to them because of this new commercial setup. Subsequently, every patient is allocated only a three- to five-minute consultation with the doctors. This unrealistic consultation time creates problems for both patients and doctors. On one hand, the patients are dissatisfied with the quick examination and conclusion and what they see as the impatient attitude of the doctors, while on the other hand the doctors are exhausted by the extraordinary workload placed on them, and of course poor diagnoses and advice ensue.

Creating exemplary-type doctors as a response to the New Left turn

The discussion above has briefly mapped out the main reasons that contribute to the worsening and hostile relationship between healthcare providers and patients in present-day China, and which then often leads to many violent incidents in hospitals. Under these dwindling conditions in healthcare in China, *Angel Heart* emerges as a pioneering TV drama work that reflects the adverse relationship between healthcare providers and patients. This TV show caters to the appeal of the official discourse in its attempt to reset or re-align the Chinese people's faith in their caregivers through establishing the doctor characters as exemplary citizens who bear the weight of responsibility for the life of the patients and for the fate of the nation alike. Moreover, through these model doctor characters who wholeheartedly serve the people, the drama restates and confirms the Chinese Communist Party (CCP) government's intentions and efforts to provide its citizens with a trustworthy healthcare service, in particular, and an effective public welfare system, in general.

The more than three decades of the Opening Up reforms led China into unprecedented capitalist market experiments, which not only commercialized a considerable amount of the previously state-owned and -run work units and public welfare enterprises such as hospitals and universities, but also engendered unequal and hierarchical social stratifications and class diversity. Consequently, social malaise, injustice and unrest have emerged, such as the widening gap between China's nouveau riche and the poor, the rampant corruption within the business and official circles and the escalating number of social violence and upheaval incidents. Therefore, "maintaining stability" has become an overriding preoccupation of the central regime and every level of the Chinese government. Starting from the rule of the Hu Jintao administration and continuing into the rein of the current Xi Jinping government, "building a harmonious society" and "realizing the Chinese Dream" have become the official propaganda slogans which sustain and endorse the ruling legitimacy and authority of the CCP Party. These governance ideas of the CCP, in particular the "building a harmonious society" concept, adopt some of the political viewpoints of the New Left intellectual school and criticize the negative social repercussions of neoliberal developments (Zhao 2008), uphold egalitarian ideals of socialism and demand social equality and justice across the entire society. One such ideal is to bridge the gap between China's haves and have-nots. Arguably, the haves not only refers to those political and business elites who through their concerted efforts realized their pursuit of quick and immense profit, but also notes a white-collar middle-class professional social stratum including doctors and lawyers, which similarly belong to the wealthy social ranks in the current Chinese society. This well-off professional social echelon is formed during the procedure of specialization and division of labor and rearranging China's social strata, and it shapes "new forms of social inclusion and exclusion" and spawns speedy courses of social stratification and class polarization (Zhao 2008) during China's post-socialist fast-tracked market reforms.

44 Angel Heart

Observably, a widening income gap between China's haves and the have-nots working-class people underwrites the formation of an uneven and prejudiced society. According to Li (2005 cited in Zhao 2008: 19), 75.8 percent of China's urban population feel conflicted due to the gap between the rich and the poor. Not only is there reciprocal enmity between the rich and the poor, but a substantial number of those who self-identify as being at the top of the social structure are reluctant to shoulder the obligation of aiding the poor (Li 2005 cited in Zhao 2008: 19). In order to counter this social disparity, the New Left urges political reforms which redirect government focus to the majority of its population and the underprivileged social groups and affirm their urgent needs, especially in public health and education (Zhu 2008: 25–26), where the funding is insufficient and unfairly distributed and is a causal factor increasing political contestation (Zhao 2008: 23). According to the New Left, the steadfast determination to reform, pursued at the expense of a social safety net, creates an overall apathy towards social welfare, social inequity, and the demolition of the public healthcare and education systems (Zhu 2008: 25–26). Based on the ideas of Wang Hui, a leading intellectual of the New Left school, political pressure by the large social force of workers and peasant-farmers is the only possible way to push the state to consider changes to its policy. It appears that democracy in China is more a matter of being a requirement for equity for the socially and economically disadvantaged groups such as workers and peasants, rather than for developing political autonomy for the middle class or generating legal and constitutional rights for a minority already significantly enabled by market transformations (Wang 2003 cited in Zhu 2008: 26). Since the beginning of the 2000s, the Chinese Communist leadership, eager to avoid social instability and keen to confirm its influence and validity, is more willing to adopt the New Left's political suggestion of rebuilding a welfare state that balances the social and economic capacity and well-being between China's haves and have-nots (Zhu 2008: 27).

Hospitals, where the standard and quality of the welfare system in China is symbolically reflected, are the focus of the narrative in *Angel Heart*, which highlights the most urgent agenda of the CCP government and the most keenly discussed social concern among the public. In the show, the middle-class doctors, who earn good salaries and enjoy a superior social status, are representatives of the "haves" group, and the ordinary patients serve as an allegory of the disadvantaged social cohort such as workers and peasants who are the "have-nots." Moreover, the belligerence between these two groups symbolizes the disharmony in much of contemporary Chinese society. Serving as a micro version of the Chinese government during the Opening Up reform, where it abandoned many of its missions and promises of building a socialist welfare state, the hospitals have had to undergo a marketizing transformation, which leads to a reduction of quality in their services and negligence of the patient's well-being. Under the impact of this paramount commercialization, doctors also have become less altruistic and prioritize their own income over the needs of their patients. Taking the gift-money phenomenon as a stereotypical example, doctors in China today free themselves from the constraints of their professional regulations and ethics, and their behavior is more akin to that of the corrupt officials who take bribes in exchange for doing favors for others. In this sense, the connections between doctors and their patients are more utilitarian and less concerned with the ethical ideals that were promoted during the Mao era of socialist China. Going against this apparent social reality, the corrupt conduct by doctors in real life is not disclosed in *Angel Heart*. On the contrary, the fictional doctors created in the show are of sublime virtue, and the hospital is well run according to regulations. Noticeably, *Angel Heart* attempts to repair and harmonize the relationship between medical staff and their patients and give the image of medical workers a positive revamp through foregrounding the noble persona of its doctor and nurse characters. Further, the ambitious goal of the show is to re-envisage the traditions of Maoist China, which is to create a welfare state through its reconfiguration of the public function of healthcare providers.

In Maoist China, doctors were promoted as exemplary citizens who not only saved lives and helped the sick but also had many noble merits such as their complete and selfless devotion and sacrifice to their career and country. Chairman Mao praised the Canadian doctor Henry Bethune for his contribution to the Chinese War of Resistance against Japan, where he sacrificed his life. Since then, Dr. Bethune has been regarded as the model of an ideal doctor, similar to the ideals of the exemplary soldier image of Lei Feng, who was admired and respected by millions of Chinese people in the socialist revolutionary period. As Reed (1995) pointed out two decades ago, although the esteem for the socialist role model Lei Feng may fade as China becomes gradually capitalistic, the enlistment of role models as an educational device will not. The idea that people emulate behaviors originated from the traditional Confucian idea that the individual emulates the actions of others, and therefore the sage has to set a positive example for others to follow (Schneider 2012: 183), is still a core tenet in China's state propaganda discourse. Today, the extravagances of "commodity socialism" call for new role models who maintain certain values like altruism that are rooted in communist thought.

For instance, in *Angel Heart*, despite the numerous misunderstandings and conflicts between doctors and their patients, the majority of doctors are fashioned as characters that are thoughtful, upright and generous and endure humiliation in order to cure their patients. They are once again constructed as model citizens of contemporary China who help the poor and those in difficult situations, and who privilege the patients' benefits over their own. They do not take any bribes and have a strong sense of responsibility. In their work, they empathize with their patients and take their exertions as their own. Without showing any condescending attitude, they try their best to save life and to help those in need, which are actions that win veneration and approval from their patients. One of the distinctive characteristics of the show is its rich employment of visual and acoustic arrangements in its portrayal of the considerate and devoted medical workers. In particular, in its portrayal of the doctors' and nurses' devotion and sympathy to those impoverished patients with mortal illnesses, the show enlists rich and poignant visual and acoustic elements, which manufacture dramatic climaxes and emotional release.

46   Angel Heart

For example, when addressing the sequence where a head nurse is informed that one of her patients, who is a poor peasant boy, has finally died, mawkish music begins, the camera employs a close-up shot and dwells on her pale face as tears roll down; however, she cries silently without making any weeping sound, which further enhances the sad atmosphere of the unfolding plot. The camera cuts to flashbacks of conversations between the nurse and the boy and then back again to the gloomy face of the nurse, which foregrounds the compassion and affection of the nurse for her patients. Thus, the sequence portrays the contemporary Chinese medical workers as compassionate and thoughtful people. In the following sequence, where the doctors and nurses console the father of the peasant boy, one of them kneels down in front of the man and sincerely questions in a low and gentle voice if he has any requirements or if he needs further help from the hospital, while others, all standing and weeping, listen to their conversation with sympathetic facial expressions. The close-up shots place the peasant father physically in a position above the kneeling doctor, which reverses the established impression most Chinese people have regarding the social status of the disadvantaged and privileged social groups represented by the peasant and the doctor respectively. The close and warm relation between the medical workers and patients conveyed by this sequence is overtly presented in a visual form.

In many similar sequences from the show, despite being often misunderstood and "maltreated" by their patients, the medical workers try hard to be considerate and supportive. The show combines the use of camera work, acting and conversation to underline the devotion and sacrifices of the medical workers made for their patients. The caring attitude, understanding and respect for patients by the doctors and nurses is often displayed through close-up shots depicting their tolerant explanations and interactions (through dialogue and gestures) with their patients. In doing so, the expanding gap between the emerging middle-class and the nouveau riche social echelons (represented by doctors) and the marginalized and underprivileged workers and peasant social class (represented by patients) is seen to be (albeit virtually and superficially) closing and weakening. In the show, the earnest and unequivocal services provided by China's haves to China's have-nots counter the discriminating and imbalanced social division caused by the unscrupulous economic conversion.

The majority of doctors created in *Angel Heart* have a gentle and compassionate disposition and are highly qualified for their positions, but they do not equate to the many avaricious and corrupt doctors in real life. The doctors in the TV drama place benevolence above professional skills, which clearly indicates that conscientiousness and integrity are the first requirements of a good doctor. Besides being caring and competent doctors, the characters in *Angel Heart* have a spirit of dedication, which sits comfortably with the expectations of official ideology. In many scenes, the male lead protagonist often says that the hospital is a place where faith, hope and love coexist. These lofty words are reminiscent of socialist revolutionary slogans and are articulated by a handsome, young and elegant male doctor and the overall effect is conducive to socialist beliefs in

Angel Heart 47

collectivism, altruism/sacrifice and even the revolutionary passions, now resurrected and re-inserted into the social life of present-day Chinese.

In a similar manner, in many staff meeting scenes where the hospital leader addresses the employees, he encourages them to uphold an unfaltering belief in their careers and their sacrifice to their patients; even after encountering abundant misunderstandings, setbacks and even physical attacks on themselves, they should still harbor no complaints and regrets.[1] According to the hospital director, only two characters will appear on the tombstones of his staff after they die: *yingxiong* (hero). In these meeting scenes, the director of the show enlists visual signs to display the doctors' and nurses' appreciation and support of the hospital director's words. A plethora of close-up and medium-range shots of the hospital director's solemn and amiable face are taken from the staffs' perspectives as they sit around their director in a large conference room. The mise-en-scènes that foreground the hospital director show his subordinates' respect for him and emphasize his authority and grip on power. These visual symbols demonstrate the courage and determination of the staff to follow the instructions of their director and to serve their patients. In its dual efforts to portray the benevolent director and the altruistic doctors and nurses, the sequences stimulate the audience's sentiments. The emotional climax is simultaneously felt by the hospital director, his underlings, and the TV viewers when the particular wording *yingxiong* is used to describe medical workers, which totally voids any misapprehension of the "mainstream" theme of the show.

Heroism is a classic theme in the lexicon of propaganda endorsed by the CCP government (Edwards 2011), and the correlation of medical staff and hero in *Angel Heart* demonstrates the reappearance of typical socialist moral education which mirrors the trend of recent CCP propaganda. In a conference scene, when the hospital leader encourages his subordinates to have faith in the righteousness of their careers and their selfless devotion for their patients, he compares them to the revolutionary forerunners who fought to win the socialist revolutions. In another scene, which depicts the mobilization meeting for earthquake relief, Party members, hospital leaders, doctors and nurses all respond actively and enthusiastically to the call without any hesitation and without consideration for their own safety. The show allocates a scene of several minutes to display the demanding conditions at the emergency sites where the doctors and nurses work extraordinarily hard to salvage the victims. Here, the doctors' and nurses' laudable performances in the earthquake relief remind us of the "SARS party line" which highlights the sacrifice of Party members, medical workers (and ordinary people alike) and builds a national solidarity in a "people's war" against a common enemy – a successful proactive propaganda approach (Fewsmith 2003: 254 cited in Zhao 2008: 46). When the female lead of the show comes back from the disaster area, the hospital leader praises her for spreading the spirit of revolutionary humanitarianism. Here, through establishing the noble and perfect image of medical workers, *Angel Heart* endeavors to retrieve the lost faith that the Chinese people had in relation to their doctors and nurses in particular, and more generally to retrieve a belief that the declining morality of the entire Chinese nation may be

48 Angel Heart

recovered.[2] In other words, medical workers are remodeled as spiritual support and moral pillars of the Chinese people, serving as an antidote to the relapse of ethics in the present-day social reality. In so doing, these highly moral medical worker characters mitigate, to some extent, the moral crisis confronting the whole Chinese society, which unless addressed hints at a political crisis as "the CCP's political claim to legitimacy has always had a moral dimension" (Bai 2015: 76).

In summary, through creating a cohort of dedicated and model medical worker characters, *Angel Heart* shoulders a mediator role between the antagonistic healthcare providers and patients. Based on Kong & Hawes's (2015: 34) observation, mediation had mutated into "an alternative dispute resolution forum," which is preferred and endorsed by the CCP's Propaganda Department as an imperative for promoting social harmony, as government officials have reasserted its belief in the conventional Chinese cultural ideal of mediation (Kong & Hawes 2015: 33). Together with a group of recent reality and talk show mediation programs, *Angel Heart* serves as a typical and pioneering televised "mediation" narrative which echoes the appeal from the government to cultivate and foster social harmony.

Moderating conflicts between healthcare providers and patients

The conflict between healthcare providers and patients is one of the most prevalent social problems of China, and there are numerous news reports of lawsuits between hospitals and patients and violent events taking place in hospitals, most of them involving patients fighting with doctors and nurses. In its representation of these conflicts, *Angel Heart* maintains its "mainstream" stand in terms of portraying medical workers as the wronged and victimized party in their disputes with the bad-tempered and sometimes provocative patients. Through exposing the difficulties faced by doctors when they deal with patients, especially when medical conflict occurs, the show acts more as an effective advocate for contemporary Chinese doctors. Even though the doctors in *Angel Heart* are virtuous and care about their patients, they are still regularly misjudged, blamed and physically attacked by their patients. There are many scenes in the show that paint a picture of the physical abuse inflicted upon medical staff from furious and agitated patients. An episode of the show exposes that six staff members in the department of medical disputes at the hospital were physically harmed in just one week. In another instance, a nurse was hit on the head by a relative of a patient, and she was so concerned for her personal safety, which could not be guaranteed in any Chinese hospital nowadays as there are more and more incidents of violence towards staff, that she decided to resign from her position. Some doctors are afraid to work in the newly built hospital office building, as there is no means of escape from the potential physical intimidation from the angry patients and their relatives. Based on these plot designs, *Angel Heart* foregrounds the increasing insecure working environment confronting Chinese medical staff, where doctors and nurses cannot work with dignity and their lives are under persistent threat. Further, this mutual distrust between doctors and patients as portrayed in the show accurately reflects the double-loss situation of both caregivers and care receivers in contemporary China.

In addition, many scenes in *Angel Heart* are designated to depict the highly controversial topic of the "medical disturbance phenomenon," which has attracted attention from the government and ordinary Chinese people alike (*New Observation*, n.d.). This phenomenon arises from the increasing and diverging disputes between healthcare providers and patients due to the various reasons mapped out in the discussion above. On behalf of the patients and their relatives who feel disgruntled with their treatment, hired hospital violators break into the hospital or the office of its director to physically intimidate and abuse the doctors and nurses, to smash and destroy the medical appliances of the hospital or to engage in a lawsuit with the hospital. Some of the medical disturbance cases are due to the negligence and mistakes of medical workers whose hospitals indeed should shoulder the responsibility; however, more and more medical disturbance events are initiated purely out of the malicious intention by the patients to blackmail the hospital, thus triggering the formation of a new profession – medical dispute profiteers.

In *Angel Heart*, there is a foot massage shop located very close to the hospital, and many patients and their relatives choose to rest and relax in the shop while they receive a foot massage. Coincidently, the owner of the massage shop also runs a "medical disturbance" business, and she encourages the patients to bargain or to go to court with the hospital, as she knows that hospitals are fearful of being sued by their patients. Driven by financial motivation, hired hospital violators have established a new type of business enterprise that has as its aim to bring trouble to the hospitals under the name of protecting the rights of the patients. By exposing the "medical disturbance" social stigma and the wicked purpose of the medical dispute profiteers, *Angel Heart* tries to curb the opportunistic practice rampant in the medical field and to educate the people on how to correctly and rationally handle their relationships and disputes with hospitals.[3]

By its one-sided account of the conflicts between healthcare providers and patients, which, according to the show, are caused largely by the ill-tempered patients and the malicious medical dispute profiteers, *Angel Heart* circumvents other key catalysts that contribute to the disputes between caregivers and care receivers, such as the raising of fees for medication, the careless examinations and impatient manner of the doctors and the doctors' unethical behaviors. However, the show's narrative briefly, but abstractly, touches upon the unfulfilled role of the government regarding providing reliable and affordable healthcare services to its people. This role of the government, which has been jettisoned since the adoption of the unsuccessful healthcare reform and the marketization of the public welfare enterprises, is the decisive factor that overrides all the above-mentioned contributing factors which may impact the deterioration of the relationship between medical staff and patients and the degenerating condition within China's medical industry.

In early 2015, the Chinese investigative journalist Chai Jing made a fiercely debated documentary titled *Under the Heavy Dome* (*Qiongdingzhixia*, 2015), which examined the smog pollution of Beijing. The documentary was banned

50   Angel Heart

just a week after its release in the mainland region for its negative impact on the general public, who doubted the capacity of the government to solve the smog problems. In the documentary, Chai Jing interviews many government officials in order to find out the reasons behind these high levels of air pollution. Consequently, the conclusion of the documentary points to the government as the main factor behind the heavy smog pollution. The desperate pursuit of economic growth steered by a state with a developmental approach and the lack of relevant laws to regulate the discharge of industrial waste are two key causes behind the documentary's suppositions. Unlike *Under the Heavy Dome*, which relates the government's mismanagement and duty quite clearly to the smog pollution, *Angel Heart* does it in a roundabout way by "envisaging" a well-functioning healthcare system within a welfare state that is under the rule of the CCP government in the future, which indirectly indicates that there is a present malfunctioning of the medical care system. Further, different from *Under the Heavy Dome*'s critical approach to the malfunction of the government, *Angel Heart* adopts a more tolerant and uplifting manner in its anticipation of a better performance of the government that would bring a more prosperous future for the Chinese people.

In the concluding episode of the show, the hospital director, a senior CCP member, who acts as a spokesperson for the Chinese government in the show, foresees the prospect for a China where hospitals will become a part of the social welfare system and a humanitarian concern. At that time in the future, everybody will be able to afford his or her medical expenses and enjoy a less burdened life. Here, the show visually and superficially revamps the image of the CCP administration as it envisages a future where the government will perform its obligation to provide reasonable and reliable medical services for its citizens. Moreover, the hospital director's words remind the audience of a previously mentioned episode of the show which tells the story of an impoverished peasant family in which one of the children is seriously ill and dies after an operation, resulting in the family owing the hospital an amount for medical costs which they could not pay. In sympathy with the poor family, the doctors forgo their fees and the debt to the hospital is waived. There is no further explanation about whether the doctors or the hospital finally paid the medical charges for the family. This plot comes across as unrealistic, as the usual practice is that if patients with a potentially fatal illness cannot pay their medical fees, they must leave the hospital and wait for their impending death at home, a fate that many poor Chinese face each year.[4] However, if this plot is set in a "future" China, as envisaged by the hospital director, it soon stops to be viewed as a fanciful tale.

Although *Angel Heart* fleetingly and hypothetically touches upon the critical cause of the conflicts between healthcare providers and patients, which is the malfunction of the state machine, it promotes a considerate and lenient manner among the public and predicts a "Chinese Dream" for them.[5] "Chinese Dream" is a political and social propaganda phrase which has been strongly promoted after the current president, Xi Jinping, took reign over mainland China, and indicates the continuity of a prosperous and harmonious Chinese nation within which everybody can enjoy an equal and happy life. The ending of *Angel Heart* (which

Angel Heart   51

is presented through the hospital director's speech) echoes the mainstream and official propaganda rhetoric that says that although at present China has many serious social problems, the government has the capacity to overcome them and therefore the people should also have confidence in their government and in their future. In doing so, the show enlists the topical social problem – the conflicts between healthcare providers and patients – to soothe the wrath of the public and to approach and examine this social problem in line with the standpoint of the official ideology.

Related topical social problems inherent within *Angel Heart*

Although the main storyline of *Angel Heart* is concerned with the encounters between healthcare providers and patients, it also touches on many other keenly debated social issues in contemporary China. Taking the left-over women (*shengnu*) phenomenon as an example, the female lead in the show is a carefully designed representative of the urban mature woman who is left behind in marriage. The left-over women phenomenon has emerged over the past two decades in the pan-Chinese region, including the mainland, Hong Kong and Taiwan, and it has been attracting much attention and controversy from the government, the public and the academy alike. "Left-over women" is a term originally coined by the Beijing Women's Federation (founded by the CCP in 1949) in 2007, which refers to unmarried females in China who reach the age of twenty-seven. The notion of a "left-over woman" denotes a financially independent professional single woman, but also one who has missed her best chance to marry, and so is seen as being "left over" and past their "use-by date." These women are reported and portrayed ridiculously and satirically in news reports and TV shows in the state-run and commercial media. Many reports vilifying left-over women have been republished through Xinhua (the official media outlet of the CCP) and other media outlets (cf. Fong & Fincher 2014), saying that these women are like "rotten food."

Fincher (2014) argues that the Chinese government exaggerates the negative side of the left-over women phenomenon in order to achieve its goals of social stability. According to Fincher, the frequent exposure and aggressive lampooning of the left-over women in state-run media is a government organized campaign aimed at instilling panic in economically autonomous and socially mobile women and causing them to rethink their predicament and to marry sooner, which will then help to address the gender imbalance which unless corrected could ultimately lead to social unrest. This reflects the Chinese state's attempt to manage the disastrous side effects of its own policy in population control – the one-child policy, which has led to widespread abortion of female fetuses in the preference for sons. Thus, in China today, there are about twenty million more men than women of marriageable age. The Party's fear of these agitated men, who have been unable to find wives, has been enhanced by the eruption over the past few years of hundreds of "mass incidents" (read: protests) throughout the country (Fincher 2014).

Apart from maintaining social stability, as Fincher (2014) argues, the CCP believes that the solving of the left-over women stigmatization can also drive

52　Angel Heart

consumption and the property boom. In order to keep its real estate boom in check, which is a key impetus of Chinese economic growth, a coalition has been formed between the Party and the property companies and dating websites. Government appraisals on marriage and property are often supported by matchmaking agencies and propagate the perception that being "left over" is the worst thing that can happen to a woman. The participants of the coalition sponsor myths such as the idea that a couple must have an apartment before they can marry. Further, Fincher (2014) observes that the government-led "derogatory" portrayal of the left-over women is a coordinated campaign leveled at improving the "quality" of the Chinese genes. The government imagines that if most educated and competent females are married, then better "quality" children – children with "superior" genetic makeup, will be born and the general quality of the Chinese population will be elevated.

In order to be in line with the government campaign on the left-over women phenomenon, many provincial TV stations have been hosting matchmaking shows for the left-over women in order to help them find their Mr Right. Also, a number of recently released TV series have featured stories about this social topic, like *Women of Marriage Age Should Get Married* (Danudangjia 2010). In *Angel Heart*, the female lead is a thirty-two-year-old single woman who is a head nurse in the hospital. She is in love with a doctor at the same hospital who is the son of a high-ranking official in the local health bureau, causing the nurse to believe that he is out of her league. In order to hold on to her boyfriend, the nurse purchases a small apartment and the doctor pays for the furnishings in exchange for occasionally staying there. The nurse attempts many ruses (such as pretending she is pregnant with the doctor's baby) in order to get the doctor to marry her. Eventually, after living together for some time, they finally wed. The show cleverly depicts how an older woman, and one who is often jokingly mocked and laughed at by her colleagues as a left-over woman, finds a wonderful husband. In this instance, both the property and the baby have a decisive function in causing the man to make his final decision, which indirectly parallels the official propaganda of the left-over women campaign.

Besides the left-over women phenomenon, *Angel Heart* also taps into the gold-digger (marry-only-for-money) social stigma. The male lead's mother, who was originally a nurse in the hospital but now, after she marries her husband, a powerful leader in the local health bureau, lives in a luxurious house and becomes an influential figure in the local medical circle with whom many people are keen to cultivate a friendly relationship. In the case of the nurse who is hit by the patient's relative, after quitting her job, she finds a wealthy husband and leads a very comfortable life. By creating these female "gold-digger" characters, *Angel Heart* probes into the dominant values upheld by contemporary Chinese people who prioritize material enjoyment and social status over morality and ideals. In other words, a person's success in society is gauged only by her material possessions and whether or not a person owns a lavish house and drives an expensive car. These types of social judgments lead to a vicious circle of competition and to the unscrupulous pursuit of money.

Angel Heart   53

In addition to creating "problematic" women characters, the show also exposes the unspoken rules and the corrupt nature within the Chinese workplace, with a focus on "connections" and the related blight of nepotism in the healthcare industry. In the show, a few nurses are promoted to chief nurses based on their personal relations with members of the upper management of the hospital instead of their professional skills. Similarly, in order to be promoted, some doctors have to find connections within the upper hierarchy of their field. A cancelled banquet that is originally planned by one of the doctors to build connections with a leader in the health bureau (which he finally gives up as he decides to accompany his wife to watch a comedy show) eventually leads to his failure in promotion, although he performs extremely well in his work and is greatly admired by his co-workers. On the other hand, some "paratroopers" (which indicates someone who "drops in" to the job through his/her connections) are given important positions for which they are usually not qualified. "Paratroopers" is a hot topic in China and it is now recognized that nepotism, "paratroopers" and connections are all part of the bigger picture of corruption in China – and corruption leads to poor government and corporate governance. These corrupt practices occur widely in China's official and business circles, but they are presented in the show as being comparably fecund and detrimental in the medical field.

Another contemporary social concern that attracts the show's attention is the decline of family values. This is highlighted by fights between family members over the inheritance (normally apartment and money) from deceased parents. One story tells about an old female patient whose children eagerly anticipate her death so they can inherit her apartment. However, due to the doctors' efforts, their mother survives the terminal illness. The old woman is so saddened by her children's unfilial conduct that she commits suicide soon after her recovery but leaves her apartment to the government rather than to her son and daughter. This tragic case sheds light on a prevalent selfish attitude towards their parents by many contemporary Chinese children, especially by those who were born under the one-child policy.[6] The indifference shown by the younger generations towards caring for their parents as they grow old is a concern not only for the parents but also for the government, as it means a huge increase in welfare payments for its aged citizens. Government media campaigns are trying to persuade old people not to give their apartments away to their children too early, in case they do not have enough to cover their own living and medication expenses when they fall sick or need to go to the nursing home, which is most likely the case when the majority of parents of the single child grow old. When the old woman bestows her apartment to the state in an expression of gratitude to the government and not her children who cared for her in her old age, the intent of the show is to improve the image of the Chinese government, even though its actual performance is inadequate for many Chinese people.

In short, *Angel Heart* turns the hospital into a micro society which epitomizes the macro society of contemporary China. Various kinds of social agonies and malaises manifest and parade themselves and interact with each other. Apart from the public focus on conflicts between healthcare providers and patients, the show

54 Angel Heart

extends its purview to other social debates and sets itself apart from many domestic and trendy dramas that are mainly concerned with entertaining the audience rather than achieving a social utility of invigorating critical thinking and spawning a virtual aesthetic public space among the viewers. In comparing the plots of *Angel Heart* with the popular American TV show *ER* (1994–2009), it is not difficult to perceive that *ER* concentrates more on the knowledge and skills of the medical professionals and the personal relationships between them in an emergency room, whereas *Angel Heart* concerns itself more with topical social problems. This suggests that although the Chinese and the American TV shows share comparable themes and content, the Chinese TV drama show engages more with the prevailing public interests and social anxieties.

Conclusion

As one of the major TV drama shows that focuses on the relationships and conflicts between healthcare providers and patients in contemporary China, *Angel Heart* fulfills its function in mollifying the contradictory needs and views between these two interdependent and antagonistic groups in particular, and in harmonizing the entire Chinese society in general by analogy. By creating exemplary models of doctors, *Angel Heart* responds to the call of the central government which currently endorses a New Left turn that promotes a more egalitarian society and tries to balance the needs and interests of China's "haves" (such as China's nouveau riche and middle-class social echelons) and "have-nots" (such as peasants and workers who have been left behind by the Opening Up reforms). Unlike the untrustworthy, arrogant and corrupt image of doctors held by many Chinese people, the majority of the doctor characters in *Angel Heart* have a spirit of altruism, heroism and sacrifice. Established as exemplary citizens of today's China, these doctors devote themselves unswervingly and selflessly to their careers, although they also have worries about their long hours with high workload expectations and their personal safety due to the increasing abuse and violence occurring at hospitals between the patients and their doctors.

In this way, the doctor characters fashioned in *Angel Heart* retune and restore the moral principles of present-day China. The drama thus perpetuates a mainstream sentiment in terms of justifying a propaganda purpose. In contrast to the plots of its Western counterpart, *ER*, which foregrounds the outstanding professionalism and skills of the healthcare workers, *Angel Heart* puts more emphasis on the lofty ethics upheld by the medical staff. In the hospital director's instructions to his employees on how to avoid being in conflict with patients and how to endure the irrational scolding and physical harm from the patients, he insists that the doctors and nurses should first build up their own virtue. Second, the director explains metaphorically that medical workers actually have two scalpels, one to cure the patients' physical wounds, and the other to repair their injuries of the heart. In doing so, the medical occupation is deftly and ingeniously enlisted by TV producers to respond to the appeal of the government propaganda, which is the so-called socialist moral education. Through creating new role models and finding novel ways to spread the ideological message of official discourse, *Angel Heart* sets the standard for similar themed "main melody" TV drama serials to follow.

Apart from the obvious propaganda utility for the government, *Angel Heart* seeks out the hidden reasons that trigger those disputes between medical workers and patients, although in a brief and abstract manner. In this sense, the show spots the weaknesses of China's malfunctioning healthcare system and of the policy and work of the national government. Taking the strains encountered by both the caregivers and the care receivers into consideration, the show ultimately points out that a final concord between healthcare providers and patients can be achieved through building up an effective healthcare system within a welfare state, which relies heavily on the performance and efforts of the state. By providing this exposé, *Angel Heart* clarifies the misunderstandings and conflict between caregivers and the care receivers; however, in doing so it may also have shaped new contradictions between the government and the people. Thus, in addition to embellishing the image of contemporary doctors as model citizens of the country, who signify the established moral virtue of socialist China in line with official propaganda, the show promotes a considerate and lenient manner among the public towards the performance of the government. In doing so, it enlists the conflicts between healthcare providers and patients to soothe the growing wrath of the public towards this specific social problem in particular and towards the overall social unfairness and discrimination in general, which verifies the show's role as a political and social critique that guides public opinion and contributes to the development of a "harmonious" society in present-day China.

Notes

1 Although the doctor characters created in *Angel Heart* have many virtues, a few of them sometimes still complain about their long working hours and heavy workload. Further, these doctors estimate that if the current situation continues into the future, China will soon be short of doctors. As the personal safety of doctors is in constant risk, some doctors also complain that they are not treated fairly by the patients. In exposing these complaints of the doctors, *Angel Heart* endeavors to instigate a sense of tolerance and commiseration from its audience for the doctors, in order to ameliorate the negative emotion of the public to the doctors and to alleviate the misunderstanding and antagonism between the healthcare providers and the patients.
2 Bai (2015: 72) observes that there seems to exist "a society-wide consensus that China is experiencing a moral crisis," and this consensus "is cemented and constantly reinforced by the multitude of sensational media scandals involving corrupt officials, fraudulent businesses, schoolteachers taking bribes from parents or doctors from patients, plagiarizing university professors, impassive crowds at scenes of heinous crimes, etc. Again and again, these scandals, when coupled with the subjective experiences of ordinary Chinese, confirm an apocalyptic sense of fear and anxiety." See Bai (2015).
3 In order to cope with the medical dispute profiteers, *Angel Heart* reveals some precautionary measures employed by hospitals in order to mitigate the risks of their being involved in medical conflicts with the patients. For instance, whenever the treatments or operations involve high risk, a hospital video records the meetings where doctors

56   Angel Heart

explain the possible perils to the patients and their relatives. Apart from adopting these countermeasures in advance, the show further highlights some other potential causes that may impact the quality of medical examination and treatment, including the use of inferior medical instruments, which is beyond the control of hospitals. As there are many fake or low quality products on the market (due to government neglect of its own directives and regulations), it is almost unavoidable for hospitals to occasionally purchase some of these potentially risky products. This situation vis-à-vis the healthcare of the people also reveals the decline of ethical conduct and good management in the government and business domains of contemporary China.

4   In the reality of contemporary China, affluent people can afford to have expensive medical examinations and drugs, but poor people struggle to afford even basic medical treatment, and hospitals have become a place where the obvious discrepancy between China's nouveau riche and ordinary people is most apparent. This clear inequity is the root of much social angst, leading to the situation where hospitals have been turned into a hotbed of social problems and violence.

5   For more discussion about the "Chinese Dream," see Callahan (2013).

6   In 1979, the Chinese government launched the one-child policy, a radical family planning project. This drastic social engineering program proclaimed childbearing to be a state directive. As a result of these sweeping birth control restrictions, there have been about 150 million children born under the one-child policy over the past almost four decades, and China has the largest only-child population in the world. In 2015, more than thirty years after the adoption of the one-child policy, the CCP has made significant adjustments to its family planning scheme in order to cope with emerging social problems caused by China's aging population. According to the current population control program, every couple is allowed to have 2 children.

References

Bai, Ruoyun. 2015. "'Clean Up the Screen': Regulating Television Entertainment in the 2000s," in *Chinese Television in the Twenty-First Century: Entertaining the Nation*, Ruoyun Bai and Geng Song (eds.). London and New York: Routledge, pp. 69–86.

Callahan, William. 2013. *China Dreams: 20 Visions of the Future*. Oxford: Oxford University Press.

Danudangjia [Women of Marriage Age Should Get Married]. 2010. TV serial, directed by Sun Hao, debut on China Central TV's Channel 8 in 2010.

Edwards, Louise. 2011. "Military Celebrity in China: The Evolution of Heroic and Model Servicemen," in *Celebrity in China*, Louise Edwards and Elaine Jeffreys (eds.). Hong Kong: Hong Kong University Press, pp. 21–43.

Fewsmith, Joseph. 2003. "China and the Politics of SARS." *Current History* 102 (665): 250–255.

Fincher, Leta Hong. 2014. *Leftover Women: The Resurgence of Gender Inequality in China*. London: Zed Books.

Kong, Shuyu and Hawes, Colin S. 2015. "The New Family Mediator: TV Mediation Programs in China's 'Harmonious Society'," in *Chinese Television in the Twenty-First Century*, Ruoyun Bai and Geng Song (eds.). London and New York: Routledge, pp. 33–50.

Li, Peilin, Zhang, Yi, Zhao, Yandong and Liang, Dong. 2005. *Shehui chongtu yu jieji yishi* [Social Conflicts and Class Consciousnesses]. Beijing: Shehui kexue wenxian chubanshe, pp. 136–138.

Mei, Fong and Fincher, Leta Hong. 2014. "If You Are Not Married by 25, You Are a Leftover Woman In China." *The World Post*, 4 April, available at: www.huffingtonpost.com/2014/04/24/china-gender-inequality_n_5207388.html (accessed 31 July 2014).

New Observation. n.d. (1996–2012). "Daji yinao buneng chengwei shangfangbaojian" [Cracking Down on the Medical Disturbance Phenomenon Should Not Become an "Imperial Sword"), no. 42, available at http://news.sina.com.cn/z/xgc42/ (accessed 30 May 2016).

Qianfu [Lurk]. 2009. TV serial, directed by Jiang Wei and Fu Wei, debut on Dongfang satellite TV station in 2009.

Qiongdingzhixia. 2015. [Under the Heavy Dome]. Documentary produced by China's famous investigative journalist Chai Jing, available at: www.youtube.com/watch?v=xbK4 KeD2ajI.

Reed, Gay Garland. 1995. "Moral/ Political Education in the People's Republic of China: Learning through Role Models." *Journal of Moral Education* 24 (2): 99–111.

People's Daily Online. 2014. "Ruhe baozheng yisheng bushou hongbao" [How to prevent doctors from taking gift money], reposted 10 December 2014, available at: http://opin ion.people.com.cn/n/2014/1210/c1003–26180919.html (accessed 25 March 2015).

Schneider, Florian. 2012. *Visual Political Communication in Popular Chinese TV Series.* Leiden and Boston: Brill.

Vision China Times. 2015. "Tuixiu yuanzhang yiyujingren: zhongguoyigai shi 'biliang-weichang'" [The Retired Hospital Director Articulates a Striking Phrase: The Chinese Health Care Reform "Compels a Female to Engage in Prostitution"], no. 465 (Melbourne edition): 10 October–16 October, p. 11.

Wang, Hui. 2003. "The 1989 Social Movement and the Historical Roots of China's Neolib-eralism," in *China's New Order: Society, Politics, and Economy in Transition*, H. Wang, T. Huters and R. Karl (eds.). Cambridge, MA: Harvard University, pp. 41–138.

Woju [Dwelling Narrowness]. 2009. TV serial, directed by Teng Huatao, debut at Shanghai satellite TV station.

Xifu de meihao shidai [Beautiful Daughter-in-law]. 2010. TV serial, directed by Liu Jiang, first put on the air on Beijing and Dongfang satellite TV stations in 2010.

Xinshu [Angel Heart]. 2012. TV serial, directed by Yang Yang, debut on Anhui, Tianjin, Zhejiang and Dongfang satellite TV stations in 2012.

Xinhua Net. 2005. "Yiyao daibiao baoheimu – jiaoshouji yisheng yue huikou da shiwan" [Medical Representatives Expose Shady Deals – Professor-Level Doctors Receive a Monthly Commission of 100,000 Yuan], reposted 21 December, available at: http://news. xinhuanet.com/politics/2005–12/21/content_3948893.htm (accessed 12 March 2015).

Zhao, Yuezhi. 2008. *Communication in China: Political Economy, Power and Conflict.* Lanham, MD: Rowman & Littlefield Publishers.

Zhu, Ying. 2008. *TV in Post-Reform China: Serial Dramas, Confucian Leadership and the Global TV Market.* London and New York: Routledge.

3 A trans-media reading of a white-collar workplace bestseller and its TV and film adaptations

A Story of Lala's Promotion and *Go Lala Go*

Introduction

In 2007, Li Ke's novel *A Story of Lala's Promotion* (*Du Lala shengzhiji*), became a bestseller among Chinese white-collar workers in joint ventures or foreign-owned (Western) companies. The novel revolves around office politics, Western company culture, the white-collar lifestyle, the "strong woman" phenomenon and middle-class aesthetics. In order to decipher the embedded cultural codes of this book, this chapter undertakes a textual analysis of the plots of *A Story of Lala's Promotion* and its TV and film adaptations, *Go Lala Go!*. In this trans-media study (from fiction to TV drama and film), this chapter examines three interrelated themes in the novel, the film and the TV serial. First, focusing on the influence of Western corporate culture on Chinese white-collar workers, the extensively followed norms of Western work culture are interpreted, and the acculturating process of Western culture over its Chinese counterpart is made clear. The chapter also asks how, on the platform provided by foreign companies and with the impact and training of Western corporate culture, intelligent and diligent young Chinese women aspire, struggle and realize their dreams in the workplace. Second, employing a feminist perspective, the analysis addresses the situation of contemporary Chinese professional women represented by the fiercely debated social phenomenon of "strong women," and how they symbolize female independence and individualism. And third, through an analysis of the film and TV adaptations and a focus on white-collar females' lifestyle and consumption habits, this chapter also highlights the modern-day Chinese pursuit of a middle-class identity and aesthetic that mirror the overwhelming consumerism of post-socialist China.

Since its publication in 2007, *A Story of Lala's Promotion* has continuously ranked at the top of the bestseller lists for eighty-eight weeks on Dangdang Web (Dangdang Web is one of the most popular online shopping websites in China). In 2008, its sequel, *As Time Goes By* (*Nianhua sishui*), was published and, in 2010, another sequel, *In This Struggling Year* (*Wo zai zhe zhandoude yinianli*), was released. Also in 2010, the film adaptation of *A Story of Lala's Promotion*, *Go*

Lala Go! by the well-known Beijing-based young actress-writer-director Xu Jing-lei was released, and the box-office revenue of the film reached 100 million RMB only a couple of days after its release. In the same year, a thirty-two-episode TV drama adaptation based on the same novel also aired and it similarly enjoyed huge popularity among the TV audience.

Compared with its film version, which is more concerned with personal and romantic relationships between the main characters and is similar in many ways to a Hollywood-style romantic comedy, the TV adaptation is closer to the content and essence of the original novel in terms of its meticulous and vivid portrayal of office politics and the trend towards globalization of workplace culture. There are many challenges for the film's director, who has to compress the rich plots of the book into a less than two hour movie, and so many wonderful elements of the novel cannot be included in the filmic version of the story. In particular, for those audiences who have familiarized themselves with the book, the movie seems to betray many facets of the novel and does not meet the expectations of these filmgoers. Therefore, the TV rendition of the novel functions as a more suitable means to untangle the cultural traits prompted by *A Story of Lala's Promotion*.

The backdrop of *A Story of Lala's Promotion* is the business and cultural landscape of a foreign-owned company that is operating in China, and includes its operational mechanisms, company culture, human resource (HR) management and interpersonal relations. Focusing on a core group of characters, including Du Lala (HR and administration manager), Wang Wei (marketing director), Lester (HR director) and Howard (CEO of the Chinese division of the company), the novel foregrounds office politics, Western corporate culture and the lifestyle and values of white-collar workers, particularly female employees. Du Lala is a good-looking woman in her early twenties and is from a small city in southern China. She is from a working-class family and has had to rely on her intelligence and hard work to make a living after graduating from university and moving to the larger metropolis. Unlike other "rich second generation" and "official second generation"[1] people who are wealthy and have various connections to help them, Lala has to rely on her own attributes and attainments to achieve what she wants and dreams of. She works in a state-run enterprise for a year, until she finds a sales job with a privately owned company. However, after working there for four years, and being sexually harassed by her boss, Lala quits. She finds a new position as a marketing assistant in a foreign-owned, global top-500 enterprise, called DB. As a result of her ability and diligence, she is promoted to administrative supervisor and then to HR and administration manager in just a few years. After years of hard work and continual struggle and when she is in her late twenties, Lala finally becomes a member of the newly formed Chinese middle class.[2]

The main characters in *A Story of Lala's Promotion* are:

Howard – CEO of the Chinese company
Lester – HR director
Wang Wei – marketing director

60 *A trans-media reading of* Go Lala Go

Rose – administration manager
Du Lala – HR and administration manager (after Rose leaves the company)
Zhou Liang – HR and administration supervisor
Pamela – HR and administration supervisor

Westernization and globalization reflected in the workplace

Since China opened up to the outside world at the end of the 1970s, and as the world economy has steadily but surely globalized, joint ventures and foreign-invested enterprises (mainly Western companies from North America and Europe) have become an indispensable part of China's market economy. The engagement of these joint ventures and foreign-operated companies with the Chinese economy is not simply a process of internationalization – "a mere quantitative increase in the contacts and flows across nation-state boundaries or an increasing outward-orientation of the nation-state" (Albert 2007: 167, quoted in Loubere 2010: 72). Instead, it represents globalization, a process which "influences and structures processes of economic production and exchange, political authority, the formation of individual and collective identities, or cultural frames of reference" (Albert 2007: 167, quoted in Loubere 2010: 72). This comparison between internationalization and globalization helps us apprehend the utility, philosophy and politics of joint ventures and foreign-invested enterprises, which signify not only an extension of the Western capitalist economic form, but also a cultural penetration of the receiving countries. According to Yu (2008: 157), "[e]conomic globalization has not only changed production, consumption, and exchange, but it has also altered modes of thinking and behavior, and has had a major impact on national cultures." China's current economic model compels foreign-invested companies to play a critical role in sustaining the prosperity of China's economy: thus, Western work modes, office politics and interpersonal relations, which are part of corporate culture, have an immense influence on Chinese workers in these enterprises.

Some scholars have offered different observations regarding this cultural globalization unfolding in foreign corporations operating in China. They indicate that traditional Chinese values such as an emphasis on the maintenance of harmonious relations among colleagues, preservation of the collective, agreement to prearranged social structures and power hierarchy, holism, contextualism, saving face and reciprocity of relationships and *guanxi* (ties and connections) influence Chinese staff working in foreign-run enterprises, particularly when settling conflicts (Kirkbride, Tang & Westwood 1991: 365–86; Ding 1997: 31–45; Chan, Luk & Wang 2005: 464). In contrast to these observations, traditional Chinese work modes and values have been replaced by Western workplace standards and culture in *A Story of Lala's Promotion* and its film and TV drama adaptations. In the narratives of the novel, the movie and the TV show, which all center on Du Lala's experiences, the operational mechanisms, management concepts and corporate culture of the foreign company is simply transplanted into the Chinese socio-economic system and cultural milieu. Consequently, they directly or indirectly critically engage with and adjust the thinking and behavioral manner of their

Chinese employees who have long been immersed into and assimilated by Western company culture. Therefore, the experience of Chinese white-collar workers affiliated to these foreign companies is a microcosm of the broader Westernizing and globalizing fashion of the world economy and culture. Despite Chinese workers encountering and negotiating with both local and international or Western values during the transformative process of localizing a transnational corporate culture, an overwhelming stimulus of Western company culture on the Chinese workforce is clearly flaunted in Du Lala's story. Through a detailed analysis of Du Lala's experiences, as a typical Chinese employee in a foreign or multinational organization, we gain a clear picture of the globalizing trends in contemporary China.

DB, a global top-500 American communications company where Lala works, is an archetypal Western enterprise; both its organizational structure and management strategy represent American-style corporate culture. According to Chan, Luk and Wang (2005: 466):

> Corporate culture refers to the values, beliefs, and principles that serve as a foundation for an organization's management system, and the set of management practices and forms of behaviour that both exemplify and reinforce those basic principles.

At DB, classic Western management ideas, such as SMART (specific, measurable, attainable, relevant and time-based) signify the high efficiency, rationalization and pragmatism of this management style. From careful budgeting to painstaking negotiations, and from thorough investigation to results analysis, Lala gradually familiarizes herself with Western management concepts and tactics, eventually becoming highly skilled at them. Shifting from a slow-paced and less effective working style in the state-run and arguably privately owned Chinese company to a fast-tempo, efficient and logical Western working approach, Lala transfigures herself into a qualified, successful and aspiring female professional at DB's management level. Here, Lala's conversion verifies the corporate culture of DB which is "keeping dynamic and forging ahead." Further, Lala personifies the impact that globalization exerts over China; in particular, its influence on young aspirational Chinese women and their work and life experiences.

According to Fan and Regulska (2008: 94–95), Chinese women's emancipation, at both the economic and physical levels, as promoted during the Mao era, did not "necessarily enrich women's identity with the desire for professional success and economic independence." Further, changes initiated under socialism "didn't eliminate gender discrimination as reflected in wages, occupational attainment and promotion." The situation has worsened in the post-socialist transition eras: when a market economy with Chinese characteristics was implemented by a state with a developmental approach, traditional gender ideology and practices in the labor market were resumed and overt gender discrimination when hiring was common (Fan 2000: 423–424; Fan 2003: 27; Fan 2004: 284; Fan & Regulska 2008: 96–100). For example, men still dominate the job market in positions

62   *A trans-media reading of* Go Lala Go

such as heads of government and enterprises, managers and senior clerical staff. Under these general conditions, Western companies provide opportunities for young motivated Chinese female staff to develop their skills and knowledge and compete equally with their male counterparts in business circles. Eventually, it is expected that many proficient Chinese women will become supervisors and managers in foreign corporations, like Rose, Lala and Pamela in the Du Lala phenomenon.

Other traits of the Western business world revealed in the novel and its film and TV drama adaptations are its cruel competitiveness, often leading to an employee's "crisis of consciousness." Within DB, there is pitiless competition among staff and departments. This is exposed when Lala is promoted to the position of HR and administration manager; however as she is not familiar with the HR routines at DB (her previous duties were mainly administrative), the HR staff are reluctant to train her for fear that Lala would perform better than them. This callous contest among colleagues is likewise revealed by Lester's non-trusting relationship with Rose and by Rose's (Lala's former boss) non-trusting relationship with Lala; as well as Lala's own defensiveness with Zhou Liang and Pamela. For example, Lala's manipulation of Zhou Liang and Pamela follows Lester's instructions to her:

> I am not saying that we are building a harmonious team and everyone needs to listen to you; what I am trying to explain is how to balance your subordinates. If they are perfectly united, it might be the beginning of a nightmare for you. Never make your subordinates too united and never trust any one of them too much. You should make them compete against each other so that you can control the whole situation. Another point is that when you are training them, you should always do it separately. Remember, you are irreplaceable.
>
> (Li 2010: 138)

In one scene of the TV serial, Lester teaches Lala a motto which is highly useful and instructive for her survival and advancement at DB, given the intense competition among colleagues. "It does not matter how well you perform, the point is which way best suits your own needs." This harsh competitiveness of Western companies fuels a sense of crisis among the employees. Lala is in constant fear of new staff members outperforming her. In order to stand out from other employees and to gain a promotion, Lala frequently works late at night and rarely takes any paid annual leave, especially when she is in charge of major projects. In the TV drama version of the novel, many scenes show Lala arriving at work earlier than her subordinates so that she can deal with the pile of documents that she must attend to. She also works extra hours without having meal breaks. Lala's desperate efforts to impress her superiors serve as a foil to the ruthless competition and unstable future of the Western business system (Hou 2010: 25).

In the TV drama, Wang Wei, the director of sales (in the novel Wang Wei's position is marketing director), is under constant stress – just like Lala. The sales division is one of the core departments of a company like DB, and its success to a large degree determines the future of the company, as well as the destiny of its executives. Thus, competition within this sector is vicious. In addition to its internal struggles, the sales department has tense relations with other departments. In one plot of the novel – seen in both the film and the TV show – Lala is directing an office-renovation project. On the day that the office area must be vacated, Wang Wei and his staff members refuse to obey the order issued by Lala's administrative department, leading to a quarrel between Wang Wei and Lala. At the outset, Lala tries to be reasonable, but Wang Wei refuses to cooperate. However, ultimately Lala's stubbornness and resolve is too much for Wang Wei and she wins the argument.

This scenario reveals not only the aggressive nature but also the openness of Western corporate culture, which encourages staff to speak out and communicate with each other. Although Wang Wei is Chinese, he has long been accustomed to Western office politics. At the beginning of their disagreement, Wang Wei wants to teach Lala – the newly promoted administration supervisor – a lesson. He tries to intimidate her so that he and his department can win the upper hand. This way, in their future dealings, Wang Wei hopes that Lala will take notice and behave. However, to Wang Wei's surprise, Lala has also gained insight into Western business culture and office politics, and instead of enduring his bullying, she speaks up for herself with confidence. In her previous job at the privately owned Chinese company, Lala only resigned when she could no longer tolerate the owner's sexual advances. Also, in another scene, when Rose intentionally finds fault with Lala not long after Lala started working in the administration department, Lala just thanked Rose for her advice; however, after becoming more familiar with Western business culture, she begins to use Western ways of solving problems. Therefore, in her fight with Wang Wei, when Lala – a junior female administration supervisor – challenges the authority of a senior male sales director, she epitomizes the assimilation that has occurred in company culture as a result of globalization. Moreover, her career struggles and successes display the contemporary Chinese female worker's sense of rights and independence in the workplace (Du 2010: 24). Here, it is worth mentioning the mise-en-scène of the sequence, in particular the acting of the performers, which renders the manners, gestures and lines of both Wang Wei and Lala dominating and aggressive, indicating their thinking and behavioral patterns have also been acculturated by the Western business culture and principles.

Another distinguishing feature of Western business culture as exhibited in the Du Lala phenomenon is its promotion of fair competition. In Chinese culture, a strict system of seniority, in conjunction with personal connections, determines whether someone – especially a newcomer – survives in a workplace. Therefore, in the Chinese workplace, it is often the case that people can survive only if they have connections and it doesn't matter whether or not they are proficient in the job. However, the Western workplace situation is different. In the globalised business world, Chinese white-collar workers like Du Lala operate in a much more independent and impartial environment than they did pre-globalization. In the case of Lala, who started from a junior marketing assistant without any connections in

64   *A trans-media reading of* Go Lala Go

DB, she relies solely on her exceptional ability and unparalleled assiduousness to gain acceptance with her colleagues and win favor from her supervisors. The open and unprejudiced working environment and performance assessment fostered by Western corporate culture make it possible for Chinese staff, especially female workers like Du Lala, to struggle, compete and succeed in the workplace. This also turns Du Lala's case into a classic example where an entry-level female clerk can become a middle-class, successful career woman.

However, despite its impartial competition and transparent management system, the foreign-invested enterprise has its own weaknesses, such as its exploitative nature, which could be detected in Lala's description about Lester's different attitudes towards her: "Whenever he wants me to work for him he treats me with the warmth of spring; whenever I ask for a promotion, he treats me with the coldness of winter." Almost every time Lala receives a promotion, her new title does not match her sharply increased workload. Furthermore, she only gains the promotion by negotiating directly with her supervisor or manager:

> Lester, the renovation project has been completed successfully. I've also managed all the administrative departments across the country over the past six months, and everything has gone smoothly. As a result, I believe I have the capacity to be an administrative manager. Is there an opportunity for promotion for me?

This speech (and Lala's behavior) demonstrates that in the Western workplace, taking the initiative and safeguarding the interests one deserves is likely to enhance an employee's opportunities for success. This is in sharp contrast to Chinese workplace culture, where an employee needs to adopt a humble manner to progress.

In today's globalized climate, joint ventures and foreign-invested enterprises operating in China bring not only advanced management technology, but also an efficient and impartial corporate culture into the Chinese economic and cultural milieu. Chinese white-collar employees of these corporations operate in a more rational, autonomous, industrious and proactive way than staff in traditional Chinese companies. The Du Lala story is about how Chinese company culture and working practices have been subsumed by global (Western) standards, through the performance and behaviors of Chinese employees in foreign firms. In addition, the characters from the novel and its film and TV renditions, like real Chinese employees, act as mediums and catalysts, transferring foreign concepts, manners and culture into the Chinese socio-economic context. In this way, cultural assimilation occurs.

The new female image and the "strong woman" phenomenon

Recently, a number of popular novels focusing on female office workers or "office ladies" (OL)[3] in foreign firms have appeared in China, and undoubtedly *A Story of Lala's Promotion* is the most successful among them. For those people actually employed by foreign and multinational corporations, these novels have become quasi-textbooks: they showcase realistic workplace issues, situations, relationships and difficulties (Guo 2010: 231; Peng 2010: 50–1). When Zhang Wei, the scriptwriter of the TV version of *A Story of Lala's Promotion*, was collecting materials for the script, she went to several multinational companies. There, she saw many young female workers using a pen to underline the classic sayings of Du Lala in the novel (Zhang 2010). For those who are simply interested in the phenomenon, these books are also informative and intriguing. Due to the massive appeal spawned by the white-collar "office lady" bestsellers, film and TV producers and investors are keen to cash in on this hot cultural sensation. An inherited focus of these "OL" themed visual narratives from the original novels is the focus given to the endeavors and accomplishments of these talented and aspiring contemporary Chinese career-oriented women. From a feminist perspective, these popular visual texts reflect the changing situation of modern-day Chinese middle-class professional women.

"White-collar beauty" (*bailingliren*) is a term which has been used since the "Opening Up" economic reforms to describe young Chinese women working in joint venture or foreign-owned companies. The phrase implies that these are attractive bourgeois women. There is a general perception among the Chinese public that these women are good looking (they are known as "flower vases"), that they earn good salaries and that they have clerical roles such as receptionists and secretaries. They are employed partly for decoration, and their duties are relatively mundane. The emergence of the Du Lala–style of gifted and ambitious female managers and executives in foreign firms provides an alternative to the traditional image of the "white-collar beauty." Lala has the looks of a "flower vase" and begins with DB as a junior office clerk. As a result of her skills and persistence she eventually makes it to the senior management ranks, which is conventionally male-dominated and females are a marginalized subclass. In this sense, Lala's career journey changes the ideas about "white-collar beauty." The more commonly accepted understanding is that the "white-collar beauty" enjoys a less stressful job, with more leisurely duties, but the Du Lala phenomenon reveals the fierce contests and the fragile job security in foreign-owned companies, and changes the image of white-collar females from "flower vase" to "super-girl." This renewed image of white-collar females emphasizes women's career performances, pursuits and desires. The customary identity of professional women employed by foreign companies is given a nuanced and positive twist, and instead of holding positions such as secretary, receptionist, typist and assistant, Du Lala and many of her female co-workers are supervisors and directors who challenge their male colleagues in the workplace.

The opening sequence of the TV drama, through strong visual and acoustic arrangements, begins a lengthy narrative arc on the Du Lala character who is a hardworking and persistent young professional woman. Via an off-screen narrative voice, Du Lala introduces herself to the viewers. She is accompanied by the theme song of the show, with lyrics which highlight the struggles and determinations of an aspirational professional woman to overcome those hardships

66 *A trans-media reading of* Go Lala Go

and setbacks in the career marketplace. The camera uses long takes and follows Lala closely to shoot one of her busy mornings during which she has to catch an extremely crowded bus to the company headquarters. Although at this time Lala works for the private local company as a junior office clerk, her diligent and tenacious manner is carried on throughout her career, even after she is promoted to the managerial level at DB. The camera shot then adopts an angle that faces the approaching bus, which runs at a high speed and creates an effect of stressfulness, competition and maybe even oppression. As Lala gets on the bus, she trips and finds herself on the bus floor, and even though she is lying on the floor in an extremely embarrassing situation she still manages to smile to all those onlookers who surround her but do not attempt to offer any help. Hesitating for a couple of seconds, Lala manages to stand up by herself, pretending that nothing has happened while smiling to others. With the help of a rich combination of visual and acoustic elements, the sequence successfully creates the image of a professional woman who has inner strength, is tough and tenacious and endures hardships, all of which invite empathy, respect and even admiration from the audience.

In addition to its function as a signifier for strong professional women, the Du Lala phenomenon has turned itself into a representative of the "strong woman"; a controversial socio-cultural phenomenon in contemporary China. Lala achieves economic independence in her early twenties and by her late twenties she has become a successful single woman in the business world. In China the phrase "shelved ladies" or "left-over women" refers mainly to independent single females who have a decent job and earn an income high enough to give them financial freedom and social respect (Cao 2010: 56). They are also autonomous in matters of love and marriage. Zhang calls the "shelved ladies" the "3S ladies," where the three *s*'s stand for "single," "seventies" (born in the 1970s, nowadays those single women born in the 1980s have joined the legion of "shelved ladies") and "stuck" (2011: 20). "Stuck" does not have a negative intent; the "shelved ladies" choose to remain "stuck" and to retain their independence and have high expectations for marriage (Zhang 2007: 8). Ma uses a more aggressive title to describe the characters of many "shelved ladies": *baigujing*,[4] where *bai, gu* and *jing* serve as abbreviations for *bailing* (white-collar), *gugan* (backbone) and *jingying* (elite) (2006: 115). According to Ning (2008: 222), the "shelved ladies" normally have three "highs" – high qualifications, high intelligence and high income – plus an above-average outlook, which increases their employment opportunities. Because of these advantages, they also have high standards when choosing a partner.

The Chinese sociologist Li Yinhe (2010) notes that economic autonomy and affluence is the principal contributing factor to the "shelved ladies" phenomenon. In Du Lala's case, as highlighted in the storyline of the TV drama, her family comes from a comparatively underdeveloped city in southern China. Her parents long to have their own home in Shanghai, the most advanced and colorful metropolis of modern-day China, where Lala is currently based. The mother urges Lala to purchase an apartment in Shanghai so she and her husband can move from their hometown to live with their daughter in their dream city. Later, without letting Lala know in advance, the parents move to Shanghai to live with her and the three of them have to rent a place temporarily. While Lala is still saving for a down payment on an apartment, her father is diagnosed with an early carcinoma of the stomach.

Her father's attending physician is moved by Lala's filial piety towards her parents as she struggles between working and looking after her sick father, and he becomes attracted to her. However, he is not Lala's ideal type and she refuses his advances. Instead of relying on a man to help her out during hard times, Lala borrows money from her best friend and works even harder to support the entire family. Later, the father recovers and Lala is promoted to the managerial level at DB which leads to a huge increase in her salary. According to the novel, when she is promoted as HR and administration manager, Lala earns 230,000 RMB per year and is now able to purchase a spacious apartment to accommodate the whole family. When she brings her parents to the display suite of their future home, the mother is surprised by the size and quality of the rooms in the show apartment, but she has doubts about Lala's long-term financial ability to pay for such an apartment in Shanghai. However, Lala replies with assurance and confidence that she earns more than enough to pay the mortgage.

Due to their economic capability, the "shelved ladies" do not need to count on others (in particular a husband) to provide a comfortable lifestyle. As such, they are not in a hurry to get married and they will not be submissive in their relationships with men. According to Fan (2000: 423; Fan 2003, cited in Fan & Regulska 2008: 99):

> In China, Confucianism designates specific roles to individuals based on their gender, social class, and position relative to others; it erects boundaries and defines relations between members of society. Thus, women are subordinate to other male members of the family and are expected to be submissive and to sacrifice their interest to those of man.

Even in today's China, these established Confucian ideas and expectations towards women are still effective and forceful in the mind-sets of many Chinese people, in particular the older generations. In one scene of the TV drama, Wang Wei is gradually moved by Lala's hard work and persistence, falls in love with her and tries to persuade Lala not to be so determined to be a strong woman. In Wang Wei's opinion, "a woman is supposed to stay at home and assist her husband and bring up children. Why are you so stubborn and copy others to become a successful professional woman? You would be better off getting married while you are still young and learn to be a virtuous wife and a caring mother." Moreover, Wang Wei warns Lala that she concentrates too much on her work, which results in her losing her femininity and charm as a woman. Based on Wang Wei's observation, Lala only becomes gentle and meek when she is worn out at work. Here, Wang Wei's words and viewpoints expose the male chauvinism embraced by many Chinese men and signify the disparagement of the general social attitude towards the "shelved ladies." However, Lala cannot agree with Wang Wei, as she has different ideas regarding a woman's role in the family and in society, even though she is also interested in him and eventually becomes his girlfriend.

68   *A trans-media reading of* Go Lala Go

A comparison of the literary, filmic and televisual embodiments and interpretations of the Du Lala figure indicates that the TV drama narrative, more than the film and novel, foregrounds the independent and strong woman persona of this character, especially regarding her opinion on marriage and other relationships. In the concluding episodes of the TV serial, when Wang Wei is leaving DB and heading for another city, he wants Lala to give up everything she has gained at DB and go with him. However, Lala declines his request, as her career advancements and prospects at DB mean more to her than her relationship with him or any other man, which forces Wang Wei to change his mind at the very end of the show.

Employment at this foreign-owned firm has already transformed Lala from a novice in the career field to an aspiring and effective professional woman, and it continues to provide a platform for her to expand her career ambitions. In sharp contrast to the Confucian-styled desirable female subjects, "shelved ladies" such as Du Lala are self-governing individuals and strong woman characters, whose experience to borrow Keane's argument, "has provided an opening in China for a new-liberal ethic of self-cultivation," which sheds a contrasting light on the Maoist-style socialism that negates the self-governing subject (Keane 2007: 62). These self-determining strong women support themselves and they choose to work hard, and compete with men in the workplace. In Lala's case, she works harder than her male colleagues and supervisors, she disagrees and argues her point with them over projects and competes with them for promotions. Du Lala symbolizes the ideal post-1970s and 1980s middle-class Chinese woman (Peng 2010: 50–51). As Qian (2010: 299) states:

> [This ideal woman is] young, beautiful, fashionable, virtuous and dutiful, considerate, strong and independent. At home, she should be able to run the automatic washing machine and intelligent microwave; outside, she should be a skilled woman, who drives a car and competes hard in the workplace.

Here, the Du Lala–style autonomous, diligent, righteous and respectable young female professionals offer a fresh and affirmative image of the contemporary Chinese woman. In present-day China, materialistic and hedonist values are popular among some young women – the "gold-digger" figures who find rich husbands or "sugar daddies." In the TV show, Daisy, Wang Wei's former wife and a marry-only-for-money woman, divorces her husband for his lack of ambition when compared with other, wealthier men and then finds a rich foreign boyfriend. In contrast to Daisy, Lala is not interested in the lavish lifestyle Wang Wei could possibly provide for her. In real life, some of these "material girls" like Daisy, willingly or reluctantly, become "second wives" or mistresses of private businessmen or bureaucrat-entrepreneurs. These new men of wealth in China, who are "both advanced productive forces and also corrupt polluters of socialist morality" (Jeffreys 2008: 232), offer a luxurious lifestyle or promotional opportunities for women in exchange for their sexual services and companionship, which suggests the moral decline within the Chinese business community and the entire society. Therefore, these "concubine" women represent lazy, parasitic and indecent female figures. Du Lala was also offered a chance to become the mistress of the manager of the privately owned Chinese company. However, she rebuffed the man's seduction and resigned from her job. Lala's continual sexual harassment in her previous job was a major factor in her determination to find work in a foreign company. According to Lala, "there is less sexual harassment in foreign enterprises, as the managers and directors are all very busy due to the fast-paced and high-efficiency working manner and environment" (Li 2010: 13). Here, Lala's choice not only highlights the effectiveness of foreign companies, but also builds an image of a self-esteemed and morally virtuous contemporary Chinese woman. In her relationship with Wang Wei, Lala never had any intention to befriend the more powerful people at the company, even when she was just a junior staff member, thus she never thought about taking advantage of her intimate bond with Wang Wei in order to advance her own career at DB. On the contrary, her career ambitions are realized by struggling through issues and challenges on her own, which gives her equal footing with Wang Wei in their romantic relationship. In seeking equality, Lala does not drive Wang Wei away from her; rather, it consolidates the man's respect for her and lays the foundation for a stable and harmonious relationship. As Lester says to Lala when he retires from the HR director position (Lala becomes his successor in the TV show adaptation):

> You are too frank and adhere to principles. I always tried to persuade you to adapt to the environment. However, you eventually changed the environment and changed everybody around you. I know that your future is full of possibility and hope.

Here, Lester's words condone the way Lala has achieved career success by her determination to avoid all the negative aspects of workplace culture. Instead, Lala transfers positive energy to her co-workers, who share upbeat feelings with her, and together they contribute to the maintenance of a positive ethos in the workplace.

Besides her high moral quality, Du Lala's career aspirations and her longing for social recognition ensure that her story is full of practical significance to the "shelved ladies" (Cao 2010: 56–57). The success of Li Ke's bestseller and the film and TV adaptations suggest their accurate and insightful reflection of the topical shelved ladies social stigma. As a representative of the shelved ladies, the Du Lala figure justifies the existential veracity of this female subject's position and defends criticisms of it from the social and cultural spheres. The shelved ladies are often equated with "left-over" women, with the pejorative reference of being "left over" suggesting that a woman has been left behind by her peers in terms of choosing a spouse and implying that the left-over women are not attractive enough or are too fastidious in picking a suitable partner. This superficial understanding of the left-over women phenomenon oversimplifies the trend, which is popular among successful single females who are highly educated and middle-class professionals working in well-paid jobs who care more about their self-value and their own career, personal success and prosperity

70 *A trans-media reading of* Go Lala Go

than conventional gender ideology that prioritizes women's duty and role in marriage and family. The left-over women are rendered absurdly and sarcastically in columns, news reports and cartoons in the state-run media, which portray them as covetous and motivated. Thus, the official media has to pressure them to be "less materialistic and ambitious and lower their criteria and hurry up to find a husband before they become unwanted" (Cooper 2014). However, the Du Lala character offers a counter-example to that created by state propaganda; one who is extremely rational and clear-minded in dealing with relationships and in choosing her future Mr Right.

Configuring middle-class identity through consumption and career choice

Apart from being self-governing in issues of career choice and development, relationships and marriage, the autonomy and confidence of female middle-class professionals is also highlighted in the TV drama and film adaptations through manufacturing pleasant viewing experiences, promoting consumerism and employing drama to depict the impediments that these women must overcome due to their career choices. In the Chinese socio-cultural lexicon, foreign companies and professional workers are automatically juxtaposed with high incomes, skyscrapers, beauty, the middle class, high fashion, luxury goods and an expensive lifestyle. Therefore, both the TV and film versions of Du Lala's story exploit the rich symbolic meanings and cultural connotations of these socio-economic signs to manufacture visual selling points. The framing of the TV serial and film provides an enjoyable and instructive viewing experience for the audience, which maps out the living and working environment and conditions of the emerging middle class in contemporary China. For instance, the interior design and decoration of the company buildings and offices reflect a modern aesthetic. The spacious open-plan working areas and the stylish staff cafe reflect middle-class employees' expectations.

Furthermore, through their visually rich and splendid narratives, the film and the TV serial cater to the illusionistic and hedonist logic of a consumer society, by seeking to continuously manufacture and promote sensual stimuli and emotional outlets for the audience (Peng 2010: 50). The filmic adaptation's highly criticized inclusion of commercial products is a good example of this hedonistic logic. Based on the enormous appeal Li Ke's novel garnered among readers, Xu Jinglei's film attracted many companies to advertise their products in it. Therefore, Xu, in part, turns the film version of the novel into a product placement show. For example, brands like Lenovo (Lenovo Group Ltd. is a China-based multinational technology company which has acquired IBM's personal computer business and Motorola Mobility), Cartier, Mazda, Lipton, Nokia, Dove and Lotto are favored by the film's characters. These include: the white Lenovo desktop on the modern office desks; Lipton tea bags in the office tearoom; the Mazda MX5 (a sports car designed for fashionable metropolitan females) driving past the business center of Beijing. These all represent the trendy and luxurious lifestyle of middle-class office workers. These product placements in the movie possibly function as "television advertisements, infomercials and shopping programs" that "bombard Chinese audiences with messages and ideas about consumption . . . informing them about the latest trends in the market, and teaching them the skills needed to meet the demands of a modern lifestyle" (Xu 2009: 151).

Additionally, through their characters' consumption of lavish brands such as Hermes, Louis Vuitton and Burberry, which designates the social strata and cultural aesthetics of their users (middle-class white-collar Chinese workers or China's nouveau riche social echelon), the TV play and film texts exhibit how globalization and Westernization influence and acculturate the collective identity, consumption customs and lifestyle preferences of the Chinese middle class. This "showing" of the newly acquired extravagant consumption habit of the emerging Chinese middle class is especially underscored in the film adaptation of the novel at an unprecedented level. The director, Xu Jinglei, invited the Hollywood fashion designer Patricia Field, the stylist of *Sex and the City*, to design clothing for the characters in the film *Go Lala Go!* Ms Field chose Gucci, Loewe, Roger Vivier, Tod's, Dior, Valentino, Moschino and Bluemarine and designed more than seventy fashionable appearances modelling for the film characters. More than fifty of them were adopted in the film by Xu Jinglie, turning *Go Lala Go!* into a filmic version of a fashion magazine. In one scene of the movie, after Lala has a quarrel with Wang Wei, she goes shopping and purchases international big brands, such as Giorgio Armani, Toga, D&G, Hermes and Agnona. Thus, the film shows that by consuming trendy and expensive international – mainly Western – brands, the Chinese female professional creates her social identity and forms her cultural and aesthetic pursuits, and this seems to validate the globalization of consumption. In addition, procuring luxurious Western brand goods highlights the economic independence and strength of female Chinese middle-class office workers and consolidates their confidence.

Here, both the TV and film renditions of *A Story of Lala's Promotion* serve as examples of a typical cultural product, which successfully transfers the Du Lala phenomenon into a popular cultural sensation. Yu (2008: 173) observes:

> With the rise of the culture industry, culture is exerting influence in many new areas besides education, including consumption, aesthetics, economy, entertainment, and so forth. Culture not only affects the ideology and value systems of human beings; it also exerts deep influence on their lifestyle, consumption style, manufacturing style, and their social psychology.

Through foregrounding the lifestyle and consumption patterns of Chinese female business professionals, and further revealing the aesthetic inclinations and collective psychology of this social stratum, the TV serial and film accurately reflect the middle-class taste and culture which have become so alluring in contemporary China's social and cultural sphere. Xu (2009: 151) comments on the tendency of

72 *A trans-media reading of* Go Lala Go

contemporary Chinese programmers to bow to middle-class taste. This trend also occurs in books, films and TV drama series in China:

> [A]lthough almost all Chinese citizens have access to television, more recent consumer programming has become increasingly specialised and upscale, addressing and shaping the growing middle-class market with programs on everything from the latest technological gadgets and foreign travel to art investment. These programs embrace icons of global consumer culture and highlight their symbolic meanings, while acknowledging the middle class's striving for empowerment and self-expression within the sphere of consumption.

The middle class's endeavors to seek empowerment and self-expression through consumption have been reflected in contemporary Chinese popular TV drama serials and films which themselves focus on middle-class life: all characters enjoy a comfortable lifestyle, residing in modern housing, driving expensive cars, dressing in fashionable clothing, using expensive foreign brand appliances, dining at chic restaurants and traveling constantly abroad. Contemporary Chinese audiences, who are no longer "members of a collective political body, but, rather, [are] individuals engaged in various stages of striving for middle-class status" (Qian 2015: 160), take their cultural cues from these televisual works.

Moreover, in their manufacturing of a middle-class flavor, the TV serial and the film adaptations cleverly enlist celebrities with an established middle-class image from their previous screen roles. For example, Wang Luodan (starring as Du Lala in the TV drama adaptation) and Xu Jinglei (starring as Du Lala in the film version) share the stereotypical appearance of female white-collar workers and may be considered independent, intelligent and intellectual. Li Guangjie (starring as Wang Wei in the TV show) and Huang Lixing (starring as Wang Wei in the movie) have a classic collection of suits that highlight their cosmopolitan image and capable and experienced personalities that are common among business elites. Chen Huishan (starring as Rose in the TV drama) and Mo Wenwei (starring as Rose in the movie) display feminine charm and elegance through their fashionable appearances and convey the traits of the effectiveness and resolution of strong professional women through their acting (Peng 2010: 50).

In addition to the above-mentioned strategies adopted by the TV serial and the movie to highlight a middle-class image and culture, Du Lala's struggles in the workplace change her from a novice to a successful professional woman and illustrate a middle-class journey for many contemporary Chinese people. Coming from an average working class household in a second-tier or third-tier city, with no connections and networks on which she can rely to find a good job in the big metropolis, Lala is a standard "ugly duckling woman" who emerges from nothing but achieves a lot in her career. For these "ugly duckling" men and women, (*fenghuangnan/fenghuangnu*) of today's China, the only capital they hold is their youth and a university qualification. By receiving a higher education and acquiring a high-profile professional job, some young Chinese with lower socio-economic backgrounds have joined the ranks of the expanding middle class. By relying on their knowledge and skills, and unremitting efforts in their chosen fields, these "ugly ducklings" realize their middle-class dream in terms of securing a high-income job in a big city, purchasing a spacious apartment and driving an expensive car. Thus, Du Lala's experiences exemplify for many the struggles of China's budding middle class. From another perspective, the Du Lala character may also be read as a modern Cinderella figure who depends on her high moral quality, virtues, humble nature and tolerance and finally wins the respect and love from the prince.

The dramatic plots of the novel and its TV drama adaptation, which foreground Du Lala's workplace struggles and achievements, and her "practical-cum-romantic" love relationship with her own fairy tale prince, Wang Wei, create a widely accepted and popular middle-class woman persona. As the novel and TV serial narratives convey, the struggle for career recognition is central to the female middle-class business professional's existence, and romance is something she dreams of but does not pursue. These traits of Lala strike a chord with many upwardly mobile middle-class professional women who count on their own ability and intelligence to gain financial well-being and social recognition. In one of Lala's classic lines in the TV drama, she reveals her belief in the significance of a career for women when she says that "a career is absolutely important for women, for if you try hard, your efforts will pay off." In other words, middle-class professional females such as Du Lala are more realistic in their expectations because they know what is required for success and what is not. Thus, romance is a bonus they want and deserve, but it is only after and in addition to their career goals. In Lala's case, her career success gains her respect from Wang Wei and she finally gains his love as well. Moreover, through transforming Daisy, an original "gold-digger" character, into a qualified female white-collar professional (after she is deserted by her rich foreign boyfriend) who follows the career path of many middle-class employees, the show inserts a positive connotation to the middle-class social identity in contemporary China, which endorses and praises hard work and independence. Daisy's realization of her errors and her change of moral direction criticize those who only seek materialism, and confirm the wise choice of the majority of young contemporary Chinese women.

In summary, the white-collar, middle-class way of life is detailed and normalized in the TV serial and film adaptations of *A Story of Lala's Promotion*. The enormous popularity of these texts and other novels, TV dramas and movies with similar themes that describe the trend towards a middle-class lifestyle and culture as both a socio-economic phenomenon and a cultural movement, verifies the status of the prevailing white-collar and middle-class value system, not only in literary and artistic creation, but also in the lives of contemporary Chinese people.

Conclusion

The success of *A Story of Lala's Promotion* and its TV and film adaptations is not accidental. The theme of the Du Lala phenomenon that is reflected in these literary

74 *A trans-media reading of* Go Lala Go

and visual narratives – the life of white-collar middle-class employees in joint ventures and foreign-invested enterprises – has recently become a prevalent subject in Chinese popular culture. Through a trans-media plot and character analysis of *A Story of Lala's Promotion* and *Go Lala Go!*, this chapter has shone a light on the overall economic and cultural trend towards assimilation and globalization, where Western economic and cultural paradigms have gained the upper hand. In addition, by examining the successful transformation of contemporary Chinese female white-collar workers from "flower vase" to "super-girl" in the workplace (on a platform provided by foreign/Western companies), this chapter has highlighted the "shelved ladies/left-over women" phenomenon and explored current trends in studies concerning Chinese women. Moreover, the globalization of consumption, lifestyle and culture has also been reviewed in this chapter. The nuanced combination of consuming habits and preferences and the lifestyles and aesthetics of white-collar office clerks further underlines the socio-cultural identity and pursuits of the contemporary Chinese middle-class reflected in the Du Lala phenomenon.

Notes

1 In contemporary China, there is what is referred to as the "wealthy second generation" and the "official second generation." The "wealthy second generation" refers to the children of the rich businessmen who became wealthy during the Opening Up reforms. And the "official second generation" refers to the children of the high-ranking CCP cadres who were in office during the Mao era. It also refers to the children of current high-level Chinese officials.

2 The main character of the novel, Du Lala, represents a typical member of the middle class of contemporary Chinese society: she has no recognized "social background," but has received a good education and struggles until she eventually achieves success. To the majority of Chinese people, her story is more valuable, due to its relevance, than the Bill Gates story.

3 Besides the Du Lala series by Li Ke, other novels with similar themes include: *Diary of a White-Collar Female Who Works in A Foreign Company* (Juewang 2008), *Niu Xiaomi's Struggle in A Foreign Company* (Hong 2009) and *The Great Little Assistant* (*Liaobuqi de xiaozhuli*) (Xiao 2010). The English abbreviation of office lady – "OL" – is widely used in Chinese literary and media texts to refer to middle-class female office clerks in both Chinese and foreign companies.

4 *Baigujing* is the name of a female demon in the traditional Chinese novel *Journey to the West (Xiyouji)* by the Ming Dynasty writer Wu Chengen. Here, using this phrase to depict white-collar female workers in contemporary China highlights their ability and intelligence.

References

Albert, Mathias. 2007. "Globalization Theory: Yesterday's Fad or More Lively Than Ever?" *International Political Sociology* 1: 165–182.

Cao, Ruixia. 2010. "Du Lala Shengzhiji: Yuzhongbutong de Meili" [*Go Lala Go!* A Different Kind of Prettiness]. *Dianying Wenxue* [Movie Literature] 16: 56–57.

Chan, Kwok-Bun, Luk, Vivienne, and Wang, George Xun. 2005. "Conflict and Innovation in International Joint Ventures: Toward a New Sinified Corporate Culture or Alternative Globalization in China." *Asia Pacific Business Review* 11 (4): 461–482.

Cooper, Marta. 2014. "Over 27? Unmarried? Female? You'd be on the scrapheap in China," *The Telegraph*, published on 31 April 2014, viewed on 31 July 2014, www.telegraph. co.uk/women/womens-life/10786321/Leftover-women-Over-27-Unmarried-Female-Youd-be-on-the-scrapheap-in-China.html.

Ding, Daniel Z. 1997. "Control, Conflict and Performance: A Study of US-Chinese Joint Ventures." *Journal of International Marketing* 5 (3): 31–45.

Du, Jun. 2010. "Jiedu Dianying Du Lala Shengzhiji de Nuxing Yishi" [Understanding the Female Sensibility in the Film *Go Lala Go!*]. *Dianying Pingjie* [Movie Review] 8: 24–25.

Fan, C. Cindy. 2000. "Migration and Gender in China," in *China Review 2000*, Chuangming Lau and Jianfan Shen (eds.). Hong Kong: Chinese University of Hong Kong Press, pp. 423–454.

Fan, C. Cindy. 2003. "Rural-Urban Migration and Gender Division of Labor in Transitional China." *International Journal of Urban and Regional Research* 27 (1): 24–47.

Fan, C. Cindy. 2004. "The State, the Migrant Labor Regime, and Maiden Workers in China." *Political Geography* 23: 283–305.

Fan, C. Cindy and Regulska, Joanna. 2008. "Gender and the Labor Market in China and Poland," in *Urban China in Transition*, John R. Logan (ed.). Malden, MA: Blackwell Publishing, pp. 89–112.

Go Lala Go! Du Lala Shengzhiji. 2010. Directed by Xu Jinglei. China: China Film Group Corporation.

Guo, Junsheng. 2010. "Zhichang Xiaoshuo Xuyao Bei Fuyu Sixiang he Wenhua Neihan" [The Career Place Novels Need to Have More Cultural Connotations]. *Meili Zhongguo* [Charming China] 13: 231–232.

Hong, Hulang. 2009. *Niu Xiaomi Waiqi Dapinji* [Niu Xiaomi's Struggle in a Foreign Company]. Beijing: Jiuzhou Press.

Hou, Shuwen. 2010. "Du Lala Shengzhiji: Xiandai Zhichang de Shengcun Tiyan" [*Go Lala Go!* Surviving in the Modern Workplace"]. *Dianying Pingjie* [Movie Review] 11: 25–26.

Jeffreys, Elaine. 2008. "Advanced Producers or Moral Polluters? China's Bureaucrat-Entrepreneurs and Sexual Corruption," in *The New Rich in China: Future Rulers, Present Lives*, David Goodman (ed.). London: Routledge, pp. 229–244.

Juewang, Canghai. 2008. *Yige Waiqi Nubailing de Riji* [Diary of a Female White-Collar Worker in a Foreign Company]. Beijing: China Friendship Publishing Corporation.

Keane, Michael. 2007. *Created in China: The Great New Leap Forward*. London: Routledge.

Kirkbride, Paul S., Tang, Sara F. Y. and Westwood, Robert I. 1991. "Chinese Conflict Preferences and Negotiation Behaviour: Cultural and Psychological Influences." *Organizational Studies* 12 (3): 365–386.

Li, Ke. 2010. *Du Lala Shengzhiji* [A Story of Lala's Promotion], 3rd ed. Xi An: Shannxi Normal University Press.

Li, Yinhe. 2010. "*Shengnu Yu Danshen Langchao*" [Shelved Ladies and the Singles Fashion], blog entry, 6 July, available at: http://blog.sina.com.cn/s/blog_473d53360100jwlf. html (accessed 8 May 2011).

Loubere, Nicholas. 2010. "Is China Conforming to a Westernized Global Culture? An Assimilation Theory Analysis of Chinese-Western Cultural Relations." *Graduate Journal of Asia-Pacific Studies* 7 (1): 70–83.

Ma, Xiulan. 2006. "Suowei 'Shengnu Shidai'" [The So-Called 'Shelved Ladies' Era]. *Xiandai Yuwen* [Modern Chinese] 12: 115.

Ning, Hong. 2008. "Shengnu Xianxiang de Shehuixue Fenxi" [A Sociological Analysis of the 'Shelved Ladies' Phenomenon]. *Lilun Jie* [Theory Horizon] 12: 222–223.

Peng, Junyi. 2010. "Cong Yingpian Du Lala Shengzhiji Kandao de" [Reflecting on *Go Lala Go!*]. *Dazhong Wenyi* [Popular Literature and Art] 6: 50–51.

Qian, Gong. 2010. "Red Women and TV Drama," in *Contemporary Chinese Visual Culture: Tradition, Modernity, and Globalization*, Christopher Crouch (ed.). New York: Cambria Press, pp. 295–315.

Qian, Gong. 2015. "Remolding Heroes: The Erasure of Class Discourse in the Red Classics Television Drama Adaptations," in *Chinese Television in the Twenty-First Century: Entertaining the Nation*, Ruoyun Bai and Geng Song (eds.). London and New York: Routledge, pp. 158–174.

Xiao, Yi. 2010. *Liaobuqi de Xiaozhuli* [The Great Little Assistant]. Tianjin: Tianjin People's Publishing House.

Xu, Janice Hua. 2009. "Building a Chinese 'Middle Class': Consumer Education and Identity Construction in Television Land," in *TV China*, Ying Zhu and Chris Berry (eds.). Bloomington: Indiana University Press, pp. 150–167.

Yu, Keping. 2008. "The Developmental Logic of Chinese Culture under Modernization and Globalization." *Boundary 2* 35 (2): 157–182.

Zhang, Wei. 2010. "Du Lala Re Zheshe Chude Zhongguo Zhongchan Jieji Xianxiang" [Du Lala Hit Reflects the China Middle-Class Phenomenon]. *Asian Weekly*, 6 June.

Zhang, Yajun. 2011. "Woguo 'shengnu' Wenti de Shehuixue Sikao" [A Sociological Reflection on the '3S Lady' Phenomenon]. *Shandong Nuzi Xueyuan Xuebao* [Journal of Shangdong Women's University] 96 (2): 20–24.

Zhang, Yue. 2007. "Xiandai Dushi 'Shengnu' Xianxiang de Shihuixue Toushi" [A Sociological Reflection on the 'Shelved Ladies' Phenomenon in Modern Cities]. *Shangxi Qingnian Guanli Ganbu Xueyuan Xuebao* [Journal of Shanxi College for Youth Administrators] 20 (4): 8–10.

4   *Honey Bee Man*

Divorced women and an elaboration of the contemporary Chinese female

Introduction

Honey Bee Man (*Woai nanguimi*, 2014) is a TV serial about romance in the city. Its backdrop is the post-divorce life of contemporary Chinese women, particularly those who were born in the 1960s, 1970s and 1980s, and it depicts many of the typical encounters experienced by these women. With a focus on the post-divorce lives of three generations of modern-day Chinese women, *Honey Bee Man* maps out a nuanced and discursive gender space which gives light to the considerable economic changes that have impacted the lives of ordinary Chinese people, and particularly Chinese women. This chapter discusses the varying relationships and marital forms and reveals the utility and value of China's divorced women in relation to the government's propaganda rhetoric, as it bids to stimulate what it defines as a competent, considerate and buoyant citizenry. By constructing an "ideal woman image," "a suitable female subject" and a "preferred femininity" via the TV screen, the state discourse creates an apt, virtuous and desirable model for its ideal Chinese woman. In doing so, official publicity promotes a particular "model" of divorced women (such as the Huiyun character in the show) as even-tempered, caring and strong females who do not complain about their fate, but instead strive to become even more tender, virtuous and generous after their marriage breakups, while it remolds those "unqualified or incompetent wives" (such as the Ye Shan and Fang Yiyi characters in the show) into a submissive and traditional Chinese good wife–wise mother figure and rewards them with a happy "second spring." Furthermore, by producing "mismatched" couples, which are politically useful, the show helps to relieve the sour taste of social disparity and wealth discrimination that is the upshot of a resurfacing class demarcation and social discord generated by the ongoing economic transformations.

The era from the May Fourth Movement to the Republican period, and the accompanying focus on women, marriage and family, constitutes a considerable amount of all the literary and filmic creations in the history of modern China. The female writers who were active and influential during and beyond the May Fourth period foregrounded women's issues, and especially their roles in marriage and family (Meng & Dai 2004). Also, in the movies that were shot during the Republican time, many filmic melodramas focus their narrative on the lives of women,

78 Honey Bee Man

their dilemmas and their misery (Pickowicz 2012). Ranging from depictions of women's anti-feudalism struggles and pursuit of individual freedom to portrayal of their personal choices and vicissitudes in an era that was undergoing a gigantic change, the representation of women and their lives in these literary and artistic texts is constantly tied to national events, politics and the social chaos of their times.

During the socialist period, revolutionary films were a major source of cultural and artistic creation, which, guided by the socialist realism paradigm, combined "entertainment with indoctrination" (Sun 2008: 97). The image of women, as presented in these revolutionary films, was used as a signifier of darkness, obscurity, the exploited and part of the poor and victimized proletariat masses, who had been saved and enlightened by the Chinese Communist Party (CCP) and the communist cause it upheld (Dai 2000: 90–93). Similarly, in much of socialist literature, "the state's political discourse translated itself through women into the private context of desire, love, marriage, divorce, and familial relations" while "it turned woman into an agent politicizing desire, love, and family relations by delimiting and repressing sexuality, self and all private emotions" (Meng 1993: 118). In these circumstances, Chinese women were projected as a national subject where their personal feelings and family lives were totally overwhelmed and appropriated by the political imperatives of the CCP government.

By the time of the Opening Up reforms, a watershed moment which marks China's transformation from a socialist revolutionary society to a post-socialist post-revolutionary society, the politicization and subsequent tragedy which befell many individuals during the Mao era was openly exposed and criticized in so-called Scar Literature novels and films.[1] In many Scar Literature books and their film adaptations, such as *Legend of the Tianyun Mountain* (*Tianyunshan chuanqi* 1980) and *Hibiscus Town* (*Furongzhen* 1986),[2] the trials and tribulations suffered by women during the socialist political movements, which reached a peak during the Cultural Revolution, and the "scars" which remain due to the political irrationality of the times are highlighted.

Within the same time period, the TV drama serial emerged as a dominant, popular cultural and entertainment form comparable to literature and film. The most common TV drama shows made at this time have a more secular and recreational intent as they shift the focus from political wounds to domestic and family matters. With the Cultural Revolution and the Opening Up reforms serving only as a narrative background, the shows reflect the daily lives, domestic issues and relationships among family members of ordinary Chinese people. The very successful TV drama *Yearning* (*Kewang* 1990), made by the Beijing Television Arts Center, is a typical example of the depoliticizing and domesticizing fashion of media products in the early 1990s and beyond. With Wang Shuo (a famous and slightly notorious Beijing-based Hooligan Literature writer) as one of its main creative minds, *Yearning* attempts to steer the attention of the mass audience away from the collective and overriding political concerns that had been crushing the social and personal lives of Chinese people for several decades towards more pragmatic and familial matters and concerns. By zooming in on the private space in social imagination and artistic representation, *Yearning* caused a paradigmatic turn in the development of Chinese TV drama narrative (Kong 2008: 75–76). In *Yearning*, the female lead, Liu Huifang, portrays a virtuous Confucian wife and wise mother character rather than the model soldier/worker and iron-girl figures of the Mao era, and the show's narratives are more concerned with Huifang's role in the domestic sphere and her relationship with her husband and other family members.

Following *Yearning*'s unparalleled success, family stories revolving around mundane quotidian concerns and the life of ordinary urbanites became the core subject matter and thematic preference of Chinese TV drama creation in the 1990s and 2000s (Yin 2004 cited in Kong 2008: 77–78). Further, the ascent and recognition of the "private space" in TV culture and public discourse has opened up more space for conveying women's narratives and demonstrating their life experiences. Disengaging from politics and national affairs, Chinese women now occupy "a room of their own," and via the cultural and media platform provided by the TV screen, their individual life matters, (especially those gender-specific ones), relationship and marriage issues, social identity and role and their ensuing emotional concerns, which are modified by the dramatic socio-economic developments, are foregrounded.

Female image and marital status in post-reform TV drama serials

Unparalleled economic transformation has produced enormous and diverse occupational, social, matrimonial and familial challenges and opportunities for contemporary Chinese women. More recently, the deepening of economic renovation and the succeeding social changes it has stimulated have caused more social stigmas and moral dilemmas for Chinese women, which in turn has attracted immense attention from TV producers. As females constitute the vast majority of Chinese TV drama viewers, the stories and hardships facing women are arguably more likely to increase audience ratings and to be more relevant to TV drama spectators. From the socio-economic vicissitudes of the past couple of decades, a new group of female icons in TV drama serials has emerged. For example, *Coming and Going* (*Lailaiwangwang*, 1999) and *Holding Hands* (Qianshou, 1999) both fashioned young, trendy, strong-willed and to some extent "morally weak" or "problematic" female characters, who are "third parties" in other people's relationships. Equally, these two popular romance serials feature the victimized wives who are middle-aged female workers and choose to sacrifice themselves for their husbands and families as they confront the balance between their careers and families and all the diverging requests from family and society. However, after their husbands achieve their first goal of career success, they then go on to develop extramarital relationships with young and pretty women, and this then leads eventually to the breakdown of their marriages, and thus the futility of the wives' sacrifices (Kong 2008: 79). One obvious effect of the immeasurable changes in Chinese society that have been the result of economic reforms is the "destabilization of the institution of marriage and the breakdown of family life

80   Honey Bee Man

in urban China," and accordingly, TV dramas reflect this social reality and "are often full of turmoil and tension, mid-life crises, extramarital affairs and marriage breakups" (Kong 2008: 78). Furthermore, TV dramas that deal with these issues often have a unique feminine viewpoint and awareness.

Another distinctive female icon, which has been varyingly labelled as "shelved ladies" or "left-over" women, is partly represented in "pink drama." As a unique Chinese cultural-media phenomenon, "pink drama" features the "single, childless urban women" who were born after the 1980s and who are "[e]ducated, independent, and enjoying Westernized lifestyles in cosmopolitan cities" and are "successful in careers but [are] nevertheless confused in [their] personal relationships" (Huang 2008: 101). Echoing Huang, my own research (see Chapter 2 and Chapter 3 of this volume) on the "shelved ladies"/"left-over" women social phenomena that are reflected in the recently broadcast TV drama series, helps to substantiate the position that instead of being passively left behind in marriage issues, many contemporary Chinese females are enabled by their newly acquired economic and social power and are in fact willing to be "left-over," "shelved" and "strong" woman figures.

One observable and debatable social outcome of China's huge economic makeover is that it has produced two distinct types of urban women: "winners" and "losers."[3] The "winners" include professional, middle-class, white-collar females who gain economic independence and social recognition out of their struggles and success in the workplace, whereas the "losers" comprise, for example, laid-off female workers and those full-time housewives who sacrifice their own career for the well-being of the entire family. Noticeably, in many cases, both types are struggling and sometimes suffer in their relationships and marriage lives. The "strong" women seek equality with their partners in their relationship, and some of them even assume an aggressive or overbearing manner towards their male partners and adopt a dominant role in their relationships, which on one hand fails to conform to the established Confucian model of a virtuous woman, while on the other hand it leads to a loss of femininity and charm in the eyes of their men. The other type of women, those who choose to fulfill a supportive role in their families, risk their own well-being on the success of their partners, who may then desert them or are very likely to lose interest in their worn-out wives and look for new partners or mistresses.

This dire situation confronting many present-day Chinese women in their relationships and marriages is further evidenced by China's mounting divorce rate. According to statistics, in 2013, China's divorce rate rose by 40 percent over the past five years, and the figure in Beijing was even higher than the national rate. In 2012, there were 3.1 million couples divorced, while in 2008 there were only 2.26 million (Chinanews.com 2013). Divorce was a sensitive topic in China a couple of decades ago, and divorcees felt discomfort and even shame when their situation was known publicly, as there was a social conception that a divorced woman or man must have some weakness(es) that had caused the failure of her/ his marriage. Although this discriminatory viewpoint has gradually changed over recent years and a more tolerant attitude towards divorce has been adopted, being a divorcee still incurs negative judgments, especially of divorced women. As a burgeoning social problem, divorce and post-divorce life (particular of women) has gained more attention from TV producers and the general audience alike.

Kong (2008: 80) has pointed out that although different from the Western soap opera, the Chinese TV serial still lacks a distinct "women's tradition"; however, the incipient subgenre of urban romances has still managed to map out a gendered space to render the various complications and worries confronting contemporary Chinese females. Notwithstanding their occasionally over-idealistic endings, these TV serials deliver relief to the audience and a feeling of social adherence with other women undergoing a comparable arduous journey. Here, Kong's argument not only clarifies that there exists a "female space" configured by contemporary Chinese TV drama works, which engages with the concerns of many modern-day Chinese women, but it also detects the social function fulfilled by these shows given that their storylines help to create a communal attachment among the viewers who have similar concerns with the shows' characters. In the light of Kong's observations, I argue that *Honey Bee Man*, the TV drama text under examination in this chapter, reveals the challenges and problems encountered by divorced women and intends to help those "unlucky" women attain a healthy and positive stance on love, marriage and life after divorce. This not only is practical support for many female viewers who have similar life experiences, but also assists to construct an "idealized woman image," "a good national female subject" and a "preferred femininity" in response to the call of the state propaganda discourse.

Honey Bee Man: three generations of divorced women

The narrative arc of *Honey Bee Man*, a thirty-four-episode TV drama serial, mainly concerns itself with the post-divorce lives of three generations of Chinese women, and their challenges, ideas and attitudes after divorce. Huiyun, Ye Shan and Fang Yiyi, the three lead characters, are imbued with different personalities, outlooks and ideals about their marriages. They represent, respectively, post-1960s, post-1970s and post-1980s Chinese females. Born in the 1960s, and now in her late forties, Huiyun is of the comparatively older generation among these three women and the one who upholds the customary and Confucian-styled principles expected of women. She grew up during the heyday of revolutionary China and received an orthodox socialist moral education which emphasizes altruism and sacrifice. Huiyun is a typical "loser" female character, as her famous painter husband leaves her and their son for one of his students, a youthful and attractive young woman, after he attained fame and wealth for his artistic work. During her marriage, Huiyun is the perfect wife and mother, who carefully and wholeheartedly "waits upon" her husband and son, and although she has done nothing wrong, her husband abandons her in her middle age. In the show, Huiyun rarely complains about her bad luck, although for a middle-aged woman, to lead a single life is by no means an easy task.

Ye Shan is Huiyun's cousin, and a representative of successful professional women born in the 1970s. In her mid-thirties, Ye Shan is a high-level manager

82   Honey Bee Man

at a world-famous Japanese cosmetics corporation. She is officious and even sometimes overbearing towards her subordinates, and at home she is domineering towards her husband, which eventually leads to the collapse of her marriage. The Ye Shan role is an archetypal strong woman figure. She competes fiercely with men, both at work and at home, which not only evokes antipathy from her male colleagues, but also causes conflict with her husband, leading to a ruined marriage.

The other main female character is Fang Yiyi. She was born in the 1980s and is in her early twenties. As an unemployed youth, she experienced a "quickie" marriage and "quickie" divorce within a month. The Fang Yiyi character represents the self-centered and happy-go-lucky personality of the post-1980s and post-1990s generations who were born under the one-child population control policy of the CCP government.[4] By contrasting and comparing the post-divorce life of these three generations of Chinese women, the plots of *Honey Bee Man* reveal how economic, social and cultural transformations have altered the lives of contemporary Chinese females.

Huiyun represents middle-aged virtuous wives who are betrayed by their husbands. The Huiyun character is in her late forties and appears to have retired (or to have been laid off) from her job.[5] Although the story does not make it clear why Huiyun stopped working in paid employment, it does make it clear that she continues to work at home in her unpaid supportive role. Huiyun is an accomplished domestic provider, and the family apartment is extremely clean and tidy. She is an excellent cook and takes good care of her son's daily life. Huiyun's integrity is reflected by her former husband's nostalgic longing for her when he compares his current wife with Huiyun. As shown in many scenes of *Honey Bee Man*, the ex-husband returns often to his old home with Huiyun whenever he has a quarrel with his new wife, in order, it seems, to find comfort, warmth and peace with Huiyun. The husband feels very relaxed at his old home and seems to yearn for the past as he casts a wistful gaze at the furnishings of the apartment. He is usually reluctant to leave the apartment and return to his new home and his pretty young wife.

There are a number of reasons for the broken marriages of the Huiyun-style Chinese women. First, they have grown up in the early decades of socialist China where women were required to play two equal roles in the social and domestic domains. In other words, in addition to acting as capable, diligent and loyal workers who selflessly contributed themselves to the construction of their country, these women also shouldered the obligation of having to be proficient and virtuous housewives according to the expectations of the entrenched Confucian covenants and socialist morality. Barlow (2004: 288) compares the situation of Chinese women and European women in their respective modernity projects (for Maoist China, it was an alternative socialist revolutionary modernity path compared with the West) and argues that while in Europe women gave up feudal social foundations and took on the challenges of the modern era, women in China just added modern roles to the feudal roles they already had inherited, multiplying their estrangement from personal being or social standing. This double payment made by Chinese women "as required by the superpositioning of their roles as citizens and housewives" is considered by Dai (2002: 123) "a type of national violence being inflicted exclusively on women." Thus, one of the compulsory roles of women is to be a housewife, and this is endorsed by the socialist modernity project that impels Huiyun-style women to take up a supportive role in their families. This then places these women in a passive and inferior role in their marriages, and for modern-day Chinese men who perhaps seek more in a marriage partner, it may lead to boredom with their wives, which then often leads to antipathy.

Since the Opening Up period, "the contradictory and double standards demanded of women in China's puritan socialist-turned-capitalist consumer society" cause those women who have grown up in pre-reform China to feel defenseless and confused (Kong 2008: 79). On the one hand, the Confucian ideals relating to Chinese women (which continued throughout the nascency of socialist China), caused these women to become convinced that it was their duty to sacrifice themselves for the benefit of the entire family, a position which also led them into a situation of dependency and lack of self-identity. However, on the other hand, the post-socialist competitive economic and social environment requires modern-day Chinese women to be independent, both financially and psychologically, and to be strong enough to survive in their chosen careers. These ambiguous and paradoxical expectations placed on middle-aged Chinese women such as Huiyun create challenges with their social and familial identities and responsibilities, which directly or indirectly lead to their broken marriages.

Furthermore, the diverging aesthetic standards relating to a woman's appearance and feminine appeal between the socialist revolutionary period and the reform eras lead to a position where the Huiyun-style middle-aged Chinese woman feels uncomfortable and unable to adapt to the rapid change of social and cultural fashions. The coming-of-age and maturation experiences of Chinese women of Huiyun's generation in the "androgynous" revolutionary society expunged their femininity and their sense of womanhood.[6] Although the appearance of Huiyun in the show has restored to some extent her feminine attractiveness, when compared with Ye Shan and her former husband's new wife, who always dress in fashionable clothes and wear stylish hairdos and exquisite makeup, Huiyun's appearance seems too traditional and conservative, which makes her somehow less competitive to these chic females in the eyes of contemporary Chinese men.

Compared with Huiyun, her cousin Ye Shan is a pretty, fashion-conscious and capable post-1970s Chinese woman who received a higher education, enjoys better material conditions and possesses more confidence. The ongoing economic transformation provides additional financial opportunities and social mobility for women of Ye Shan's generation and opens up extra space for young, intelligent and ambitious Chinese women to obtain better careers. Consequently, many of the Ye Shan–style "strong women" struggle and compete vigorously in the workplace and turn themselves into middle-class, white-collar professionals or managers in local corporations, joint ventures or international enterprises. They are less immersed in traditional gendered role cultivation and in socialist moral coaching – plus, due to their economic autonomy, social status and self-assurance, the Ye Shan–style women rarely assume a subservient or secondary role in relationships or marriage; instead, they are more often than not dominant leaders, which is opposite to Huiyun-style housewives.

In the narratives of the show, Ye Shan is painted as an authoritarian manager who seldom smiles and is overbearing and gruff in manner to her underlings. She is often seen yelling at her employees and speaking to them in a pompous and condescending way as she stands in judgment with her hands on hips. Ye Shan's domineering manner is further accentuated by her rude and irrational behavior, and it was this sort of conduct that created pandemonium at the wedding ceremony of her former husband and his new wife. Unlike her cousin Huiyun, who presents a peaceful mood and strives to keep in contact with her ex-husband and his new family, Ye Shan's comportment is often outrageous and violent. She is quarrelsome and aggressive towards the newly married couple and turns the wedding party into an uproar when she finds out that her ex-husband's new wife has become pregnant. However, rather than portraying Ye Shan's husband as an immoral and heartless man, the plots instead foreground the unfeminine and overbearing nature of Ye Shan as the catalyst for the breakdown of their marriage. As the narrative of the show unfolds, the audience gradually realizes that it is Ye Shan's preoccupation with work and her career success, and her ensuing arrogance, that has caused her to overlook her family life and the feelings of her husband and has led naturally and understandably to her husband's infidelity.

By polarizing the Ye Shan and Huiyun characters, with Ye Shan being a strong, aggressive and inconsiderate career woman, as opposed to the Huiyun character, which is that of a humble, forgiving and thoughtful housewife, *Honey Bee Man* ingeniously reveals the moral dilemmas and social complications imposed on contemporary Chinese women in their attempts to adjust and balance their roles between work and family life. This equivocal and awkward situation that confronts many contemporary Chinese women is created by the huge and ongoing economic and social changes in China today. The work-or-family dilemma is oversimplified in the show text, as it is not just an overemphasis on work or a retreat to domestic duties that can provide the answer for how to overcome the relationship difficulties that many modern-day Chinese women find themselves in. For instance, neither Huiyun, a virtuous wife and caring mother, nor Ye Shan, a smart and accomplished professional woman, succeeds in managing her marriage.

Similar to these fictional characters, a growing number of contemporary Chinese women end up with broken relationships or marriages and have to face the consequences of these failures. In Ye Shan's case, even though her career prospects are constantly rising and she lives a comfortable and materially affluent lifestyle, her after-work single life is sad and lonely. As demonstrated in recurring sequences throughout the show, after she finishes work and returns to her large and stylish apartment, Ye Shan always has a bowl of instant noodles for dinner and after that she habitually sits back on the sofa to watch TV until she falls asleep. Ye Shan's forlorn and tedious after-work life is seen in ironic contrast to her successful career. After all the years she has spent working long hours, struggling to overcome all the obstacles that have come her way, it seems that she deserves a happy life. However, her solitude betrays her seemingly contented and pleasant life. When Ye Shan's mother comes to visit her from their hometown, the old woman finds that her beloved daughter has become a single woman again and her heart is broken by this shocking news. The mother understands exactly the hardships her daughter has gone through over the past years while she was struggling in the competitive and fast-paced metropolis. She is aware that Ye Shan's workplace accomplishments cannot counterweigh the deficiency of a normal family life. In summary, the Ye Shan role in the show serves as a foil to the time-honored Confucian ideal and to the mainstream state prospect of a good woman.

Different from Huiyun's virtuousness and devotion, and Ye Shan's charm and career success, Fang Yiyi is the stereotypical post-1980s and post-1990s young woman who has been unleashed from many traditional and socialist moral constraints. The young Chinese people of these generations are self-centered and willful in action, as most of them have been spoiled by their parents and grandparents throughout their childhoods. It is common knowledge that they are pampered children of adoring parents, and they are usually the only child in the family. Different from many other one-child-generation children who have been spoiled by their elder family members, Fang's mother died when she was little and her father abandoned her and her then teenage big brother. Thus, in order to compensate for her perceived harsh childhood, her brother is the one who spoils his little sister, although he has to work extremely hard to support the entire family. Spoiled, without the practical knowledge of day-to-day life and the skills to do housework, capricious and self-centered, the Fang Yiyi character represents a certain type of post-1980s and post-1990s woman. In particular, her avant-garde appearance, (she always dresses like a punk, wears strange hairstyles and rides a big black motorbike) and rebellious personality provide a counter-example of "a good woman" according to the Chinese standard. Fang Yiyi–style women contribute equally with their usually one-child male counterpart to the looming epidemic of marital crisis facing China's young people.

For example, these young people are seen as selfish, often lack responsibility and are reckless in marriage-related choices and issues. The fiercely debated and controversial social phenomenon of the "quickie" marriage and "quickie" divorce of modern-day China is exposed by the show's plots. "Quickie" marriage and "quickie" divorce are widespread and even "fashionable" among the youth of post-1980s and post-1990s generations of China. These young Chinese men and women act on impulse and emotion: a very unconventional way of settling one of the main affairs of one's life in China. An opening sequence of *Honey Bee Man* shows Fang Yiyi, who is about twenty years old, and her husband, who is of a similar age, during their divorce proceedings. The two of them were just married a month ago and their rush to marriage is a clue of their false maturity. In comparison to "left-over" women and older single youths who have become huge social concerns of the current Chinese society, Fang Yiyi and her husband enter into marriage at a much earlier age; however, their pretentious early maturation not only sees them marrying early, but also results in their early ("quickie") divorce. During their divorce proceedings, the couple show no signs of regret or

86 Honey Bee Man

sadness for their actions, and their childish quarrel over who should pay the 7.5 RMB divorce fee only reveals their irreverence towards marriage, which is like child's play. Their nonchalant attitude towards marriage confuses the staff at the Bureau of Civil Administration who deal with their divorce case. In this sequence, close-up shots of the two youths' indifferent faces constantly occupy the center of the camera frame, which shows the director's focus and concerns. The youths' apathetic approach towards one of the most important events and institutions of their lives is highly likely to cause much contemplation among the TV viewers about the current situation and the potential risks of married life for China's younger generations.

In another scene, Fang Yiyi returns to her former husband's family to collect her belongings, but the young man's mother does not allow her to enter the apartment. Fang Yiyi calls her older brother to come over to help and this nearly leads to all-out physical conflict between the two families. Eventually, Fang Yiyi and her brother manage to enter the apartment, and after some intense verbal clashes between Fang and her ex-husband about who has ownership of their previously shared possessions, which are all cheap toys or small appliances, Fang Yiyi finally leaves with two parcels of goods that she claims belong to her.

Here, the couple settle accounts in every minute detail, once again denoting their egocentric personalities, which is a common trait of their generation. Further, the couple's actions throw light on some reasons for the unsustainability of their marriage, but, more importantly, it is also an indication that the time-honored Chinese conjugal bonds and family values, which are based on mutual support and mutual sacrifice, are crumbling and vanishing. In other words, the old-fashioned family relationships and matrimonial ties are now being challenged or replaced by the pursuit of personal gains, a prevailing mark of this developing individualistic and materialistic society. The transformation of spousal relationships in contemporary China not only is a metaphor for the divergence of Chinese society from a mutually caring collective to a self-interested and materialistic gathering, but is also the result of this divergence.

In summary, by presenting the stories of three generations of China's divorced women, the televisual narrative of *Honey Bee Man* engages with and centers on the current concerns of the viewers about a number of topical social issues regarding Chinese women, and has created an emotional outlet for those females in the audiences who may have had similar experiences in marriage and life.

Configuring divorced women: defending and upholding the state discourse

In her discussion about the portrayal in TV dramas of China's laid-off female factory workers who seek reemployment in domestic service jobs, Sun (2008: 96) points out that TV drama shows are a politically useful device. Sun (2002, 2008) further argues that the economic difficulties facing those laid-off female workers "are constructed in the state discourses as individual rather than social problems." Similarly, in *Honey Bee Man*, the marriage breakups of the three women are configured as personal predicaments instead of social stigmas. However, it is not difficult to discern that Huiyun's betrayal by her husband is a symbolic instance of the widespread marriage crisis between China's emerging wealthy males and their first wives. Based on Kong's (2008: 77–78) observation, the economic reforms and the associated divisive social problems lead to the disruption of the foundation of marriage and the collapse of family life in urban China. A number of China's nouveau riche men are those who "plunged into the sea" as self-employed entrepreneurs during China's economic makeover and thus became wealthy due to the economic policies. A characteristic of these new "rich men" is their loss of interest in their first wives and family and their penchant for extramarital affairs with pretty young women. Following this need to "stray" outside the family is the rise in the frequency of divorce, and in Huiyun's case, she is the sidelined and ostracized woman in her marriage who is finally discarded by her rich husband. The comparison between Huiyun and her husband in their economic and social status, their roles in the family, together with the outcomes of their divorce, is indicative as to how the market economy (with Chinese characteristics and implemented by a state with a developmental approach) eventually impacts on the lives of ordinary Chinese people. In other words, Huiyun's unfortunate situation does not suggest a simple personal failing or dilemma, but is really an indication of a social malaise caused by unrestrained economic changes and the immense growth of the economy.

In the case of Ye Shan, one of the main catalysts for her unsuccessful marriage, which is her desperate pursuit of a successful career, is also an indication and an indictment of the ferocious competition in the employment market and the unrestricted economic development. Likewise, the failure of the post-1980s and post-1990s generations of young Chinese people such as Fang Yiyi and her husband, who are not competent wives and husbands in their marriages, may be largely attributed to the side effects of the one-child population control policy, which turned out overindulged, incapable and irresponsible citizens. Through highlighting their personal weaknesses and problems, the narrative of the show shuns the economic, social and policy incentives that act as the underlying driving force behind the failed marriages of Ye Shan and Fang Yiyi. In doing so, the show adopts a conformist stand in its defense of the state discourse regarding its input in and impact on the broken marriages of contemporary Chinese females.

Besides avoiding the issues pertaining to lack of government accountability and its links to the marriage difficulties of the three protagonists, the show also deliberately eschews the financial and psychological strains and effects that divorced women must face and endure. Living in the spacious and comfortable apartment left to her by her ex-husband as compensation for his extramarital affair that led to their divorce, Huiyun enjoys a middle-class standard of living. Ye Shan is similarly well-off, as she has a high income. Fang Yiyi also encounters no financial problems after she returns to live with her single brother (as she did before she got married), who takes good care of her. Just as they have no economic concerns, these three divorced women also seem to not have been harmed too much emotionally, which is in contrast to the reality of the situation confronted by the

88 Honey Bee Man

majority of divorced women in China. Living as three "happy" women, the characters all find their "second springs," in which they either become more virtuous and generous (in the case of Huiyun) or are transformed into qualified and desirable females (in the case of Ye Shan and Fang Yiyi).

In *Honey Bee Man*, the Huiyun figure is enlisted as a metaphor for the established righteous image of Chinese females endorsed by Confucian thought and socialist mainstream moral discourse, which promote the "good wife–wise mother" female in the domestic sphere. By creating the Huiyun character, the show intends to compare the "older" generation of Chinese females with their younger counterparts. In one scene of the show, Huiyun's former husband complains to her about his current wife, who continuingly pushes him to paint and sell more works, which puts great pressure on him and makes him feel worn out.[7] He expresses his wish to reunite with Huiyun, who he believes truly understands him and never causes him stress by urging him to make money (however, his request is denied).[8] Here, the comparison and contrast between the money-oriented value system upheld by the young wife and the non-utilitarian faith in life maintained by Huiyun reflects the evolution of Chinese people's mentality during the transformation of Chinese society, from one that promoted a non-materialistic ethos of the socialist era to a covetous and pragmatic social entity of the post-socialist epoch.

Besides being portrayed as a traditional and simple female figure, Huiyun has been used as a representative of an "ideal woman," "a suitable female subject," with the "preferred femininity," a woman who symbolizes gentleness, tolerance, devotion, resilience and positive energy. Compared with other popular TV urban romance dramas that focus on recounting the perplexity and agony brought about by the marriage breakups of middle-aged women, *Honey Bee Man* shifts its narrative core from portraying "the anger, confusion, frustration, jealousy and even hysteria of middle-aged women" Kong (2008: 80)[9] to depicting a positive, placid and comfortable mood that is adopted by the Huiyun character as she manages to cope with post-divorce life. Here, Huiyun's tender, generous and peaceful attitude towards her former husband, and her divorce and post-divorce life, mirrors the official propaganda discourse as it engages with and attempts to soothe and negate the growing discontent of the public and possible social unrest. The Opening Up policy has been in place for around thirty years, and now, when the negative repercussions of the reforms are becoming clear (including political corruption, social inequality and the collapse of morality), many Chinese people who have been left behind in the rapidly changing economic times feel confused, discriminated against, disgruntled and uneasy about the future. Yu Dan opines[10] that those without a peaceful mind feel continually dissatisfied, jealous, cynical and melancholy and that conversely, those with a positive mentality feel undisturbed by the life difficulties that they are encountering and adopt a cheerful and optimistic temperament towards their future. In addition, according to Yu Dan, "a thoughtful citizenry with 'settled hearts' makes for a more secure society that will eventually achieve the greatest good for the greatest number" (Nylan & Thomas 2010: 221). The Huiyun character in *Honey Bee Man* exemplifies those even-tempered, optimistic and "strong" citizens, who are fostered by the CCP government as valued highly in the construction of social stability and harmony in today's China. Alternatively, the various dispositional and ethical merits embodied by the Huiyun character act as a spiritual painkiller to mollify the emotive unrest and frustration confronted by modern-day Chinese as they deal with a society ravaged by corruption, moral deterioration and the collapse of family bonds and values. In repaying her kindness and virtues, the script rewards Huiyun by arranging her marriage to Mr Right in its concluding sequences. Through a matrimonial agency and its most experienced dating consultant, Fang Jun, a warmhearted and sincere young man who is Fang Yiyi's brother and becomes Ye Shan's boyfriend in the second half of the show, Huiyun is introduced to a widowed and retired factory worker who is extremely thoughtful and mild, and the two later become husband and wife.

Different from her cousin Huiyun, Ye Shan's post-divorce life and her quest to find a new husband convert her from a "strong" professional woman to a devoted female who is willing and happy to sacrifice her own career for love. On the same day she has the tremendous row at the wedding function of her former husband, Ye Shan registers her name at the same matrimonial agency where Huiyun is enrolled. Dressed in fashionable clothes and wearing sunglasses, Ye Shan walks into the agency in her own arrogant manner and immediately attracts the attention of the staff. The mise-en-scène centering on Ye Shan's narcissistic demeanor and haughty personality indicates that she looks down upon those dating agents and will most likely be a very difficult client. Fang Jun, the most experienced and popular dating agent of the company, aware of the potential for trouble, volunteers to conduct the first consultation with her. Not surprisingly, Ye Shan's condescending manner and the harsh preconditions she sets for her future partner irritate Fang Jun and lead to a quarrel between the two. For his unprofessional behavior, Fang Jun receives a stern warning from his manager, and furthermore, Ye Shan must pardon him, otherwise he will be sacked. During his home visit to apologize to Ye Shan, Fang Jun, frankly but with humor, points out the likely reasons for Ye Shan's marriage breakdown. He mentions her overcommitment to her job, her negligence of household duties, her narcissism and unbearably haughty manners and her thoughtless attitude towards her husband's feelings. Again, Fang Jun's outspoken words infuriate Ye Shan, who has a strong and positive self-image and is unable to bear any criticism. Although this meeting between the two ends up in a verbal conflict, Ye Shan starts to realize the truth of Fang Jun's words and begins to be moved by the man's honesty and unpretentiousness. In their following meetings, Fang Jun fulfills his duty as a dating agent impeccably and he sets Ye Shan up with many excellent possible suitors; however, for various reasons, Ye Shan does not like any of them. As they continue to meet regularly, Ye Shan gradually comes to know more about Fang Jun's past and slowly falls in love with the man. Perhaps due to his quasi-parental role in caring for his sister, Fang Jun's gentle approach to Ye Shan, his patient and considerate personality, plus his strong sense of responsibility for family members shed a satirical light on those "strong" woman figures such as Ye Shan, who are thoughtless and aggressive workaholics and lack the traditional feminine qualities.

90   Honey Bee Man

In one episode, Fang Jun calls to see Ye Shan at her apartment and finds out she is having instant noodles. He swoops up the noodle box and throws it into the rubbish bin, quickly dons an apron and in about ten minutes has cooked two bowls of delicious noodles. Ye Shan is absolutely shocked by what she sees and suddenly senses what it was that made her so unqualified to be a good wife in her prior marriage. Here, the appearance of Fang Jun in Ye Shan's life awakens her womanly instinct and activates her conversion from a "masculine," "strong" and domineering woman to a "normal" and desirable Chinese female. As mutual feelings of affection develop between the two and they start thinking about getting married, Ye Shan's company unexpectedly gives her notice that she will be transferred to Hong Kong soon, which means that she and Fang Jun have to endure long-term separation, as they will be living singly in two cities. Without letting Fang Jun know in advance, Ye Shan makes a risky decision to quit her job, as she does not want to be parted from her fiancé. In this plot, Ye Shan ultimately reexamines the values of work and marriage, which is a significant shift in thought from privileging career success to favoring her role as a virtuous wife.

Before formally resigning from her job, Ye Shan starts to attend interviews for future employment opportunities. While waiting for a job interview, Ye Shan coincidentally meets her ex-husband, and they finally have a chance to speak calmly and candidly about their previous marriage. Ye Shan's former husband asks her why she gave up such a promising opportunity to advance her career in Hong Kong, as he presumes that the only thing that could bring contentment to her life is a successful career. Ye Shan replies that she now considers that the most important thing in her life is to live with Fang Jun. In a previous scene, when Huiyun points out Ye Shan's shortcomings that led to her failed marriage, Ye Shan disagrees with her, expresses outrage and retorts that Huiyun's way of treating her husband and running her family was outmoded and abhorrent. Thus here, Ye Shan's reorientation regarding a woman's duty in relation to family and life matters illustrates how a once "avant-garde" and "modern" woman may come to conform to established social mores and gender norms; a way of thinking which fits neatly into the expectations of the mainstream and official discourse on Chinese women's role in domestic space and in society.

Compared with Huiyun and Ye Shan, Fang Yiyi's post-divorce life does not contrast with her pre-marriage and post-marriage life. One obvious reason is that her marriage only lasted for less than two months, and there is no child and no distribution of valuable property between herself and her husband. Ironically, Fang Yiyi even comforts her brother after her divorce, as he is more distressed than she is, for in her opinion, it only cost her less than 20 RMB (the total amount of money she spent on the marriage and divorce certificates) to complete these two most important events of one's life. Fang Yiyi becomes unemployed not long after her divorce; however, this does not cause too much trouble to her life due to her brother's support. Fang Yiyi meets with Huiyun's son, Mo Xiaokang[11] when the young man's car knocks her off her motorbike. Luckily, Fang Yiyi is not seriously injured and Mo Xiaokang takes her to hospital for treatment. Later, Fang Yiyi and Mo Xiaokang become friends and Fang helps Mo with his business. Mo Xiaokang's parents expect, and are of the belief, that Xiaokang is in the UK to continue his studies, but he fails to board his plane as planned and is hiding from his parents in Beijing, where he starts a small advertising business. Mo Xiaokang and Fang Yiyi's relationship is just starting to blossom when Fang finds out that she is pregnant with her ex-husband's baby. Due to a problem of her uterus, she has to keep the baby, as an abortion would risk her ever again getting pregnant. Mo Xiaokang, however, remains faithful to Fang Yiyi and decides to marry her and raise the baby with her as his own. At their wedding ceremony, Fang Yiyi's speech to the guests gives the impression that she knows that she has transformed from a willful, unruly, irresponsible and immature girl to a dutiful and virtuous woman. Here, the most defiant woman figure in the show transforms into the most conformist. With both Ye Shan's and Fang Yiyi's transformations, it does not matter whether they are successful professionals, or unemployed and rebellious youths, the show puts an ideological closure to their stories as they have finally become "good Chinese women" and virtuous wives.

The "mismatched" couples in *Honey Bee Man*

Compared with their first husbands, all three divorced women, Huiyun, Ye Shan and Fang Yiyi, remarry "unsuitable" men, whose conditions regarding economic capacity (in Huiyun's case), career achievements (in Ye Shan's case) and family background (in Fang Yiyi's case) are either inferior or superior to those of themselves. Huiyun is considered to be above-average in appearance and retains a graceful bearing in her middle age. She also has a spacious and modern apartment left to her by her former husband that secures her a comfortable and middle-class lifestyle; she is certainly not a "left-over" woman in the dating market. Based on her conditions, Fang Jun sets her up with many successful men, including engineers, government officials and high-profile professionals. After many failed dates, for various reasons, Huiyun is left without a potential husband. However, by chance or fate, Fang Jun, her marriage agent, meets a widowed and retired hairdresser, Liang Shuyou, a working-class man with a humble outlook who runs an open-air barber stall at a public park. The two men get along well, and Fang Jun intends to find a new wife for the old man. First, he arranges Liang to do the hair of some of the female customers of the dating agency, including Huiyun. Huiyun is very satisfied with Liang's workmanship and she slowly comes to see that Liang is a considerate and friendly person and that she is growing fond of him. They develop a romantic relationship, which Huiyun's former husband does not like, as he believes that Liang's social status is too low. He is also concerned for himself, as he is worried about loss of face if others know that his former wife is married to an old worker. He tries hard to persuade Huiyun to quit the relationship; however, Huiyun does not care about Liang's lowly background and she eventually marries him.

92　Honey Bee Man

In the relationship of Fang Jun and Ye Shan, Ye is a senior manager at a foreign company, which means that she earns a very good salary and enjoys an elevated social status; however, Fang is only a dating agent at a small local company. Ye lives in a modern and lavish apartment; however, Fang only lives in a back-lane courtyard in Beijing *hutong* (a traditional Beijing-style compound with many families living together). Ye dresses in trendy and expensive clothes, but Fang only dresses casually, except when he is at work, where he wears a uniform-styled suit. Ye dines out in posh restaurants and Fang eats at the roadside food stands. Ye drives a luxury car and Fang uses public transport. All of the above disparities imply that Fang is out of Ye's league and that Ye is too good for him. However, Ye loves Fang deeply and almost gives up a wonderful job opportunity in order to be with him. However, Fang does not want Ye to sacrifice too much for him and he asks her to give him some time to better his own career, which according to him, is not for Ye's sake but to satisfy his own self-esteem as a man. At the end of the show, Ye finally takes up the new position in Hong Kong, and one year later she is transferred back to Beijing and promoted to the marketing director of the pan-Chinese region of her company. Also, Fang Jun is promoted to the manager of the dating agency, and the two of them are finally together even though Fang is still far left behind Ye regarding their respective career achievements.

Fang Yiyi and Mo Xiaokang are also of disparate status. Although Mo's parents are divorced and he lives with his mother, his wealthy father, a painter, still supports Mo and plans to send him to study in the UK, a very expensive educational option for a Chinese household. In present-day Chinese society, Mo is a standard "rich second generation" character; however, Fang, coming from a modest family background with poor career prospects, and as a single mother with a young baby, is certainly the "Cinderella" character in the show. Despite the huge disparity of rank between the two young people, they are deeply in love with each other and eventually become husband and wife. From the stories of these three "unmatched" couples, it is not hard to discern that family background and history, economic ability and career success are not the decisive factors that influence the marriage choices of the characters in *Honey Bee Man*. Superficially, the cessation of old norms and conjugal patterns and the advent of new matrimonial models and trends produce upbeat effects and bring about fresh prospects for people regarding their nuptial options and inclinations. In this sense, "mismatched" does not simply have the negative connotations often expected; on the contrary, it provides innovative opportunities for people to make "risky" and "adventurous" choices. These purposely designed "mismatched" couples are politically useful, as they help to close the widening gap, or at least mask its existence, between China's new wealthy social class and ordinary people. These "mismatched" couples also help to mitigate the bitter taste of social inequality and wealth discrimination that is the result of re-emerging class differentiation and social division created by the ongoing economic reforms.

Conclusion

By analyzing the post-divorce lives of three generations of contemporary Chinese women as presented in *Honey Bee Man*, this chapter has examined the fresh and discursive gendered space provided by TV drama narratives in order to give light to the momentous socio-economic transformations that have impacted on the lives of ordinary Chinese people, and specifically on Chinese women. Through plot and character analyses, this chapter has delved into the life conditions and emotions of divorced women in order to highlight the apparent links between contemporary Chinese women and the ever-changing economic and social reality of China today. As demonstrated in the above discussion, it does not matter whether they are virtuous housewives, successful professionals or unemployed and rebellious youths, many present-day Chinese women, irrespective of which generation they belong to, encounter setbacks and failures in their marital lives which have been caused in part by the huge socio-economic modifications in current China.

The show's narrative has presented the dilemmas and difficulties faced by many Chinese divorced women as individual circumstances rather than broad social problems, while at the same time it promotes a particular "model" of divorced women, such as the Huiyun character in the show, as being even-tempered, considerate and resilient females who do not complain about their fate, but instead strive to become even more gentle, virtuous and generous after their marriages fail. This "perfect" divorced woman image serves as a metaphor for a thoughtful and optimistic Chinese citizenry as envisioned by the CCP government. Further, the storyline of the show remolds those previously "unqualified (or incompetent) wives" (such as the Ye Shan and Fang Yiyi characters in the show) into submissive and traditional Chinese good wife–caring mother figures and rewards them with a happy "second spring." In addition, those "unmatched" and "unequal" couples created in the show fit neatly into state propaganda as they help to assuage the sour taste of social disparity and wealth discrimination that is caused by the re-emerging class discrepancy and social rift created by the ongoing economic makeover.

Notes

1 Scar Literature and Scar Films were meant to be therapeutic and to help the "sent-down youths," banished Party cadres, and intellectuals reconcile the psychological abrasions inflicted upon them during the disorderly years of political struggles under the reign of Mao and his followers.
2 *Legend of the Tianyun Mountain* (1980) is a film directed by Xie Jin, the Chinese film melodrama master, which was adapted from writer Lu Yanzhou's novel, *The Red Azaleas over the Mountain*. *Hibiscus Town* (1986) is also a Xie Jin film which was adapted from Gu Hua's same-titled novel.
3 Here, the notion of female cohorts of "winners" and "losers" does not refer to the "gold-digger," "mistress" or "second wife" female figures who depend on others or through indecent means seek to gain a better life or a better job.

94 Honey Bee Man

4 The one-child policy was terminated by the Chinese government on 1 January 2016, and every couple is now allowed to have a second child according to the current population policy.

5 In contemporary China, many Chinese women retire at a very early age, sometimes in their early forties; others are simply laid-off by their work units in middle age due to the privatization trend of state-run factories and enterprises or because of the bankruptcy of their work units.

6 Socialist revolutionary protocol urged the wearing of simple, revolutionary attire and Chinese citizens were encouraged to "struggle for political correctness and to put aside the pursuit of self-adornment" (Ip 2003: 350). Through combined "coercion, negotiation, propaganda and education" women were gradually politicized and desexualized; moreover, during the Cultural Revolution, "traces of femininity and sexuality were further sanitised and nearly erased" (Qian 2010: 296–297). For more discussion, see Chen (2003), Larson (1999) and Cai (2014).

7 Huiyun's former husband is a renowned painter and he and his current wife run a gallery to exhibit and sell his works, which are quite expensive and sought after.

8 When Huiyun's former husband tests her about their possible reunion, Huiyun reminds him of his young wife's contribution to his career and success. Here, Huiyun's dispassionate comments consolidate her positive image and reveal her gentle state of mind, even after her own adversity in her marriage.

9 Kong (2008: 80) observes that the emotional status of the dependent and "weak wives" who are stuck in relationship crises with their husbands is reflected in urban romance TV drama shows.

10 Yu Dan is a professor and Associate Dean of the School of Arts and Media at Beijing Normal University. Yu and her well-known book *Yu Dan lunyu xinde* (Yu 2006) are controversial topics in cultural discussions of modern-day China. James Leibold notes that in mainland China today, "one cannot enter a bookstore without encountering Professor Yu Dan's depoliticized, self-help musings on the *Analects*, which has sold ten million legitimate and another six million pirated copies, inviting comparisons with Mao's little red book" (Leibold 2010: 18). For more discussion, see Cai (2015).

11 Huiyun's son has been living with her since the divorce. Until her son becomes an adult Huiyun does not consider remarrying. According to typical Chinese custom, potential stepmothers or stepfathers are reluctant to cope with potential stepchildren, thus many divorced men and women refuse to remarry for the sake of their children left behind from their previous marriages. As discussed above, the Huiyun type of Chinese women are old-style and virtuous, they are thus usually compassionate and generous and think about others first.

References

Barlow, Tani E. 2004. *The Question of Women in Chinese Feminism*. Durham and London: Duke University Press.

Cai, Shenshen. 2014. "Rhetoric and Politics of the Female Body and Sex in Two Contemporary Chinese TV Drama Serials: *The Place Where Dream Starts* and *Blow the North Wind*." *Journal of International Women's Studies* 15 (1): 151–166.

Cai, Shenshen. 2015. "Academia and Cultural Production: Yu Dan and Her Confucius from the Heart: Ancient Wisdom for Today's World." *Sungkyun Journal of East Asian Studies* 15 (1): 89–108.

Chen, Tina. 2003. "Female Icons, Feminist Iconography? Socialist Rhetoric and Women's Agency in 1950s China." *Gender & History* 15 (2): 268–295.

Chinanews.com. 2013. "Zhongguo lihunlu jinwunian zengzhangjin baifenzhisishi Beijing zengfu chaopingjunzhi" [China's Divorce Rate Rose by 40% over the Past Five

Years, and the Figure in Beijing Was Even Higher than the National Rate]. Posted 15 November, available at: www.chinanews.com/sh/2013/11-15/5509637.shtml (accessed 10 February 2016).

Coming and Going (Lailaiwangwang). 1999. TV drama serials, directed by Tian Di, produced by Hubei Economics TV station and Zhongbo Company.

Dai, Jinhua. 2000. *Wuzhong Fengjing* [Scenes in the Mist]. Beijing: Peking University Press.

Dai, Jinhua, 2002. *Cinema and Desire: Feminist Marxism and Cultural Politics in the Work of Dai Jinhua*, eds. Jing Wang and Tani E. Barlow. New York and London: Verso.

Dwelling Narrowness (Woju). 2009. TV drama serials, directed by Teng Huatao, first broadcast via Shanghai TV drama channel.

Hibiscus Town (Furong zhen). 1986. Feature film, directed by Xie Jin. Shanghai: Shanghai Film Studio.

Holding Hands (Qianshou). 1999. TV drama serials, directed by Yang Yang, produced by China Central Television and Beijing Golden Pond Film and TV Corporation.

Huang, Ya-chien. 2008. "Pink Dramas: Reconciling Consumer Modernity and Confucian Womanhood," in *TV Drama in China*, Ying Zhu, Michael Keane, and Ruoyun Bai (eds.). Hong Kong: Hong Kong University Press, pp. 103–114.

Ip, Hung-Yok. 2003. "Fashioning Appearances: Feminine Beauty in Chinese Communist Revolutionary Culture." *Modern China* 29 (3): 329–361.

Kong, Shuyu. 2008. "Family Matters: Reconstructing the Family on the Chinese Television Screen," in *TV Drama in China*, Ying Zhu, Michael Keane, and Ruoyun Bai (eds.). Hong Kong: Hong Kong University Press, pp. 75–88.

Larson, Wendy. 1999. "Never This Wild: Sexing the Cultural Revolution." *Modern China* 25 (4): 423–450.

Legend of the Tianyun Mountain (Tianyunshan chuanqi). 1980. Feature film, directed by Xie Jin. Shanghai: Shanghai Film Studio.

Leibold, James. 2010. "The Beijing Olympics and China's Conflicted National Form." *China Journal* 63: 1–24.

Meng, Yue. 1993. "Female Images and National Myth," in *Gender Politics in Modern China: Writing and Feminism*, Tani E. Barlow (ed.). Durham and London: Duke University Press, pp. 118–136.

Meng, Yue and Dai, Jinhua. 2004. *Fuchu lishi dibiao: xiandai funu wenxue yanjiu* [Emerging from the Horizon of History: Modern Chinese Women's Literature]. Beijing: People's University Press.

Nylan, Michael and Wilson, Thomas. 2010. *Civilization's Greatest Sage through the Ages*. New York: Doubleday.

Pickowicz, Paul G. 2012. *China on Film: A Century of Exploration, Confrontation and Controversy*. Lanham, MD: Rowman & Littlefield Publishers.

Qian, Gong. 2010. "Red Woman and TV Drama," in *Contemporary Chinese Visual Culture: Tradition, Modernity, and Globalization*, Christopher Crouch (eds.). New York: Cambria Press, pp. 295–315.

Sun, Wanning. 2002. "The Invisible Entrepreneur: The Case of Anhui Women." *Provincial China* 7 (2): 178–195.

Sun, Wanning. 2008. "Maids in the Televisual City: Competing Tales of Post-socialist Modernity," in *TV Drama in China*, Ying Zhu, Michael Keane, and Ruoyun Bai (eds.). Hong Kong: Hong Kong University Press, pp. 89–102.

Yearning (Kewang). 1990. TV drama serial, directed by Lu Xiaowei and Zhao Baogang. Beijing: Beijing Television Arts Center.

96 Honey Bee Man

Yin, Hong. 2004. "Zhongguo dianshiju yishu chuantong" [The artistic tradition of Chinese television drama], in *Zhongmei dianshiju bijiao yanjiu* [Comparative Research on Television Drama in China and America], Qu Chunjing and Zhu Ying (eds.). Shanghai: Sanlian chubanshe.

Yu, Dan. 2006. *Yu Dan Lunyu Xinde* (published in English in 2009 under the title *Confucius from the Heart: Ancient Wisdom for Today's World*). Beijing: Zhonghua shuju.

5   *See without Looking*

From vulnerable people to competent and respectful citizens

Introduction

See without Looking (*Tuina*, 2013) is a pioneering TV drama serial which focuses on the lives of people with disabilities and explores their vulnerability within Chinese society. This chapter highlights the plight of a group of blind masseurs, and it studies how they have been presented by the mainstream rhetoric as "useful" and "respectful" citizens, due to their strong work ethic and their positive attitude, which enable them to be self-supporting in the competitive and pragmatic contemporary Chinese society. By analyzing the characters and plots of *See without Looking*, this chapter explains how the traditional social mores, family values and romantic love, which are generally declining in today's China, are maintained and practiced by this group of blind people. Moreover, this chapter investigates a distinguishing feature of the show as it foregrounds the sex lives of people with a disability and employs body politics in an attempt to garner more attention to the needs and rights of this disadvantaged social group.

Through their vibrant and poignant portrayal of the life of ordinary people and their interaction with society-at-large, contemporary Chinese TV dramas often function as propaganda conduits and are rich in political utility. Anti-corruption dramas convey a message of the government's intent to carry out its anti-corruption campaign and to reestablish a clean image of officialdom. Urban youth dramas highlight standards of neoliberal subjectivity that are concerned with self-accountability, obligatory attainment in work and self-renovation, which, as a type of governmentality, are particularly useful for China, as the creation of a novel type of market subjectivity is key to China's socio-economic transformation (Zhang and Ong 2008 cited in Zhang 2014: 174). Family-values dramas endorse the comparatively moderate aesthetics and moral canons that "tie in with the mainstream state ideology of 'social stability' and building a 'harmonious society'" (Kong 2008: 83).

Furthermore, a number of TV dramas that reflect the lives of public servants (such as public security servants)[1] and middle-class high-income professionals (such as medical workers, law specialists and white-collar office clerks associated with joint-venture or foreign companies) all focus on the life of the upwardly mobile social groups in China and outline the prosperous prospects of Chinese

98   See without Looking

society.[2] Arguably here, contemporary Chinese TV serials seem to implement "self-discipline" in terms of choosing themes, subject matters and social groups in order to be in line with the intent of state propaganda. Even in their depiction of the "left-behind," marginalized and disadvantaged social groups, such as laid-off workers and migrant workers who were victimized during the economic great leap forward in the post-socialist period, TV drama serials adopt a conformist approach by transforming these economically and socially underprivileged groups into "useful" citizens and "model" workers and entrepreneurs for the state. Furthermore, these financially and socially deprived groups are used by the state and its propaganda apparatus to prove the appropriateness of China's neoliberal turn while China joins the ranks of global capitalism.

Based on her observations about the portrayal of "maid" characters in contemporary Chinese TV drama, Sun (2008a: 96–98) argues that through depicting the training, discrimination and setbacks received and encountered by the maids in their journey of job seeking and becoming a person with high personal attributes, the show plots chart the transformation course of this deprived social group from having "incompetence, uncleanness, or untrustworthiness – thus becoming objects to be modernized, civilized and educated" to "a modern, cosmopolitan subjectivity" and "useful" citizens for the modern state. In her examination of laid-off female workers who became model domestic helpers and entrepreneurs, Sun (2008a: 96) remarks that they are frequently enlisted in both state and popular media narratives as politically useful and meaningful figures and devices in constructing considerate, conscientious and suitable citizens of contemporary China, who "while not contending with fellow national subjects over access to economic and political resources . . . [are] still doing [their] bit for [their] country and state."

In a similar way, Kong (2014: 112) notes how these middle-aged laid-off female workers were reconfigured as successful entrepreneurs relying on their unremitting efforts to improve themselves in the proliferation of "dramas of bitter emotion" (*kuqingxi*). According to Kong (2014: 112–116), the "media's efforts to write the issue of laid-off workers into an aspirational story of neoliberalism" is an ideological practice that is " 'masking' and 'whitewashing' a huge social scar." In addition, the inspiring reemployment stories of the laid-off workers serve as evidence of China's wise reorientation from a socialist planned economy to a capitalist market economy and its developmental approach in economic makeover. In so doing, the TV drama serials "used former laid-off women workers to promote the officially approved concept of economically rational individuals who succeed through their competitive and entrepreneurial spirit," and through this " 'reemployment star discourse,' the massive failure of socialism is thus transformed into an inspirational story of self-salvation, and painful retrenchment is welcomed as an opportunity for regeneration and new life" (Kong 2014: 116).

Following the studies of Sun (2008a) and Kong (2014), this chapter investigates how a disadvantaged and sidelined social group represented by blind masseurs is recruited by the televisual media to construct competent, "useful" and respectful citizens for the government to further its preferment of neoliberal subjects for the market economic reality, and to reduce the gap and assuage the antagonism and enmity between China's upwardly mobile social groups and those who remain on the lower rungs of the socio-economic ladder. Furthermore, by presenting an account of a situation where traditional human relationships and family ethics are being gradually jettisoned by many average Chinese people but being maintained by the cohort of blind masseur characters, the drama fashions a virtual and emotional refuge for the audience, who are bewildered and perplexed by the moral predicaments and ethical divergences caused by an ever-growing utilitarian and materialistically covetous society.

Life is hard for people with a disability

China has 82.96 million people with a disability, and this constitutes 6.34 percent of the country's total population. The Chinese demographic of people with a disability contains 12.33 million people (14.86 percent) who are visually disabled, 20.04 million people (24.16 percent) who are hearing disabled, 1.27 million (1.53 percent) who have speech disabilities, 24.12 million (29.07 percent) who have physical disabilities, 5.54 million (6.68 percent) who have intellectual disabilities, 6.14 million (7.4 percent) who suffer from mental disabilities and 13.52 million (16.03 percent) who have multiple disabilities (CDPF 2006a cited in Chau 2009: 19). Consequently, due to these enormous numbers, the Chinese government faces a massive task if it is to meet the special needs of its large population of people with disabilities and to accommodate them completely in social and economic life (Chau 2009: 19); therefore an effective social welfare system for disabled persons is of immense strategic importance.

There are many problems that China's current social welfare arrangements for people with a disability must address, including medical rehabilitation, employment, education and basic living requirements (Zhou & Zhang 2008).[3] According to a recent report, of Chinese disabled persons 12.3 million live below the poverty line in rural areas, and 2.6 million urbanites are classified as having "life difficulties" (*Xinhua Economic News* 2015). In regard to employment, people with disability, as a vulnerable social group, endure long-term discrimination in terms of not receiving equal education and employment opportunities, and this hinders their efforts to effectively participate in social life and share its achievements (Hu 2010: 45).

The Chinese government recognizes that employment is the key issue for any plans to improve the lives of people with a disability, as it permits them to be autonomous (*Xinhua News Agency* 2010), and it regards employment as a vital means for disabled people to integrate into the community and to be contributing members of society. Numerous regulatory and policy initiatives in regard to education and employment for people with a disability have been introduced over the past two decades[4]; however, the veracity of these measures is inadequate. Under the intense competition of the market economy, many enterprises and welfare services that are supposed to provide disability employment and play a significant role in safeguarding the right of employment and other rights of disabled people (Liu 2014) do not have the ability or means to foster employment for disabled

100 See without Looking

groups (Chau 2009: 19). Thus, more than half of those people with a disability are still forced to seek employment through their own personal associations and networks (*Xinhua News Agency* 2010). For those people with a disability who are lucky enough to find a job, they will most likely end up with a low-paying and manual labor position, such as working as a packer at a plant producing copper bars and cables, a job that pays 1,600 yuan (240 US dollars) per month (*Xinhua News Agency* 2010). A recent news report says that the Chinese central government has published a new document that outlines its plans to promote the well-being of the country's 85 million or so disabled people through "taking measures to better their livelihoods and employment opportunities while ensuring public services for disabled people to allow them a prosperous life at the earliest date" (*Xinhua Economic News* 2015).[5]

See without Looking is TV drama serial of thirty-one episodes adapted from the well-known contemporary Chinese writer Bi Feiyu's 2011 novel of the same title, which was broadcast in primetime via CCTV's Channel One in 2013. Although the show did not receive any negative comments for its rich exhibition of the emotional world of persons with a disability and it was applauded by cultural critics, it was not favored by the general viewing public. After its first-round broadcasting via CCTV's Channel One, it was purchased by only a few local satellite TV stations for re-running due perhaps to its solemn theme and plots. Compared with the sober and heavy subject matter in *See without Looking*, more light-hearted and less serious costume and youth idol dramas are more popular as they are more relaxing for an audience that wants to reduce the pressure of their daily lives (Xiao 2013); however, the director of *See without Looking*, Kang Honglei, is confident that the solemn and meaningful subject nature of the show will not be changed just because it has poor audience ratings (Xiao 2013). Bi Feiyu's novel was also adapted into a same-titled film (English title: *Blind Massage*) by director Lou Ye in 2014. The movie won many awards and nominations at mainland, Taiwanese and international film festivals. As the original author of the novel, Bi praised Lou's adaptation for presenting a loyal and convincing view of the life of people with a disability, which is a blend of warmth and cruelty, complexity and paradox (Li 2014). The TV drama shares the core storyline with the novel and the film versions, which all recount the life stories of a group of blind masseurs working in a massage center.

Finding reasonable and sustainable employment in China for people with a disability is difficult, and the jobs are scarce. Some of these people work at neighborhood factories or social welfare enterprises and earn a small wage – a pittance; others are simply unable to find a job due to widespread discrimination. A popular occupation among the visually impaired is traditional Chinese massage, and this would often include some form of therapeutic or osteopathic type of manipulation or simply massage for relaxation. Blind masseurs are normally well trained and skilled in the various methods of massage therapy and are considered adept at locating the problems on their clients' bodies. As visually impaired people manage their daily lives through feeling, their fingers and hands are usually more nimble and sensitive than other people's. In his novel, Bi Feiyu attempts to map out a complete world of the people with a disability; however, the narratives of the book are mainly concerned with a group of blind masseurs who are actually the "elite" cohort among the disabled population, and they earn a comparatively good salary and enjoy a moderately better social status than most other people with a disability. Bi is anxious that the Chinese audiences will be given the wrong impression that people with a disability live a better life in China than they actually do and what may be wrongly put forward by his book. Because of this, in a recent interview with the *Southern Weekly*, he said that the life of the disabled in China is extremely difficult and that they lead a totally unequal life compared with normal persons, and so people with a disability must be treated differently as a group due to their vulnerability (Li 2014). Similar to other disadvantaged and devalued groups such as peasants, workers and rural migrants, who have long been neglected by media attention (Sun 2008: 44 cited in Qian 2015: 170), the hardships and issues faced by people with a disability is not publicly visible, as media outlets that disobeyed censorship orders and report on the vulnerable social groups have invariably been punished (Zhao 2008), which might be another reason why Bi is so concerned. From the following discussions of the show's plots, it may be seen that Bi's appeal is ambiguously and paradoxically echoed by the show's director and producer.

In *See without Looking*, Sha Fuming and Zhang Zongqi run a massage center collaboratively in Nanjing, a southeastern provincial capital city. Sha is completely blind but Zhang has vision in one eye. A group of very skilled young blind masseurs work in the center. Masseur Wang Quan and the manager, Sha, are from the same hometown and befriended each other while they were co-workers in a massage shop in Shenzhen, the first special economic zone in China. Both are outstanding masseurs and are highly regarded by their customers. After saving some money from his work in Shenzhen, Sha returns to his hometown, Nanjing, and opens the massage center in partnership with Zhang. Later, Wang returns home as well with his girlfriend, Kong Jiayu, who is also a blind masseur, and both of them join Sha and Zhang's massage clinic. Their dream is to one day open their own massage shop and to purchase a house.

Besides the senior masseurs such as Sha Fuming and Wang Quan, there are also young junior blind masseurs working in the massage center. Qu Manglai and his girl friend, Xiaomei, are both employed there. However, Xiaomei is later forced to marry another man and she leaves Qu and the massage shop, a move which deeply hurts Qu. After Xiaomei leaves, Qu sings sad songs continuingly for a whole day until he coughs blood. This does not go unnoticed and his tragic love story is transmitted via media reports and becomes a sensational news item. Jin Yan, a pretty blind girl, who is also a masseur, becomes aware of Qu's tragic love story and goes to meet him in Nanjing from Dalian, a city in northeastern China. Jin is deeply moved by Qu's love and devotion and she falls for him, thus in order to be with Qu, Jin joins Sha's massage center.

Other masseurs at Sha's massage clinic include Ma Yue and Du Hong. Ma is a teenage boy who lost his sight as the result of a car accident when he was young. Du is a young blind woman who plays piano; however she cannot support

102 See without Looking

herself by her piano playing so she goes to Sha's massage center to learn massage. Due to her good looks, pleasant personality and exceptional skills, Du is popular with the customers. Besides these blind masseurs, Gao Wei, a beautiful and extremely capable young woman in her mid-twenties, is one of the only two staff members who do not have a disability. Gao simultaneously shoulders the duties as the receptionist, manager and accountant of the center. Zhang Zongqi's wife is another main character in the show, although she has no disability. She is an astute and aggressive street vendor who is also employed as the cook at the massage clinic.

In *See without Looking*, the hardships and challenges faced by the blind masseurs, the so-called elite disabled cohort, are displayed poignantly through their work and life encounters. Sha Fuming is the top masseur in the center, and he is trusted by and popular with the customers; Sha is also the one who actually manages the clinic with all his heart and soul. In sharp contrast, Zhang Zongqi, who only had one good eye but was not really disabled as such, seldom came to the clinic, and rarely attended to the business side of the enterprise. However, as he contributed some of the seed money for the massage center, he was entitled to a share of the annual profits. Besides the massage shop, Zhang is also involved in other businesses, such as an organic vegetable plantation from which he sells his products to the massage clinic. The shrewd and business savvy Zhang takes advantage of Sha, not only in their jointly run massage business, but by persuading Sha to invest together with him in the stock market. Because of Sha's absolute trust in him, Zhang cheats Sha and embezzles the money Sha spends in the stock market for other investments. Sha believes at first that he has lost all of his investment because of the stock market crash, as told to him by Zhang; however, he later finds out that Zhang had sold the shares before the crash and reinvested the money into other business as his own money. When Zhang needs even more money for his new venture, he mortgages the massage center building. However, his new business scheme fails and the massage center, it seems, will be lost to his creditors. This is a catastrophic and final blow for Sha, who is crushed by these cruel facts, and he becomes very ill and falls into depression. However, all is not lost, and with the assistance of Gao Wei's boyfriend, Sha saves the massage clinic from bankruptcy and saves the jobs of all the blind masseurs. Apart from his immoral earnings from the massage center profits, Zhang's wife also embezzles money from the board's expenses. In the encounters between Sha and the Zhang family, between disabled and non-disabled people, it is apparent that the disabled are in a disadvantaged position.

In Wang Quan's and Kong Jiayu's case, their difficult living situations and the discrimination they receive from others in the community are even more obvious in the show's plots. In order not to burden his parents and brother, the teenage Wang moves out of his family's apartment and goes to Shenzhen to seek job opportunities to support himself. He eventually finds a job and after saving some money and meeting Kong, he and Kong decide to return to Wang's home city, where they hope to open their own massage center. During their short stay at Wang's parents' place, the blind couple is treated with contempt by Wang's brother. He believes that the couple intends to lead an idle life in his parents' home and to contest the inheritance right of their parents' apartment. The brother's continuing enmity causes Wang and Kong to move out from Wang's family home and to join Sha's massage center, which provides separate male and female dorm accommodation for staff members.

People with disability are also victimized and mistreated with regard to issues pertaining to marriage. In the case of Qu Manglai and his girlfriend, Xiaomei, the separation is caused by the fact that Xiaomei is "sold" to a man from the village who admires her good looks and is willing to buy a blind wife at a high price. In some of the more remote areas of rural China, it is still hard for poor male farmers to find a wife and so many are forced to purchase a wife from even poorer households. In addition to her impoverished family, Xiaomei's unfortunate predicament is largely due to her disability, as her family members consider her to be useless and a burden on the rest of the family. From their perspective, to marry her to a person of sound body in exchange for a large sum of money is the best outcome for her and them, regardless of the young woman's feelings and affections. Xiaomei's disability is only relevant in that it reduces her exchange value and automatically puts her into an inferior situation compared with non-disabled people in the matter of marriage. For her boyfriend, Qu Manglai, another person with a disability, this means intense grief and sadness, as his beloved girlfriend is forced to leave him for another man and he could do nothing more than cry and sing sad songs.

Du Hong, the young and pretty blind woman who is also an award-winning pianist, is the most unfortunate of the show's characters. Soon after she starts to work as a masseur at Sha's massage center, Du wins the admiration of both her co-workers and her customers. However, Du also encounters many troubles during her work as a blind masseur. During one home-visit massage service, Du is sexually harassed by a bedridden old man who gropes her during his massage, and while she is fending off his advances, the man falls from the bed. The old man is not reprimanded in any way, but Du must suffer the complaints of the old man's wife. Du's embarrassing encounter foregrounds the vulnerability of people with a disability and the unsympathetic and aggressive attitude of others towards them. In one harrowing scene from the show, Du's fingers are jammed in a door when it is closed suddenly by a gust of wind. Due to the injuries to her fingers, Du is doubly disabled; she is unable to do any massage, nor can she play her beloved piano. Du's dual incapacity underlines her misfortune and provides an image of the disability that is pitiful. However, Du does not want to be pitied by others and she does not want to burden Sha and the other blind masseurs, so she unselfishly leaves the massage center and seeks employment elsewhere. She eventually finds a receptionist job at a company; however, when she knows that Sha and his massage center are experiencing hard times, she returns to Sha. Through an arduous routine of practicing massage with her feet, Du again becomes a skilled and popular masseur.

104 See without Looking

Configuring an image of competent and respectful citizens through blind masseurs

As a person with a disability who is doubly incapacitated, Du Hong's determination and courage to make a living in the competitive society of contemporary China corresponds with the state propaganda discourse which fosters a neoliberal subject who values self-responsibility and self-reinvention. Du Hong, a twice disadvantaged woman, serves as an allegory and sets an example for economically and physically underprivileged social groups to count on themselves rather than on the state to solve their problems. The economic difficulties facing laid-off female workers "are constructed in the state discourses as individual rather than social problems [and] the figure of a laid-off worker who is prepared to accept losing jobs as natural and inevitable, to accept downward social mobility and seek alternative ways of making a living without much subsidizing from the state is both desirable to the state and useful to the market" (Sun 2008a: 96–97). This pragmatic approach adopted by the government towards the laid-off workers, which I think is indifferent to the needs of the individual and is irresponsible, is reoriented and reconfigured in many programs released through the official media channels and in many contemporary TV drama narratives into an optimistic and supportive manner of the CCP administration in its promotion of the reemployment project and self-cultivated entrepreneurship.

In *See without Looking*, this superficial attitude of encouragement by the government towards the employment and financial viability of disadvantaged groups is reiterated and reaffirmed through the portrayal of a group of self-reliant and self-reassuring blind masseurs. Besides the Du Hong character and her story, Sha Fuming's story about a competent and respectful blind small entrepreneur is the narrative core of the entire show. Based on his (and other blind masseurs') consummate massage skills, rigorous work ethic, and generous personality, Sha's massage business is booming. The massage center not only supports Sha but also provides work for his blind peers, and through hard work and the creation of a positive, honest and law-abiding corporate culture, Sha's massage center has transformed the once "useless," discriminated against, marginalized and disparate people into a cluster of highly efficient, disciplined and socially valued professionals.

From the high personal and professional qualities displayed by the group of blind masseurs, to the clean and tidy massage rooms and to the disciplined but impartial working regulations and management policies of the center, *See without Looking* exemplifies a perfect small enterprise staffed and managed by people with a disability. Without mentioning any government subsidies or community donations received by the center, Sha and his blind employees maintain a profitable business and support themselves through their skills while being contributors to the well-being of the rest of society. Besides doing business, Sha Fuming further engages with the fast-paced and profit-oriented market economy of post-socialist China by investing in the stock market, even though he is cheated by Zhang Zongqi and almost loses the massage center due to Zhang's careless business adventure. Sha's active participation in the ever-growing and promising market economy of present-day China proves that disabled and disadvantaged groups can adapt and be effective in the intense market competition. This outcome conveys a clear message from the state; that instead of giving up and surrendering to their misfortunes, socially, economically and even physically challenged people should prove to the rest of the society that by relying only on their own intelligence, hard work and courage, they are able to overcome their difficulties and become useful, competent and respectful citizens in a modern and competitive society.

Besides the Sha Fuming character, the Wang Quan character is another model of disability with potential to be both a good citizen and a signifier of a political message. Compared with his brother, a parasitic single man, Wang Quan works hard and sends money back from Shenzhen to his parents on a monthly basis. In doing this, Wang does not burden his family, but conversely he shoulders the "burden" of the household. Due to his skills and diligence, Wang stands out from the other blind masseurs and becomes a highly sought-after masseur who earns a good salary. Using the money he saves up in Shenzhen, Wang supports his parents, saves for his own massage clinic, and even allows himself to dream of purchasing a house for himself and Kong Jaiyu after they are married. Wang's plan to establish a massage center in his hometown is temporarily aborted due to his unwise investment in the money market and his current lack of business acumen; however, his drive to be financially independent exhibits a neoliberal ethos that invites admiration from all people, disabled or not. By comparison to those referred to as NEET (which means elderly-devouring young adults [not actually but metaphorically]), Wang Quan's story is impressive and inspirational and deserves veneration and applause. Through disseminating positive values, Wang exemplifies those criteria required for a person to be an independent, valuable and devoted modern citizen; an image and ideal that is fostered and sponsored by recent CCP administrations.

Another self-sustaining and self-improving blind masseur character created in *See without Looking* is Ma Yue, an innocent but naturally competitive person. After becoming visually impaired in the car crash, Ma endeavors to turn himself into a socially useful and valuable person, and he leaves the comfortable life provided to him by his businessman father, learns to become a masseur and then finds a job at Sha's massage center. Different from many of the rich second generationers who flaunt their wealth, depend solely on their parents to live an extravagant lifestyle and utilize "connections" to do business, Ma Yue provides a counter-example that values self-attainment and self-respect.

Traditional relationships, family values and love for people with disabilities

Kong (2008: 83) argues that the writers and producers of dramas about ordinary people and their lives, an emerging TV drama subgenre, have recognized the emotional anxieties faced by Chinese people, particularly by the less well-off, "in an

106 See without Looking

increasingly aggressive and individualistic society where morals and family values, whether traditional or socialist, have collapsed." In *See without Looking*, and especially in the relationships between those with and those without a disability (such as those in the stories of Sha Fuming and Zhang Zongqi, of Wang Quan and his brother and of Du Hong and the old man and his wife), the ethical deterioration and increased utilitarian ideals between friends and family members are underlined. By polarizing the non-disabled with the disabled people into moral offenders and moral defenders, respectively, the show maps out the ethical dilemmas and conflicts in a progressively materialistic and money-oriented society (the real world) and a more conventional and harmonious social entity maintained by the disabled groups (in the imagined world).

In Sha Fuming's case, although he has been tricked and taken advantage of by Zhang Zongqi many times, which has resulted in enormous economic loss for him personally and for the massage center collectively, and even that his health has been seriously impacted by Zhang's cruel and thoughtless behavior, he graciously pardons him in the closing episodes of the show. He does this, we presume, as he values their previous friendship and has confidence in rebuilding a traditional, virtuous and harmonious relationship based on mutual trust, mutual understanding and mutual support. He is even able to do this while living in a society that is extremely competitive and greedy. Sha's benevolence and virtue is also reflected in the help and support he offers to other blind people, especially to the young blind masseurs working in his massage center. In order to help them secure a reasonable income, Sha teaches Du Hong and Ma Yue the skills and techniques of massage patiently and carefully. Consequently, Sha's righteousness and generosity are repaid by almost all his friends, disciples and employees when he himself is in difficulty, and they offer him their unconditional and unreserved help. These unselfish acts of kindness provide the audience with the illusions of just how much power morality still exerts in Chinese society, in terms of building a congruous and mutually caring society. In the closing episode of the show, Sha and all the blind masseurs gather together at the massage center for a reunion party, which serves as a metaphor for an imagined harmonious community and brings ideological closure to the show. During the party sequence, the acoustic arrangements lift the buoyant atmosphere to its peak when Manglai sings the classic Italian opera aria "Nobody Shall Sleep!"

Wang Quan, like Sha Fuming, is another character who epitomizes high social morality. His character is meant to convey the ultimate understanding and appreciation of time-honored family values such as filial obligations and preservation of domestic concord. His relationship with his brother serves as a typical example of this type of traditional morality, as Wang never takes his brother's hostility towards him and his girlfriend to heart, and he does not blame his brother for what he has done to him; instead, he replaces evil with good. When he finds out that his brother is getting married, he gives him 20,000 RMB as a wedding gift, a not insignificant amount for a man with a disability who works extremely hard to support himself and his family. The most spectacular representation of his responsibility and love for family occurs when Wang confronts the loan sharks who are chasing his brother for bad debts he owes them. He acts chivalrously and courageously towards the gangsters hired by the loan sharks. Holding a big meat cleaver in his hand, he unbuttons his shirt and slices the skin on his chest and stomach in order to show he is not afraid to die to save his brother. As blood oozes out from the cuts, even the violence-hardened gangsters are shocked, as they had never seen or even imagined that a blind man, who they thought of as weak and pathetic, could act so fearlessly and with such frenzy.

In so doing, Wang saves his brother's life and shows his bravery and how much he values familial affection. In this scene there seems to be an absurd swapping of expected behaviors. Wang Quan assumes a gangster's role in his dealing with the real hoodlums, who are intimidated by the "criminal-like" demeanor of a weak and blind person. Wang's desperate attitude and conduct in this particular act serves as a double-coded signifier, which generates a subversive reading of the show's text that originally echoes the state propaganda paradigm in its promotion of a gentle, "orthodox" and conformist disabled subjectivity. On one hand, being stuck in an awkward and powerless position in a corrupt and utilitarian society where most advantage and favor goes to the more privileged social groups, and rather than compete and confront the more privileged on an equal footing and in a rational way, vulnerable groups, such as people with a disability in particular, and all China's underprivileged social echelons in general, need to adopt unconventional and extreme methods in order to safeguard themselves. On the other hand, Wang's violent behavior, as illustrated in the show, serves as a particular instance of the growing phenomenon of social violence in China.

Noticeably, the Wang Quan role in *See without Looking* is reminiscent of the "criminal knight" (Cai 2015) characters created in Jiang Zhangke's recent film, *A Touch of Sin* (*Tianzhuding*, 2013). *A Touch of Sin* consists of four separate stories, all of which are based on recent real-life events of social violence in China. Due to the ever-expanding gap between China's nouveau riche and China's poor, and the ever-present corruption in both business and government circles, contemporary Chinese society is a reservoir of social evils and malaise. Accordingly, the increasing upsurge of social violence has become a major domestic concern for the CCP and its goal of sustaining a stable and harmonious society. Most of these cases go unreported in the official media, which remains state-controlled and subject to censorship at many levels, although many cases of social violence are now coming to light through social network media such as *weibo* (microblog) – a popular news source for many urban Chinese. Through revealing the nexus between personal hardship and social violence, Jia Zhangke explores the catalysts behind the violent scenes of Chinese social unrest, such as economic inequality, social discrimination, and bureaucratic corruption. Jia Zhangke creates a plethora of "criminal knight" characters and revives the traditional chivalrous ethos of ancient China which was also found in the 1980s and 1990s Hongkongese movies that adapted customary concepts of gallantry and brotherhood to stories of contemporary crime and violence.

In *See without Looking*, the Wang Quan role is similar to the "criminal knight" character created in Jia Zhangke's cinematic world, who emerges from a corrupt

108   See without Looking

and unjust social reality and espouses violence as a means to defend the disadvantaged group he belongs to and restore justice for the social factions he represents. As noticed by many scholars, the "disadvantaged groups" (such as sent-down youths, laid-off workers, migrant workers and urban poor), who are identified by the Chinese central and local governments as the "problematic groups" of contemporary Chinese society, have become the most common originators of the increasing social protests and petitions since the 1990s (Perry 2002; O'Brien 2008; Cai 2010; Yang 2014: 46; Bai 2015, Kong & Hawes 2015: 43). Furthermore, some of these desperate anti-social acts end up as violent homicides and suicides. A recently released mainland film, *Mr. Six* (*Laopaoer*, 2015), starring China's most famous New Year film director, Feng Xiaogang (who plays the lead character Mr. Six in the movie), provides the latest visual reflection of the growing dissatisfaction within China's "disadvantaged groups" and their subsequent protests. The concluding sequence of the film is about an impending armed fight between China's "haves" and "have-nots" – a large riot, which filmgoers in China can empathize with, and was a very lively topic on social media sites.

Besides the "Confucian sage" morality embodied by Sha Fuming, and the "criminal knight" righteousness represented by Wang Quan, moral perfection is also signified by the Qu Manglai role in *See without Looking*. Qu's love for Xiaomei serves as a foil against the prevailing pragmatic and materialistic philosophy about love that is embraced by many contemporary Chinese people. Being constant in love and cherishing unchanging love is a desirable character of a person by his or her lover or spouse – however, there are an increasing number of Chinese men and women who have no qualms with temporary and utilitarian affections and who do not take the matter of love seriously. Thus, from a certain perspective, Qu's faith in the traditional meaning and mode of love that focuses on constancy and eternity underlines the established moral mores treasured by conventional Chinese thinking and values, which are defended and retained by the people with a disability in the case of *See without Looking*.

In addition to successfully conveying the personal virtues of people with a disability through intriguing and poignant dramatic plots, the theme song of the show – "Seeing"/"Kanjian" (which is played at the beginning of each episode), with its "musically conveyed expression," manifests rich sentiments (Zhong 2010: 144) which, to borrow Zhong's (2010: 149) words, "help set not just the mood of the entire drama but, more important, the poetic tone." According to Zhong's (2010: 146–147) observation, the use of music and songs has played an important role in meaning making when it is blended into filmic or TV drama narratives. In this sense, the lyrics and melody of the theme song of *See without Looking* highlight not only the hardships of life as experienced by the disabled group, but also their romances and their moral virtues, and "brings out the theme of the drama (*dian ti*)." In line with the show, the sentimental lines of the theme song paint the loneliness, suffering and helplessness of the disabled group, together with their optimistic, mutually caring and mutually supporting manner, and present the difficulties and hopes of people with a disability.

Love and sex serve as a field of combat for people with a disability

Love is a rarely mentioned and perhaps even taboo topic in regard to the life of people with a disability in China, as there are few films or TV shows that depict this facet of their life experiences. *See without Looking* engages freely with this infrequently touched theme and provides a poignant rendering about the usually hidden aspect of life of people with a disability. In a love triangle between Qu Manglai, his ex-girlfriend Xiaomei (who in the second half of the show escapes from her husband's family and returns to the massage center for Qu) and his current girlfriend Jin Yan, Qu oscillates between the two women, as he does not want to hurt either of them. On one hand, Qu's infatuation with his first lovemaking experience with Xiaomei on the day the girl leaves him for her upcoming wedding causes him to feel that he is a heartless man if he declines the girl's advances. However, he also suspects that Jin Yan is more likely to become his soulmate, as she is well-educated (at least compared with himself and Xiaomei), intelligent and independent of thought. When the two girls compete to win Qu's favor, Xiaomei claims a "corporeal right" of Qu, due to her sexual involvement with him; however, Jin Yan gradually becomes the winner because of her independent thinking and assertive manner.

Jin's resolute self-determination is not only apparent in her uncompromising attitude during the contest with Xiaomei for Qu's love, but is also displayed in her valuable help to Xiaomei when she is forced to return home with her husband who "purchased" her. When Xiaomei, a poorly educated young woman, is wavering between pursuing her true love or fulfilling her duty as a virtuous wife, Jin's behavior enlightens her as she confronts the husband on Xiaomei's behalf, even though Xiaomei is her rival in love. Jin's support for Xiaomei frightens the husband and, for the time being, he leaves his wife at peace. Jin's courage in the face of paternalism, and her generosity towards her rival in love, provide a construct of self and mutual co-operation and reliance between people with a disability. In this sense, the show further criticizes the social inequality between disabled and non-disabled people, as presented in the mercenary marriage between Xiaomei and her husband.

The show's meticulous and captivating exploration of the love experiences of people with a disability is also revealed in the story of Ma Yue. Ma Yue's love for his beautiful but deceased mother may be read as Ma having an Oedipus complex. When Ma hears that Kong Jiayu is also beautiful he begins to correlate her with his dead mother and develops an infatuation with Kong, which engenders misunderstanding and jealousy from Wang Quan. This quasi–love triangle substantiates the intricacy of the emotional world of people with a disability and juxtaposes their love experiences with those of people without a disability who also confront various and similar love complexities.

In a similar theme, Sha Fuming becomes romantically involved with Cui Yun, a divorced but non-disabled woman who has been abandoned by her husband. Cui's husband was a philanderer with a tendency towards violence, especially towards

110   See without Looking

Cui. He divorces Cui and leaves their son and Cui for a pretty young woman. At first, Cui and her son are allowed by her former husband to stay in their old apartment, which belongs to the man; however, when he starts to suspect that Cui is developing a relationship with a blind man, he feels ashamed about Cui's choice and forces her to leave the apartment. Cui and her son have little choice but to live temporarily in a small restaurant, where she works as a casual kitchen hand. Cui is one of Sha's customers and he has a chance encounter with her outside the massage center after she was beaten by her husband. Sha commiserates with Cui's situation and wants to help her. Thus, apart from waiving her treatment fees, Sha also hires her as a cook in the massage center so she and her son can stay in the staff dorm. In the relationship between Sha and Cui, there is the reversal of the normal or expected role between a person with a disability and a person without a disability. Sha (a person with a disability) provides shelter for Cui (a person without a disability) when she becomes homeless; and when Cui is bullied by her husband, Sha steps forward bravely to defend the woman and fight the man if necessary, as Sha had learnt Chinese kungfu when he was young and could easily overpower Cui's husband.

Apart from being the "hero," in a similar manner to Qu Manglai, Sha Fuming is also the forlorn and lovestruck figure. In repetitive flashback scenes, Sha is tormented and obsessed with a girl's voice. This cherished memory is of a romantic encounter between Sha and an unknown girl when he was young. As a teenage boy with no vision, Sha was very sensitive to sound and especially voice, and the strange girl's voice was very pleasant, captured Sha's attention immediately and caused an infatuation and longing for the girl. A couple of days after their first encounter, Sha bumps into the girl accidentally on the street and again he recognizes her from her voice. The girl helps Sha to cross the road and the two end up chatting. The girl has just broken up with her boyfriend and in order to make her former boyfriend angry, she asks Sha jokingly to be her temporary boyfriend. This short and "fake" romance is Sha's only romance so far and he has never forgotten the girl since their "breakup." The reason why Cui Yun attracts Sha's attention is because her voice is similar to that of Sha's sweetheart lover in his dreams. Like Qu Manglai, Sha Fuming is a stubborn believer in true and everlasting love, something which is slowly being replaced by extramarital affairs and one-night stands in much of Chinese society. Therefore, the fixation with notions of romantic love by people with a disability is ironic in light of the widespread and negative views about love held by the general population.

Further to its close consideration of the love stories of the blind masseurs and its candid reading about the love triangles among them, *See without Looking* also features sensual love scenes between vision-impaired people, something which is rarely seen on TV shows or in movies about people with a disability. As a marginalized social group during the entire period of economic transformation in contemporary China, and as an absent collective subjectivity in televisual and cinematic narratives, the quality of life and emotional status of people with a disability has never become the focus of public attention and concern. However, in *See without Looking*, love, the body and sex serve as a discursive conduit to foreground the rights of disabled groups in China. Here, the equivocal and somehow contradictory deliberations of the life experiences of people with a disability are exposed. In the show, people with a disability are constructed as being on the one hand a suitable, self-reliant and self-esteemed modern citizens whose image is congruous with the neoliberal subjectivity proposed by the CCP government, while on the other hand they are portrayed as a neglected and discriminated-against social group whose lives and emotive states need attention and concern from the rest of the society.

To openly expose the body and the sensuality of people with a disability may be seen as a derivative pattern of "body politics," to use a term coined by Foucault and as espoused by Lu (2007: 54) in his discussion about contemporary Chinese artistic and cultural works as "biopolitics." This display of "revealing" the erogenous body of a person with a disability aims to challenge the recognized and dominant foci of "normal and healthy" people, and in so doing, it gains more perception and contemplation on the life circumstances of impaired, disabled and underprivileged social groups. "Body or biopolitics" has been widely enlisted across an array of social, cultural and artistic domains in China, such as in feminist discourse. The utility of feminine desire, body and sexuality has become a fertile ground in terms of articulating individual opinion, appealing to gender suppression and inequality, questioning social establishments, rewriting history and challenging the orthodox discourse and grand narratives of a CCP-led China (Cai 2014). In the erotically suggestive scenes in *See without Looking*, the use of body politics in terms of disclosing the sexual body figures/features of people with a disability opens up a novel space for the "bodily" and "sexually" rich visual texts in representing and reflecting the life situation and emotive condition of people with a disability.

For instance, Qu Manglai's captivation with his first lovemaking experience with Xiaomei, on the day she leaves him for her forthcoming wedding, becomes a haunting memory. Whenever his secret and forbidden lovemaking memories with Xiaomei come to his mind, the audience sees scenes of an almost nude Qu and Xiaomei who cuddle up together. With their eyes full of bewilderment and helplessness, the exhibition of the half-naked body of two disabled people demonstrates the uneasy and dismal emotional situation of the disadvantaged groups of people in China and sheds a contrasting and satirical light on the buoyant outlook on people with a disability as fostered by state propaganda.

In the case of Wang Quan and Kong Jiayu, the lack of a domestic and private love space of their own (which is partly due to their healthy relatives' shunning, repulsion and derision of them) results in the suspended release of their sexual desires, and of the incomplete fulfillment of their rights as a human being. As the massage center only provides separated male and female staff accommodation, Wang and Kong cannot live together. Kong complains to Wang that she cannot endure the separation from him (due to her sexual needs). In one scene of the show, Kong boldly goes to the male dorm where Wang lives and impulsively begins hugging and kissing him, as she is driven by an intense sexual desire. They then undress each other hurriedly as they fear the imminent return of Wang's roommates.

In this way, *See without Looking* reveals the sexual encounters and explores the emotional wounds of people with a disability, which have long been avoided and even hidden from public notice and media illustration. Here, the nonexistence of a private space for Wang Quan and Kong Jiayu to fulfill their sexual needs and desires leads to them being denied the common enjoyment as human beings and serves as an allegory of the discontented rights of the underprivileged faction of Chinese society. Moreover, their "outrageous" and desperate seeking of love and sexual gratification suggest their determined and undying quest of their rights as "normal" individuals. In one sequence of the show, the intimate relationship between Wang and Kong is perfectly illustrated by the combination of visual and acoustic dynamics, which manufactures a massive emotional crescendo. The sentimental melody of the lyrical theme song of the show, which is sung as an Italian opera aria, accompanies the sequence in which the camera uses consecutive close-up shots to catch Wang and Kong's deep feelings and affections for each other. Covering themselves under white bed linen, the foreheads of the two touch, talk excitingly, tease and flirt with each other, laugh, shout and cry. Although all these sounds have been overwhelmed by the theme song, the audience is still able to feel the strong affections and passion of the two characters. Here, the white bed linen offers a shelter for the two within which they can enjoy their private and intimate moments together.

Conclusion

As a groundbreaking and highly acclaimed televised narrative about people with a disability, *See without Looking* focuses on the day-to-day work and romances of a group of blind masseurs. By modifying this "unusable" and "discriminated against" social group into "useful" and "respectful" citizens, the show echoes the mainstream discourse which adopts a superficially caring and encouraging approach (but an actual indifferent and irresponsible attitude) towards the socially and economically disadvantaged groups in contemporary China. Through its careful and intentional portrayal of a group of self-supporting and positive-thinking blind masseurs, with their high moral standards and exceptional massage skills, some of whom are successful small entrepreneurs and high-income professionals, the show exemplifies the government-driven neoliberal ethos of modern-day China. This role transformation of a disadvantaged social group not only promotes a "strong," "enduring" and "competitive" citizenry, but also camouflages the unfulfilled duty of the government towards socially and economically vulnerable groups.

Moreover, by creating the disabled characters as the believers and practitioners of traditional Chinese family values and ethical mores, *See without Looking* sheds a sarcastic light on the weakening morality within the entire Chinese society. Interestingly, in order to safeguard these customary values, some people with a disability act as "criminal knights," which not only subverts their established destitute and weak image, but also reveals the expanding social unrest and violence in China today.

In *See without Looking* an unprecedented focus on the body and sexuality of people with a disability enlists body politics to foreground the rights and expose the emotional status of people with a disability who deserve to live an equally "normal" life with other people. The exposition of almost nude bodies and the bold depiction of the sexual life of blind people provide some subversive reading to the mainstream rhetoric on people with a disability and invite more attention to and exploration of disadvantaged social groups in contemporary China.

Notes

1　Public servants in China earn much more than ordinary workers and are also entitled to state welfare such as public housing.
2　For example, see *The VI Group of Fatal Case* (*Zhonganliuzu*, 2001), *Angel Heart* (*Xinshu*, 2012, discussed in Chapter 2 of this volume), *Divorce Lawyers*, (*Lihunlushi*, 2014) and *A Story of Lala's Promotion* (*Du Lala shengzhiji*, 2010, discussed in Chapter 4 of this volume).
3　Disabled people constitute an extensive and unique vulnerable group in China. The government has made efforts to provide employment and social security for them via some suitable schemes. Although the system has made considerable impact in delivering the help of employment, medical aid and communal convalescence, it still has several difficulties including the scarcity of security substances, the incomplete coverage and subsidy, the limited source of funds and the low security level (Liu 2011). For example, as Loyalka et al. (2014) have noted in their collaborative research, although the quantity and coverage of social security for households with disabilities is mounting steadily, it is still not enough to overcome the income variance between households with and without disabled persons, specifically when we account for the additional expenses of disability.
4　Due to these measures, it is reported that the figure of disabled workers in urban China increased to 4.4 million by the end of 2009. In rural areas, there are 17.6 million disabled persons who have secure jobs (*Xinhua News Agency* 2010). The recorded unemployment rate of disabled people in urban areas has slumped from 13.6 percent in 2009 to 8.6 percent in 2010, according to a report announced by the China Disabled Person's Federation (*Xinhua News Agency* 2010).
5　The document further pledges to enhance social support, stipend, pension and basic medicare coverage programs for people with a disability and assist both individuals and their families in employment to raise their incomes (*Xinhua Economic News* 2015).

References

Bai, Ruoyun. 2015. "'Clean Up the Screen': Regulating Television Entertainment in the 2000s," in *Chinese Television in the Twenty-First Century: Entertaining the Nation*, Ruoyun Bai and Geng Song (eds.). London and New York: Routledge, pp. 69–86.

Cai, Shenshen, 2014. "Rhetoric and Politics of the Female Body and Sex in Two Contemporary Chinese TV Drama Serials: *The Place Where Dream Starts* and *Blow the North Wind*," *Journal of International Women's Studies* 15 (1): 151–166.

Cai, Shenshen. 2015. "Jia Zhangke and His *A Touch of Sin*: Social Violence, Criminal Knight and Chilling Fantasy," *Film International* 13 (2): 65–76.

Cai, Yongshun. 2010. *Collective Resistance in China: Why Popular Protests Succeed or Fail*. Stanford, CA: Stanford University Press.

114   See without Looking

Chau, Ruby. 2009. "Socialism and Social Dimension of Work – Employment Policies on Disabled Groups in China." *Hong Kong Journal of Social Work* 43 (1): 19–29.

China Disabled Persons' Federation (CDPF) (2006). "Communique on Major Statistics of the Second China National Sample Survey on Disability," available at www.cdpf.org.cn/english/.

Bi, Feiyu. 2011. *Tuina*. Beijing: People's Literature Press.

Hu, Rong. 2010. "Lunwoguo Canjiren Jiuyepingdengquan Zhidu de Wanshan" [To Perfect the System of Protection for Equal Employment for the Disabled in China]. *Journal of Guizhou University* (Social Sciences) 28 (3): 44–47.

Kong, Shuyu. 2008. "Family Matters: Reconstructing the Family on the Chinese Television Screen," in *TV Drama in China*, Ying Zhu, Michaek Keane, and Ruoyun Bai (eds.). Hong Kong: Hong Kong University Press, pp. 75–88.

Kong, Shuyu. 2014. *Popular Media, Social Emotion and Public Discourse in Contemporary China*. Hoboken, NJ: Taylor and Francis.

Kong, Shuyu and Hawes, Colin S. 2015. "The New Family Mediator: TV Mediation Programs in China's 'Harmonious Society'," in *Chinese Television in the Twenty-First Century*, Ruoyun Bai and Geng Song (eds.). London and New York: Routledge, pp. 33–50.

Laopaoer (*Mr. Six*), 2015. Feature film, directed by Guan Hu, Beijing: Huayi Bros. Media Group.

Li, Yilan. 2014. "Tuina dianyingpian 'mangren de shijie jiushi canrende': dianying tuina de gaibiannanti" [The Filmic Version of *See Without Looking* "The World Is Cruel For Blind People": The Difficulties of Adapting *See without Looking* into a Movie], infzm. com, available at: www.infzm.com/content/99716 (accessed 10 February 2016).

Liu, Jing. 2014. "Literature Review on Employment of the Disabled in Mainland China." *China Tongu* 16 (2): 193–234.

Liu, Qingrui. 2011. "Zhongguocanjiren Shehui Baozhang de Wenti Yu Duiceyanjiu – Jiyu Shenyangshi de Diaocha" [On Social Security of Disabled People in China – Based on the Survey of Shenyang City]. *Journal of Liaoning University* (Philosophy and Social Sciences Edition) 39 (6): 108–113.

Loyalka, Preshant, Liu, Lan, Chen, Gong and Zheng, Xiaoying. 2014. "The Cost of Disability in China." *Demography* 51 (1): 97–118.

Lu Sheldon, 2007. Chinese Modernity and Global Biopolitics: Studies in Literature and Visual Culture. Honolulu: University of Hawaii Press.

O'Brien, Kevin J. (ed.). 2008. *Popular Protest in China*. Cambridge, MA: Harvard University Press.

Perry, Elizabeth. 2002. *Challenging the Mandate of Heaven: Social Protest and State Power in China*. Armonk, NY: M.E. Sharpe.

Qian, Gong. 2015. "Remolding Heroes: The Erasure of Class Discourse in the Red Classics Television Drama Adaptations," in *Chinese Television in the Twenty-first Century: Entertaining the Nation*, Ruoyun Bai and Geng Song (eds.). London and New York: Routledge, pp. 158–174.

Sun, Wanning. 2008a. "Maids in the Televisual City: Competing Tales of Post-Socialist Modernity," in *TV Drama in China*, Ying Zhu, Michaek Keane, and Ruoyun Bai (eds.). Hong Kong: Hong Kong University Press, pp. 89–102.

Sun, Wanning. 2008b. "The Curse of the Everyday: Politics of Representation and New Social Semiotics in Post-Socialist China," in *Political Regimes and the Media in Asia*, Krishna Sen and Terence Lee (eds.). London: Routledge, pp. 31–48.

Tuina [See without Looking]. 2013. TV drama serial, directed by Kang Honglei, first broadcast via CCTV's Channel One.

Xiao, Yang. 2013. "Tuina jiaohao bu jiaozuo, yenei: guanzhong peiyu xu guocheng" [*See without Looking* Is Applauded but Cannot Draw a Large Audience: It Takes Time to Cultivate the Audience]. *Liaoning Daily*, available at: www.ce.cn/culture/gd/201309/04/t20130904_1383818.shtml (accessed 19 February 2016).

Xinhua Economic News. 2015. "China Pledges to Promote Well-being of Disabled People." 5 February.

Xinhua News Agency. 2010. "China strives to promote employment of the disabled," posted 3 December, available at: www.china.org.cn/china/2010-12/03/content_21473208_2.htm.

Yang, Jie. 2014. "The Happiness of the Marginalized: Affect, Counseling and Self-Reflexivity in China," in *The Political Economy of Affect and Emotion in East Asia*, Jie Yang (ed.). London: Taylor and Francis, pp. 45–61.

Zhang, Yi. 2014. "Untangling the Intersectional Biopolitics of Neoliberal Globalization: Asia, Asian, and the Asia-Pacific Rim." *Feminist Formations* 26 (3): 167–196.

Zhao, Yuezhi. 2008. *Communication in China: Political Economy, Power and Conflict*. Lanham, MD: Rowman & Littlefield Publishers.

Zhong, Xueping. 2010. *Mainstream Culture Refocused: Television Drama, Society, and the Production of Meaning in Reform-Era China*. Honolulu: University of Hawaii Press.

Zhou, Qingxing and Zhang, Xinjin. 2008. "Lunwoguo Canjiren Shehuifuli Cunzai de Wenti Jiqi Fazhan de Lujing Xuanze" [The Issues and the Developing Pathway of Social Welfare for the Disabled Persons in China]. *Journal of Chongqing Technology and Business University* (Social Science Edition) 25 (5): 68–72.

6 *Parents of the Single Child*
China's one-child policy and its social repercussions

Introduction

The TV serial *Parents of the Single Child* (*Dushengzinu de popomama*, 2013) is a family-based drama that engages with a number of topical social issues about people from the one-child generations. By portraying the domestic and workplace-related conflicts in the one-child generations, the show foregrounds the harm inflicted upon this whole generation of people in particular and Chinese society generally, as all of China was affected by the demographic policies of previous national governments. However, by exposing only some of the harmful social effects of the one-child policy, the show narrows the topics and neutralizes some of the debates and concerns about the deleterious outcomes of the one-child policy. The drama takes a superficial approach towards the more disturbing social problems caused by the one-child policy, such as the sex ratio imbalance and the "shidu" family, issues which might cause public discontent and even social unrest.

The Chinese government launched the one-child policy in 1979. It was a radical family planning project which was, however, incongruously incompatible with much of China's reform policy adopted at the outset of the Opening Up period, a time that witnessed the beginning of the state's gradual withdrawal from its extensive involvement in every facet of family and social life. This drastic social engineering program directed that childbearing was a state concern; childbearing was essentially "collectivized" at a time when the economy was heading down a reverse path (White 2007). China's population reached around 1 billion in 1980, and the then Chinese leaders believed that unless a rigorous policy of population control were implemented, China would not realize its economic goals by the year 2000 (White 1992; Greenhalgh 2008) and that a family planning strategy was required to correct China's demographic dilemma (Tien 1991). As a result of these sweeping birth control restrictions, there have been about 150 million children born under the one-child policy over nearly four decades, and China has become the country with the most single-child families in the world.[1] In 2015, more than thirty years after the adoption of the one-child policy, the CCP government made significant adjustments to its family planning scheme in order to cope with emerging social problems caused by China's aging population – a costly outcome of the one-child policy (Wang 2005). According to the current population control program, every couple is allowed to have two children.

Although the one-child policy has finally come to an end, the social problems caused by it will continue to impact Chinese society. Those people who were born into one-child families during the first two decades of the one-child policy have matured and are now ready to assume their social roles and fulfill their social responsibilities. There are, however, growing concerns as to whether this group of "sibling-less" adults has the practical abilities or the psychological and social skills to achieve "normal" expectations in regard to family, work, and society in general. It is widely observed and much discussed that a significant proportion of young people who belong to the single-child generations are not equipped to carry out even the mundane domestic necessities and household duties such as cooking and doing laundry, as they have been "spoiled" by their parents or grandparents, who treat them as "little emperors" or "little princesses." These "social and practical impairments" appear to be even more prevalent with children raised under the "4+2+1 family pattern" (meaning a household comprising four grandparents, two parents and one child). One satirical, but apt, depiction of these children is that they are often treated by their parents like "pets," and they, vice versa, treat their parents as "slaves" (*World Today* 2015). As the main beneficiaries of the Opening Up economic reforms, the single-child generations grew up in a period with less political intervention and with more material affluence, and, acting as the most active consumers in the market, they are the first generations to openly embrace materialism (Kong 2014: 206–207).

In 1983, the American journal *Newsweek* was the first to label China's one-child generations as "little emperors" in its reports which were later reproduced by many Chinese newspapers (Bao 2012). In 1986, Chinese writer Hanyi's reportage about China's "little emperors" garnered broad attention across Chinese society concerning the education and upbringing of the only-child generations (Bao 2012).[2] A 1993 report by the famous children's literature writer Sun Yunxiao added to the debate about the only-child generations when Sun compared the performances of the Chinese children and their Japanese counterparts at a summer camp, thus exposing the many shortfalls of China's single-child cohort and its potential impact on Chinese society. The report created collective concern and anxiety within Chinese society as it focused on the character defects of the only-child generations. The debate continues today with an ongoing concern about the efficacy of those from single-child families to perform acceptably in the domestic and employment realms, including caring for their elderly parents and grandparents (Bao 2012).

The one-child policy and its outcomes have become unavoidable social topics, and TV drama serials, together with other media, play an active role in participating in and providing a forum for these debates and discussions. This chapter will examine *Parents of the Single Child*, a recently released TV drama play, which represents many of the typical problems encountered by the single-child generations, mainly those born in the 1980s and early 1990s. The show selectively focuses on some of the distinctive concerns and challenges for only-child

118   Parents of the Single Child

youths. In the domestic sphere it engages with issues such as cohabitation with parents and grandparents after marriage, in-law relationships and the preservation of family congruence in an extended family; in the career field it confronts problems relating to lack of social skills and the inability to adapt to workplace culture and its "unspoken" rules. However, the show intentionally shuns some other more sensitive topics fostered by the one-child policy, such as the sex ratio imbalance and missing girls, and the unbearable pain of "shidu" families. In its efforts to avoid these complex and negative social results, the show risks being an accomplice to a "whitewash" of the one-child policy and the government's lack of remedial measures.

Parents of the Single Child: story of an extended single-child family

Parents of the Single Child was first broadcast on channels of Beijing and Hubei satellite TV. The popularity of the show is attributed not only to the star-studded cast, but also to its clever handling of the intense public debate and interest about this important social phenomenon. The storyline of the show is centered mainly on the "extra-extended" ordinary household consisting of four couples: Li Xiaoman and her husband Shu Yile (both belong to the single-child generation); Shu Yile's parents Wang Xizhen and Shu Qianjin (who are coincidentally also single children of their respective families, although they do not belong to the government mandated only-child generations); Wang Xizhen's parents; and Shu Qianjin's parents.

Xiaoman is a journalist at a private news agency and Yile works as a civil servant at a state-run corporation, thus both are of the salary-earning social rank. After their marriage, and due to their economic situation, Xiaoman and Yile live with the other three couples in an 80-square-meter apartment belonging to Yile's parents. There is also a side narrative that weaves a contrasting plot about a wealthy single-child couple, Shang Weizhi and Ai Yu (Yile's ex-girlfriend and Xiaoman's colleague). Weizhi is an only child from a prosperous background and Ai Yu marries him for his money. In one scene of the show, when Yile and Weizhi meet their girlfriends at the entrance of the news agency, Yile rides a bicycle and carries some vegetables he purchased on his way, while Weizhi drives a BMW and brings a bunch of roses to please Ai Yu. This contrasting situation accentuates the materialistic and hedonist lifestyle of Weizhi and Ai Yu in comparison with the vast majority of ordinary Chinese people, such as Yile and Xiaoman.

With its focus on Yile and Xiaoman's post-marriage life as they live with three older couples under the same roof, the show's narrative highlights the usual domestic conflicts and predicaments facing those of the one-child generation when they enter into marriage. Xiaoman, for instance, is often seen in debate with Xizhen over whether she should give her monthly income to Xizhen; when she and Yile should have a baby; and if Yile should quit his civil servant job and open his own restaurant. These conflicts between the younger and older members of a single-child family reflect the generational gap and changing values towards family relationships, cultural traditions and career expectations. These family arguments slowly modify the single-child's thoughts, behavior and values, which in turn are also gradually changing established relationships, family ethics and socio-cultural beliefs within Chinese society. The show also underlines the one-child generation's challenges and shortcomings in the workplace as it foregrounds their general unsuitability, their lack of social skills and their acrimonious relationship with the workplace norms and culture.

Conflicts within the domestic sphere

In contemporary China, the extended family pattern with married couples (young and middle-aged alike) living with either of their parents is not uncommon, thus ongoing habitual themes such as filial liabilities, in-law relations and preservation of family accord in an extended family constitute a certain amount of TV drama narratives (Kong 2008: 83). In recent times, as young people of the single-child generations born in the 1980s and 1990s enter into marriage relationships, domestic conflicts and crises are more prevalent and concerning, and so the TV drama about this situation is more compelling and controversial for contemporary audiences. Growing up within different political, economic and social circumstances, the people from the single-child generations and their parents usually have diverse attitudes, values and outlooks on family, consumption habits and lifestyles. In many cases, only children do not act in accord with the standards and expectations of their parents.

For instance, filial piety is one of China's most important traditional virtues, and one which is intensely promoted by the CCP government in its efforts to maintain a harmonious social environment. However, many of those Chinese born under the one-child policy do not follow these customs when dealing with their elderly relations. Chinese parents have always embraced the customary expectation that their children will look after and support them when they grow old; however, in the recent decades, there has been a growing and fashionable "NEET" cohort (NEET stands for elderly-devouring young adults), who, rather than caring for and supporting their parents, depend instead on their parents for support. These "elderly-devouring" young people lead a parasitic life, without regular incomes or jobs. Often, after marriage, they rely heavily on their parents to raise their children for them, not just by babysitting their grandchildren, but also by paying for their living costs, kindergarten fees and school tuition fees. In this way, these parents of single children are doubly enslaved.

In *Parents of the Single Child*, although Xiaoman and Yile have stable jobs and are not members of the NEET group, their filial piety towards their parents and grandparents is seldom displayed. They are not thoughtful and rarely help with household routines such as cooking, cleaning and shopping for food and groceries, and it is left to the two elderly women, Xizhen and her mother-in-law, to do almost all the housework. Xizhen is often seen preparing the meals for the entire family, mopping floors and doing laundry, and consequently she always feels tired and unwell. She visits the doctor regularly for various reasons, and on one occasion she is misdiagnosed as having a life-threatening cancer, a great concern for the family. After her recovery from the illness, she continues doing a substantial amount of domestic chores for the other family members and is eventually overcome with exhaustion and once again is admitted to hospital for rest and recuperation. In traditional Chinese familial and cultural conventions, the younger people in the family are expected to wait upon and follow the orders of senior family members in obedience to the established and strict domestic hierarchy of Chinese households. There is, however, a perceivable relapse of these habitual family relationships and ethics within the single-child families, where those time-honored family values and operating modes are gradually fading. In presenting the lack of filial piety in those of the single-child generations, the director adopts numerous visual signs and verbal statements. For example, many close-up and medium-range shots are of Xiaoman and Yile enjoying a comfortable family life without doing any housework. When they are at home they usually lie on their bed, drink coffee, listen to music, read magazines, or surf on the Internet without helping the elders out in doing house chores. Further, an extensive amount of the show's dialogues between Yile and Xiaoman and their parents and grandparents concern their arguments and various attempts to resolve the contested situations.

Besides Xiaoman and Yile's lack of participation in household duties, which has increased the workload and stress on other family members and shows their lack of filial piety, Xiaoman's refusal to declare her salary details to Xizhen so that she can manage and allocate their expenses leads to a considerable amount of tension between the in-laws, and Xiaoman's overreaction exhibits her inconsiderate attitude towards the elderly family members. Chinese parents are known for their devotion and generosity towards their children and would certainly not take advantage of them; they will do whatever they can for their children, including paying costly education fees, purchasing housing for them and helping to raise their grandchildren. Thus, when Xizhen offers to help Yile and Xiaoman by managing their money, she actually wants to save money for them in case they spend the money on frivolous things. However, Xiaoman claims that she would rather eat separately from other family members in the household in exchange for Xizhen's concession to allow her to keep her salary for her personal use.

Xiaoman's bargaining with Xizhen exposes the self-centered utilitarian approach towards life that is espoused by many from the single-child generations. Although Xiaoman states that she would purchase her own food, she neglects to mention that she must pay rent as their share of the apartment costs, and she also fails to mention all the labor costs that Xizhen deserves for cooking and doing laundry for herself and for Yile, and this does not even consider that she does not give Xizhen and other elderly family members any extra money as an expression of her filial piety. Furthermore, instead of thinking about how to make their parents' life more comfortable, Xiaoman and Yile are saving money to purchase, for themselves, a modern apartment so that they then can move out from their parent's place and lead a 5 + 2 lifestyle. This popular lifestyle arrangement means that on weekdays the young couple enjoys life at their own home, and on weekends they go to their parent's home for a regular visit.

In addition to conflicts about salaries and the separation of food expenditures, another dispute that breaks out within the Shu family is whether a man should keep some "personal funds." Both Xizhen and her mother-in-law urge Yile to keep aside some funds for personal use, and the two old women provide some detailed and careful instructions for Yile to achieve the goal, which provokes more severe tension between Xiaoman and her mother-in-law and grandmother-in-law. However, the fight over the "personal funds" between the only-child couple ends up with both Xizhen and her mother-in-law finding out that their own husbands have been keeping secret money for ages behind their backs. Therefore, the original disagreement between the single-child couple escalates into an all-out argument among the whole family. If these family disputes continue within the domestic sphere concerning both the only-child and the non-only-child generations alike, the social obligation facing contemporary Chinese people, such as caring for the aging parents and carrying on the family ancestral line, will be exacerbated in the case of the one-child generations.

For example, Yile's ex-girlfriend Ai Yu left him for Weizhi because she was afraid that if she married Yile, the two of them would have to shoulder the obligation to take care of their own parents plus Yile's grandparents on both his mother's and father's sides when they get old. Ai Yu confessed to Yile that she did not want to be burdened by the elderly and that she just wanted to lead a happy and carefree life. This example reflects the typical situation that many of China's only-child couples find themselves in, which is that every single couple, under normal circumstances, will be required to look after at least four elderly family members. In the show, this situation is further exacerbated by Yile's parents as they are both single children themselves, which is not very common for their generations: usually, people from Xizhen and Qianjin's generations have more than one sibling. During the Mao era, people were encouraged to have children, as Mao believed that "there is strength in numbers." Thus, in those times, each couple often had four or more children, and the burden of caring for aged parents, both financially and physically, was shared among the siblings. However, for those from the single-child generations, their burden of caring for the elderly has increased enormously with no siblings to share the filial responsibilities.

This heavy burden carried by only-child couples is a hard fact which cannot be ignored. The show reveals and confronts the impending difficulties encountered by the single-child generations; however, it fails to probe into its solutions. Here, the side effects of the collectivized childbearing policies of the Chinese government during the past several decades start to impact upon the family life of the single-child generations. The prosperity of the nation is achieved at the expense of individual families, and now the official promotion of filial piety towards parents has about it a hypocritical flavor, as it was actually the government and its policies which caused the massive burden for those children to shoulder; a burden which is beyond their capacity and wishes. In the closing of the show it is indicated through the conversation between Yile and Xiaoman that their "troubled" life would never end, which directly implies that their life will continually be "burdened" as the family elders grow old.

122   Parents of the Single Child

Another domestic matter and social duty that is highlighted in the show concerns the single-child generations' familial obligation to carry on their family's ancestral line, which in the Chinese socio-cultural context means to give birth to a son. The grandparents of the only-child generations did not have to worry whether they would have a son to carry on the family line, as they were not encumbered by government policy and could have as many children as they wanted. For the single child's parents' generation, they have been given only one chance to give birth, therefore many women living in both rural and urban China are looked down upon and even seen as worthless in their husbands' families if they fail to give birth to a son (Chu 2001). However, this unfortunate situation could be lessened if, as in previous times, their husbands' brothers give birth to a son. In the case of the only-child generations, there are no remedial measures available if the wife gives birth to a daughter, as the husband has no siblings and so the family line on the husband's side is suspended at the birth of a baby girl. In the case of the Shu family, as both Yile and his father are single children, Xiaoman has the responsibility to give birth to a son to carry on the ancestral line of the Shu family.

At first, Xiaoman and Yile do not want to have a baby until they achieve some career success; however, Xiaoman, unexpectedly and without planning, becomes pregnant. After the birth of her baby son, and in order to test the Shu family, Xiaoman tells them that it was a baby girl. Upon hearing the news, both Xizhen and her mother-in-law are extremely disappointed, which makes the already inharmonious relations between the in-laws worse and further leads to the deteriorating relationship between Xiaoman and Yile, pushing the young couple's marriage to near collapse. At the moment when Xiaoman and Yile are about to sign their divorce agreement, Xizhen, after changing the baby's nappy, finds out that Xiaoman actually gave birth to a son, thus the conflict and antinomy between the couple and the two families is immediately over and Yile apologizes to Xiaoman. This dramatic plot foregrounds the rigorous socio-cultural situation confronted by single-child couples in terms of carrying on the ancestral line of the husbands' families, which was an unexpected and unforeseen consequence of the CCP government's one-child policy. The recent adjustments to the population control plan, which allow every couple to have a second child, negate to some extent these confined circumstances for only-child couples, so long as their second child is not also a girl.

In summary, the Chinese government's strict birth control policy directly or indirectly leads to various conflicts and contradictions within the domestic sphere of the single-child families, including inharmonious in-law and conjugal relationships, and the biases and mistreatment of women in their husbands' families. From another perspective, rather than removing the remnants of feudal thoughts that were passed down from pre-modern Chinese society, the state's mandatory birth control restrictions coincidentally reconfirm old-fashioned patriarchal thinking, which has been exploiting and suppressing Chinese women for thousands of years.

Struggles and adventures in the career field

Compared with the generations of their parents and grandparents, who were allocated jobs by the socialist state within a planned economy, the single-child generations have lost their "iron bowls" and have to seek opportunities in the unprecedentedly competitive job market generated by the Opening Up economic reforms.[3] Furthermore, they confront huge peer pressure to eschew being left behind in the "rat race" (Kong 2014: 213). During the early decades of socialist China, there was not much career-related corruption in the workplace, which is in contrast to the widely circulating corruption in the career field of modern-day China. Consequently, there is more stress on the one-child generations to find suitable employment and to establish successful careers. In *Parents of the Single Child*, the Yile character serves as a representative of the single-child generations as they enter the workplace; it portrays their passions and ambitions and shows the lessons learned and setbacks encountered. Yile is a public servant, working in the propaganda section at a state-run enterprise. When he first begins his career, Yile is naïve, lacks social experiences and is unfamiliar with workplace cultural rules (most of them "unspoken rules"), as are most of his single-child peers. In the competition for position of propaganda chief at his company, Yile does not believe that he has much chance to succeed or that he will stand out from his colleagues, as he is comparatively young and lacks experiences although he does have excellent skills and proficiency. However, his father-in-law, an accomplished businessman (Xiaoman's divorced when she was young, but her father takes good care of her in order to compensate for her "incomplete" childhood), informs Yile that he has a very close personal relationship with the general manager of his company and he can help Yile obtain this position by asking the manager to do him a favor. After Yile's father-in-law talks with his manager ("oils the wheels of industry") and invites him to an extravagant banquet, the manager hints to Yile that if he performs well he will have a great opportunity to get the propaganda chief position. The manager's appreciation of Yile is quickly noticed by his colleagues, and even his competitors for the role are sure that Yile will finally get the position, as he has reliable connections. Therefore, those potential underlings of Yile start to pay him visits at his home, bringing gifts in order to build a good relationship with their future supervisor. Amongst them, there are colleagues who used to look down on him and even bullied him because they had senior status at the company; there are also co-workers who compete with him for the position.

In regard to his own efforts to secure this propaganda chief position, Yile also brings all his skills into play in order to please his manager. For example, during a business banquet, he accompanies the manager as his drinking "companion." Audiences who are familiar with the culture of Chinese officialdom will know the importance of a person's capacity to consume alcohol during business banquets. In China many business agreements and outcomes are achieved during banquets at restaurants and hotels instead of during formal meetings and negotiations held in conference rooms, and the more alcohol the two parties consume, the more the

124 Parents of the Single Child

chance they will achieve acceptable business outcomes. There are always constant rounds of proposing toasts between the two parties, and the underlings of the managers have to drink the alcohol for their leaders whenever the leaders cannot handle anymore during the banquet. Thus, the most intimate and trusted underlings of the leaders usually have to be adept at consuming large amounts of alcohol. In this business banquet scene of the show, when the other party proposes another toast, and Yile has reached his limit, one of his colleagues persuades him to drink more by saying: "are you currently running for the propaganda chief position? This is a good opportunity for you to perform in front of our leader! So whether you drink this cup of alcohol determines your future!" Here, the colleague's blunt words reveal the simple truth of the unspoken cultural rules pertaining to China's business and government circles. These rules can, to a considerable extent, restrict and even block the career development and prospects of China's young generations, while they also reform their system of value, moral beliefs and outlook on life.

In another scene, in order to demonstrate the result of his work, Yile intends to expose the names of staff members who are frequently late for work; however, his plan is halted by his supervisor, who later explains to him that if he had gone ahead with his plan, he would have offended those who enjoy privileges (such as arriving late for work), as they have various kinds of connections to the leaders of the company. These plots divulge the naiveté, foolhardiness and idealism of contemporary Chinese youths when they begin their careers, in particular those youths from the single-child generations who have been spoiled by their parents and are lacking in social skills. The storylines also show that the unique life experiences as a single child, to some degree, may lead to their unsuitability and inadequacy in the workplace.

For diverse reasons, Yile does not succeed in his application, and all those co-workers who paid him visits at home ultimately turn their backs to him. However, in the next round of applications, Yile eventually gains the position due to his officially recognized and award-winning work performances. This concluding and unpredicted triumph of Yile seems far-fetched, as the reality in China works in the opposite way, where connections and "unspoken rules" permeate every aspect of the workplace and dominate job competition and advancement. Though Yile has been promoted to the chief in the propaganda section, and it seems that he has promising career prospects, he has become fed up with the corrupt ecology in the workplace, as he confesses to Xiaoman: "the workplace culture is too complicated and I do not want to become a 'sophisticated' and 'tactful' person like your dad when I am still young." Here, Yile's complaint about the perverse culture in the workplace exposes and suggests the discontent and disillusionment felt by many young Chinese people (most of them from single-child families) about the underhanded and sometimes illegal socio-political environment they live in. Unfortunately, Yile's unpleasant encounters represent those of the majority of China's young population who do not have connections to support them in their struggles in the career field and who find themselves often in helpless and hopeless situations. Their choice is usually to either adapt to this crushing and depressing environment or seek other, "fairer" opportunities to make a successful living. In Yile's case, he wants to quit his current job and open his own restaurant, and he wins support for his proposal from Xiaoman; however, it meets strong resistance from all the older family members, who think his idea is unreasonable, fatuous and crazy. According to the older generations, to give up a public service job, which is almost as stable as an "iron bowl" position, is ridiculous and imprudent. Further, a civil servant job signifies one's loyalty to the Party, which counts a lot in the mindset of socialist citizens of the Mao eras (such as Yile's parents and grandparents).

After many rounds of quarrels and negotiations, Yile eventually resigns from his propaganda chief job at the state-run enterprise and becomes the owner/manager of his own restaurant. Yile's "plunge into the sea of business" has altered connotations when juxtaposed with those adventurous decisions made by previous self-employed entrepreneurs who abandoned their "iron bowls" at the beginning of the Opening Up reforms. Those early private entrepreneurs joined the business ranks primarily out of their desire to make a lot of money, but Yile's risky choice to escape from the convoluted and problematic Chinese official circle is his first imperative. This indicates that China's younger generations' perceived ineptitude for survival, and their frustration with work, is tied to what they see as the bigoted socio-political arena of contemporary China. Yile's unconventional decision is also indicative of his determined, non-conformist and defiant attitude, an attitude which is also adopted by the young generations towards their impending assimilation into a gloomy social reality. This problematic social condition is the result of inadequate government resources and corruption within the workplace, which cause those young people without connections or money to struggle to survive in an unfair environment. The excessive charges for education and healthcare, the constant pressure and inability to find stable jobs and soaring house prices in the first-tier cities are what young people face, and it is aggravated by increasingly lopsided access to resources and opportunities because of maneuvering by power and money interests (Kong 2014: 214).

Yile's risky endeavor is furthermore indicative of the self-centered and self-pleasing nature of people from the one-child generations. Under the impact of the Opening Up reforms and ongoing globalization, together with the influence of the one-child policy, the young generations of Chinese have become more individualistic, which is reflected in their lifestyle choices, attitudes towards work and personal expression (Kong 2014: 206–207). Unlike those pioneering private entrepreneurs who emerged at the outset of the economic transformations and set their eyes largely on profits, the single-child self-employed entrepreneurs prioritize their own interest when choosing and developing their careers and businesses. For example, Yile has an interest in cooking and promoting his homemade cuisine, thus, through opening his Happy Homemade Cooking Restaurant, Yile combines his interest with work and lives a life that is what he pursues.

From Yile's case, we see that those "willful" and "egocentric" characters of the only-child generations not only raise concerns and criticisms from the older generations, but, simultaneously, they also engender inspirational ideas for these

126   Parents of the Single Child

youths in their career and life domains. Yile's restaurant does not seem to have many customers, which might lead to the failure of his business venture. However, the value of establishing the restaurant basically lies in its symbolic meaning in that it demonstrates that China's young generations eventually have broader life choices than their parents' and grandparents' generations. Neither believing in revolutionary or socialist causes as their grandparents did nor making unconditional and unreserved contributions to their countries' modernization project as their parents did, nor making money and living a materialistic and luxurious life counts as the ultimate goal of life of the modern-day young Chinese people; rather, for many young Chinese, to follow one's own senses and to live an unrestrained life have become the dominant determinants when they make important decisions regarding career and life.

Social repercussions of the one-child policy

After more than three decades since the implementation of the one-child policy by the Chinese government, the "little emperors" and "little suns" have grown up, and the first generations of single children, who were born in the 1980s and in early 1990s have become the "backbone" of the society. Because of the inappropriate education and spoiling from their parents, together with the "lonely" environment in which they grew up, it is believed by many that a considerable percentage of the only-child generations show many ostensible flaws concerning their character, living aptitude, emotional adaptability and values. Commonly, these youths from single-child households lack a sense of family duty and traditional values (which are demonstrated in the above discussion), although they are accustomed to meticulous care and absolute devotion and sacrifice by their parents. These "pampered" groups thus become selfish and deficient in social skills and perform comparatively poorly in domestic and career situations. These undesirable traits of the single-child generations are damaging and will continue to damage the overall standard of the Chinese population, which can be considered a long-term negative social result of the one-child policy.

The UK-based Chinese writer Xue Xinran's newly released book, *Buy Me the Sky: The Remarkable Truth of China's One Child Generations* (Xue 2015), provides us with a vivid and, for some, shocking glimpse into the lives and emotional world of people from these generations, who are not only the future of China, but also partly the future of the world (*World Today* 2015). Xue's book comprises nineteen independent case studies of China's only-child children, who according to Xue are the lonely generations who grow up in households without siblings. Because they have no brothers or sisters, these people do not know how to get along with, share with and take care of others. And because of their parents' thorough caring and extra-devotion, some of these only children cannot do simple chores, such as Xue's friend's son, who couldn't even open his suitcase and tidy up his clothes when he arrived at Xue's place to pursue his studies in the UK. These "inherent" defects of the single-child generations worry Xue when she considers their future, their romances, building a family and participating and contributing to society (*World Today* 2015). In the show, Yile and Xiaoman provide some evidence to back up Xue's qualms. Usually, when the family finishes their meals at home, the young couple go into their own room and close the door behind them. Even in their own private world of two people, they do their own things: Yile either keeps working or surfs on the Internet, and Xiaoman reads news or lifestyle magazines. In the workplace, Yile's lack of social skills and his naiveté of worldly issues and concerns also contribute to the incongruous relationship between himself and his colleagues.

Apart from the only-child generations' lack of practical life acumen and social proficiencies, their "distorted" value system concerns all of Chinese society. The Yao Jiaxin case, which is one of Xue's case studies, is controversial and fiercely debated in China, and exemplifies the public's anxiety. In 2011, Yao Jiaxin, a piano student from a one-child family, ran over a peasant woman as he drove his girlfriend home, and despite the woman's pleas for help, Yao did not take the injured woman to hospital for treatment; instead, he pulled out a knife and stabbed the injured woman to death. Not surprisingly, this murder shocked the Chinese public; however, more shocking than this horrible and violent case itself is the support of Yao's actions from a group of similarly minded only-child student netizens, who believe that their lives are more valuable than that of a peasant (*World Today* 2015). This depleted view of human life and human values represented by some of these single-child educated youths poses a huge threat to the entire moral system of contemporary Chinese society. However, the public's unease about the twisted values harbored by the single-child cohort attracts no attention from, or perhaps it is deliberately avoided by, the show's producers, as they may not want to engage with such a sensitive subject.

Another thought-provoking debate concerning the Yao Jiaxin case is about whether or not he should be given the death penalty (he eventually was executed in 2011), for this would generate more dilemmas for single-child families. If Yao is sentenced to death, which was called for by many netizens, the Yao family (in particular his parents) would also be "given a death penalty", as he is their only child (*World Today* 2015). Accordingly, Yao's death would turn his mother and father into "shidu" parents, the term for parents who have lost their only child. The "shidu" family is another emerging social problem resulting from the one-child policy, and this growing social concern is also avoided in the show's narratives. In avoiding or sidelining these issues, the show risks being seen as "whitewashing" the one-child policy, in terms of covering up and circumventing those deep and deleterious social outcomes of this cruel policy. In other words, through cherry-picking and narrowing down the topics, debates and concerns about the one-child policy, the show reflects this policy and its damaging social effects in a superficial manner and shuns those more disturbing and merciless social stigmas and problems which might cause public agitation and social strife.

There were about one million "shidu" families in China, and that number is growing by about 76,000 per year. All the parents of these only-child generations have taken a huge risk when they responded to the national call to have only one child, as they have been taught to believe the government's propaganda that

128   Parents of the Single Child

their country's affluence counted on reining in population growth (Milwertz 1997; *China Daily* 2013). These parents, in particular urban worker couples, were in many cases persuaded and "forced" to have only one child, as the government used coercion to enforce the policy, and this included compulsory sterilizations and abortions (Aird 1990).[4] They were "walking a tightrope," as their children were exposed to deadly risks at all times and if their children died, there was nobody to take care of them when they got old (Yi 2013 cited in *China Daily* 2013).

For those unfortunate single-child parents who did lose their only child, they face many difficulties when they grow old and live in an "empty nest," as the majority of them have lost their ability to have another baby. However, the government policy has not evolved quickly enough to offer these parents any adequate or necessary support. One news report showed that the parents in a shidu family started to receive only a meager 22 US dollars a month compensation from the government in 2010 following their daughter's death in 2008. This skimpy assistance delivered by the government to the shidu families, where parents or even grandparents count on their descendants to support them after they retire, is a devastating financial outcome for these families. Thus, these shidu parents who have sacrificed themselves in order contribute to the prosperity of the entire country, and who shoulder the consequences created by the national birth control restrictions, require more government support in their twilight years (*China Daily* 2013). This scenario is similar to the government's careless attitudes towards laid-off female workers and their difficulties, which are categorized by the state as being individual problems instead of social problems, and this unsympathetic manner of the government may further exasperate the suffering of shidu parents.

Loneliness is one of the pains that shidu parents bear, and some of them spend hours each day chatting online with others who share the same unfortunate experiences. Shidu parents also suffer from self-condemnation for failing to carry on the family lines. Accordingly, some of the shidu mothers even propose that they divorce their husbands so that they may find a younger woman and have a child together; an unfortunate situation which would lead to the breakup of originally solid marriage relationships. In a more tragic case, one shidu mother, who was once a successful businesswoman, committed suicide after she lost her only child, a daughter, for she could no longer endure the unbearable pain from the emotional wound caused by her death (*Beijing Youth Daily* 2015). These traumas and tragedies, the adverse effects of a merciless and mandatory population control policy, verify again the compromises and sacrifices made by many Chinese people for the collective causes and national missions enforced by the CCP.

In addition to the shidu family, another growing social problem caused by the one-child policy is the sex ratio imbalance (Ebenstein 2010). Many Chinese households, in rural and urban regions alike, which are influenced or dominated by older generations who still have feudal thoughts, treat women as inferior to men and value the male-only child. This has led to the widespread abortion of female fetuses in preference for sons given that every couple is allowed to have only one child (Banister 2004; White 2010). Thus, in China, it is estimated that there were about 32 million excess males in 2005 (Wei, Li & Therese 2009). According to a more recent estimate, there are about 20 million more Chinese men than women of marriageable age. The Party's alarm about this issue is that now these stressed men who cannot find wives are beginning to protest and there have been many "mass incidents" (read: protests) across the country during the past few years. The Chinese government is trying to cope with this damaging side effect of its own population control policy by, for instance, launching a state-led campaign against the "left-over" women (Fincher 2014; Cai forthcoming). The state inflates the unfavorable side of the left-over women phenomenon in order to attain its objectives of social and political control. The recurring coverage and aggressive satirizing of the left-over women in state media outlets is a state-planned campaign levelled at infusing fear in proficient, socially mobile women and causing them to reconsider their quandary and to marry sooner, which will then assist to tackle the gender imbalance which if not addressed could lead to social instability.

Last but not least, the enforcement of the one-child population control policy results in the heavy burden of the single-child generations concerning taking care of their parents when they are aged. As clarified in previous discussions, Yile's ex-girlfriend, Ai Yu, is worried by the number of elderly family members she and Yile have to look after if she marries him, and it is this fear which leads to their breakup. Moreover, the show leaves the issues unresolved when Yile and Xiaoman intend to move out from their parents' place, as they have purchased their own apartment, and the audience is left unsure whether Yile and Xiaoman are willing to, or have the ability, to take care of their parents and grandparents when they get old. In the opening episode of the show, Yile's parents are sued by his grandparents (on his father's side) for failing to come to visit the old couple regularly, which forces Yile's parents to invite his grandparents to live with them. This plot design foregrounds the conflicts between an only-child and his or her parents regarding supporting the aged parents, which has become an issue and concern for the single child, their parents and the government alike. The latest adjustment to the family planning policy allows each couple to have two children and reflects the government's intent to solve the problems of caring for its aged population.

Conclusion

Parents of the Single Child provides a timely reflection on the social concerns and problems caused by the one-child policy and the single-child generations. By identifying the conflicts and relational challenges faced by the only-child generations in the family and in the workplace, the show engages with issues that are observed by the wider community and the majority of the single-child generations, including their self-centered outlook on life and their poor social and practical skills, which result in their comparatively less satisfactory performances in the domestic domain, the career field and the social arena. Further, by displaying the disputes and arguments between the single children and their parents and grandparents over various family and social matters, the show demonstrates the

130   Parents of the Single Child

generational gap and changing values towards family bonds, cultural customs and career prospects. Growing up within different political, economic and social conditions, the single-child generations and their parents develop dissimilar mindsets towards family ethics and cultivate diverse consumption habits and lifestyles based on different value systems and outlooks on life.

The show's narratives describe a conspicuous decline of traditional family associations and codes within households comprising single-child generations, where those long-standing family values and operating modes are slowly being cast aside. The waning of filial piety amongst the single-child generations provides a clear measure of this deteriorating situation. Due to both the subjective reasoning, which is their self-centered personality, and the objective difficulty which makes them almost incapable of realizing their duty to look after their parents when they grow old, China's only-child generations have a lethargic type of attitude towards supporting their elderly relatives. Consequently, this heavy burden regarding caring for the aged population has become a concern for both the individual families and the Chinese state alike. By engaging with just some of the typical and detrimental social repercussions caused by the one-child policy, and in a cursory manner, the show avoids comment and engagement with other equally or more harmful social effects of the birth control restrictions. In so doing, the show tends to whitewash the one-child policy through concealing and dodging the more complex and adverse social outcomes of this callous policy; such as the sex ratio imbalance, and the shidu family. By its calculated choices of subjects and its pruning of the themes, discussions and fears about the one-child policy, the show exposes this policy and its social ramifications in a feigning method and eschews those more harmful social problems which might instigate public dissatisfaction and social discord. In this way, the show's narratives remain at a reasonable distance from the more sensitive topics and side effects of the one-child policy and protect the government from public questioning and criticism. Further, it disguises the tragedies caused by the birth control policies which attest to the concessions and sacrifices made by Chinese individuals to the collective causes and state missions enforced by the CCP administration. In short, *Parents of the Single Child* sheds some light on those disturbing social consequences related to the one-child policy; however, further research is needed to investigate how the predicaments and dilemmas of the single-child generations and their families are being addressed by the state. In other words, are they being treated as individual difficulties or social quandaries in the official rhetoric?

Notes

1   For more detailed and comprehensive discussions about the one-child policy and its implementation, see Scharping (2003); Croll, Davin and Kane (1985).
2   As reflected in Hanyi's reportage, it is widely observed that the education and upbringing of the only-child generations seem to turn out pampered children and inept citizens who lack traditional virtues and civism.
3   Although many of the single-child generations receive higher education, the shortage of white-collar and well-paid positions on the job market is still a huge problem

they face when they graduate from universities. According to statistics, the number of college graduates multiplied eightfold, from 830,000 in 1998 to 6.8 million in 2012, while the figure for well-paid jobs hasn't kept pace with this huge increase. Therefore, in the previous decade, growing numbers of college graduates struggled in poorly paid transient jobs and lived in overcrowded apartments in the suburbs, which turned them into a socially underprivileged group (Kong 2014: 214).

4   For more discussion about the variety of government controls that urban workers were subjected to regarding forcing them to obey the one-child birth limit, see Li (1995).

References

Aird, John S. 1990. *Slaughter of the Innocents: Coercive Birth Control in China.* Washington, DC: AEI.

Banister, Judith. 2004. "Shortage of Girls in China Today." *Journal of Population Research* 21 (1): 19–45.

Bao, Leiping. 2012. " 'Dushengzinu' de Xianjing yu Tiaozhan" [The Traps and Challenges of the One-Child Policy]. *Shehuiguanch*a (Social Outlook) 9: 29–30.

Beijing Youth Daily. 2015. "Shidu nushangren zisha: shengqian yufu lihun liubaiwan paidiao fangzi" ["Shidu" businesswoman commits suicide: divorced and sold her house for six million before her death], posted 27 December, available at: www.wenxuecity.com/news/2015/12/27/4824288.html (accessed 28 February 2016).

China Daily. 2013. "Shidujiating: zhongguo shehui zhi tong" [Shidu: When Chinese parents forced to have one child lose that child], posted 12 August, available at: http://language.chinadaily.com.cn/news/2013–08/12/content_16887215.htm (accessed 28 February 2016).

Cai, Shenshen. Forthcoming. "Talented Celebrity Rene Liu: Spokesperson of the Left-over Women (*Sheng Nu*)." *Frontiers: A Journal of Women Studies.*

Chu, Junhong. 2001. "Prenatal Sex Determination and Sex-Selective Abortion in Rural Central China." *Population and Development Review* 27 (2): 259–281.

Croll, Elisabeth, Delia, Davin and Penny, Kane (eds.). 1985. *China's One-Child Family Policy.* New York: St. Martin's.

Dushengzinu de popomama [Parents of the Single Child]. 2013. TV drama serial, directed by Ding Hei, first broadcast on channels of Beijing and Hubei satellite TV in 2013.

Ebenstein, Avraham. 2010. "The 'Missing Girls' of China and the Unintended Consequences of the One Child Policy." *Journal of Human Resources* 45 (1): 87–115.

Fincher, Leta Hong. 2014. *Leftover Women: The Resurgence of Gender Inequality in China.* London: Zed Books.

Greenhalgh, Susan. 2008. *Just One Child: Science and Policy in Deng's China.* Berkeley: University of California Press.

Kong, Shuyu. 2008. "Family Matters: Reconstructing the Family on the Chinese Television Screen," in *TV Drama in China*, Ying Zhu, Michael Keane, and Ruoyun Bai (eds.). Hong Kong: Hong Kong University Press, pp. 75–88.

Kong, Shuyu. 2014. *Popular Media, Social Emotion and Public Discourse in Contemporary China.* Hoboken, NJ: Taylor and Francis.

Li, Jiali. 1995. "China's One-Child Policy: How and How Well Has It Worked? A Case Study of Hebei Province, 1979–88." *Population and Development Review* 21 (3): 563–585.

Milwertz, Cecilia Nathansen. 1997. *Accepting Population Control: Urban Chinese Women and the One-Child Family Policy.* Richmond, VA: Curzon.

132 Parents of the Single Child

Scharping, Thomas. 2003. *Birth Control in China, 1949–2000: Population Policy and Demographic Development*. London: Routledge.

Tien, H. Yuan. 1991. *China's Strategic Demographic Initiative*. New York: Praeger.

Wang, Feng. 2005. "Can China Afford to Continue Its One-Child Policy?" *Asia-Pacific Issues* 77: 1–12.

Wei, Xingzhu, Li, Lu and Therese, Hesketh. 2009. "China's Excess Males, Sex Selective Abortion, and One Child Policy: Analysis of Data from 2005 National Intercensus Survey." *British Medical Journal* 338: 920–923.

White, Tyrene. 1992. "The Origins of China's Birth Planning Campaign," in *Engendering China: Women, Culture and the State*, Christina K. Gilmarthin, Gall Hershatter, Lisa Rofel, and Tyrene White (eds.). Cambridge, MA: Harvard University Press, pp. 250–278.

White, Tyrene. 2007. *China's Longest Campaign: Birth Planning in the People's Republic, 1949–2005*. Ithaca, NY: Cornell University Press.

White, Tyrene. 2010. "Domination, Resistance, and Accommodation in China's One-Child Campaign," in *Chinese Society: Change, Conflict, and Resistance* (3rd ed.), Elizabeth J. Perry and Mark Selden (eds.). New York: Routledge, pp. 171–196.

World Today. 2015. "What Power Balance Has China's One-Child Policy Created?" Eleanor Hall interviewed Xinran Xue, The (ABC), 16 December.

Xue, Xinran. 2015. *Buy Me the Sky: The Remarkable Truth of China's One-Child Generations*. London: Rider Books.

Yi, Fuxian. 2013. *Daguokongchao: fansi zhongguo jihuashengyuzhengce* (Big Country with an Empty Nest: Reflections on China's One-child Policy). Beijing: China Development Press.

Conclusion

In contemporary China, where state power and market force intertwine and interact with each other in the media sphere, TV drama production, without exception, has been subject to the needs and constraints of this special condition. Neither official discourse nor market dynamism is able to singly monopolize the manufacture of TV serials as either a propaganda apparatus or a money-earning enterprise, and so TV drama producers have had to accurately consider these two influences. As audience rating has become imperative in deciding whether a TV drama series is purchased by a TV station or not, the entertainment value of the show seems to become the more important motive for the decision makers. Therefore, TV dramas informed by state propaganda and utilized for their intellectual thoughts and moral education have to be entertaining first in order to attract the viewers' attention before they can probe deeper into the contents and themes of the show.

The popular TV drama subgenres that have emerged over the past couple of decades provide convincing evidence to the above argument. For example, the very popular and acclaimed dynasty dramas do not interest the audience for their conformist plots and character designs which endorse the official rhetoric that promotes a strong central government and cultivates an antidemocratic civil ecology through the exaltation of dictatorial power. The audience is more fascinated by inspirational display of the calculated and ferocious court infighting among the rulers and the ministers. In another example, the revolutionary espionage-themed TV drama does not gain its popularity through portraying devoted and impeccable Communist spies and their patriotic and nationalist spirits, but through its enlistment of suspense and mystery and its portrayal of highly skilled professionals and the thrills and fantasy associated with the dangerous job of spying. Similarly, revolutionary nostalgia TV serials do not achieve success through their rehabilitation of the revolutionary heritage and ethos, but through their erratically cannibalizing styles and images from the past and their creative mixture of the casual romances, love affairs and brutal fights among a group of youths with an idiosyncratic revolutionary enthusiasm and fanaticism who grew up during the heyday of the Mao era(s).

The effective incorporation of the mainstream or main melody ideology into popular TV drama subgenres, as shown above, illustrates a "recreation plus propaganda" formula in modern-day TV play production. This formula is a trend and is

134   *Conclusion*

further demonstrated when TV drama is enlisted to reflect fiercely debated social phenomena and sensitive social topics. For instance, in its foregrounding of the employment and re-employment situations of laid-off female workers and domestic helpers, TV drama narratives create poignant and captivating stories revolving around some of these intensely discussed public concerns while following the life trajectory of those self-reliant and self-renovated female characters who are representatives of the useful and respectful citizens for the modern state. Likewise, in its timely reflection of the medical welfare system and the growing con-·flicts between healthcare providers and patients, one of the main concerns of the Chinese public, TV drama not only fashions touching and enchanting encounters between medical workers and patients, but also cleanses the image of the Chinese government through creating exemplary model doctors. Pioneering TV drama series that focus on depicting the life experiences of the disadvantaged social cohorts in China, such as people with a disability, create emotionally moving and motivational stories and attempt to turn this originally marginalized and discriminated social faction into highly skilled professionals and small private entrepreneurs whose struggles mirror the merits of a neoliberal subject, as promoted by a Chinese government that espouses a developmental approach. In regard to those TV dramas that paint contemporary Chinese women's life stories, they embrace a re-emerging Confucian way of thinking that features submissiveness and the devoted female personality, as promoted by the official discourse for its contribution to harmonious family relationships and a stable social and political entity. Contemporary Chinese TV drama's deliberation on the life of China's one-child generations caters to the viewing expectations of the general audiences, who all, to varying degrees, are associated with one-child families. Although the shows' narratives superficially engage with the negative familial and social results caused by the implementation of the one-child policy, they intentionally shun those more sensitive phenomena and side effects of this birth control policy, and by doing so, these TV drama texts remain in line with the official paradigm. At first glance, the above-mentioned TV serials all seem to be apolitical recreational plays, as their plots and scenes are not explicitly propagandistic or linked to government policies; however, embedded in their narrative arc, their plot design and their character building have many didactic elements and instances where state-sponsored mainstream ideological opinions work in a state of mutual "antagonism" between proselytization and popular culture.

In another subtle twist to how these "propaganda-informed and inspired" TV drama subgenres are "read" by the audience, there also exists "purely entertainment-oriented" TV dramas which contain highly coded political interpretations which shed an inspirational light on the reality within the realms of Chinese government and big business. *Empresses in the Palace* is an example where an analysis of the show (in Chapter 1) reveals that although the show's narrative has shifted its focus from court wrangling among the emperors and rulers and government ministers to power struggles among imperial concubines in the royal harem – its candid exposé of the devious tricks, fierce competition and cruel infighting among the concubines – still taps into sensitive topics such as corruption, nepotism and factional brawls in contemporary China. However, the plot and character design of the show fall in line with the state propaganda discourse through creating a strong, determined, iron-fisted and upright head concubine, which is intended to mirror Chinese president Xi Jinping and his own solid and indomitable approach in combating corruption within the higher ranks of China's bureaucracy. Through in-depth observations and an examination of a group of representative and prevalent TV drama serial texts that have been recently aired in mainland China, the conclusion is that there is a distinctive characteristic of contemporary Chinese popular media and cultural works which is reflected in TV drama narratives, and that is their subtle and natural intermingling with official discourse and their performance in the role of propagating government policy and thought. It is this feature, more than anything else, which best defines the contentious nature of today's Chinese media as a hybrid of the government publicity machine and lucrative private enterprise.

While it seems that the official propaganda rhetoric has permeated into different TV drama subgenres and narrative patterns, its effect is still difficult to gauge, as the contemporary Chinese audiences are not cultural dupes, nor are they devoid of any immunity towards diverse kinds of metamorphic propaganda. Rather, they are dexterous enough to read between the lines of the show's texts and act as critical thinkers in their reaction to the government's hidden coaching. In the past, some TV drama texts have provided an alternative and even "seditious" reading of the orthodox mainstream discourse, even though they risked being censured and banned by state propaganda institutions. As a result, various campaigns have been enlisted, ostensibly against the excesses of entertainment, immoral affairs/sexual encounters and unrestrained violence on Chinese TV screens (the usual strategies used to remove those sensitive topics and themes that threaten social stability and the government's authority). The government is very vigilant towards any harmful or intimidating cultural and media works and is ready to pounce on these rule violators using any means available to them. The tightening control over the contents of media and cultural works also applies to comments and entries posted by China's netizens on different online social-networking platforms and communities. In present-day China, the Internet and its derivative mass communication channels have become the foremost outlet where the public can exchange views on a variety of subjects and concerns. Web-based fan clubs allow for and provide forums for their members to share and interchange their sometimes inspiring and often critical comments on public concerns and civic issues, which are often based on their viewing experiences of media products. In this way, the association and communication between virtual reality and the actual world have infiltrated into the various facets of social life and have influenced the Party and its ideological ecology. Having sensed the popularity and power of the new media, the Party publicity machinery is determined not only to refurbish and improve itself in order to become adept at recruiting new media tools and tactics in its spreading of state discourse, but also to recognize the necessity to curb the detrimental and

136 Conclusion

destabilizing forces generated by online information sharing and exchange and wired socio-political and cultural commentary and criticism. Together, these two actions contribute to the CCP propaganda discourse's adaptation to the cyberspace environment within which different rounds of public opinion struggle to be heard and battles to gain influence are launched.

Index

accomplices *(gongmou)*, TV characters 2
"alternative reading" 9, 12
Angel Heart (Xinshu) 40; debut 40–1;
    doctors, characters 45; creation 46–7;
    healthcare service 43; heroism 47–8;
    hospital, micro society representation
    53–4; mainstream stand 48; medical
    disturbance phenomenon, controversy
    49; medical drama 13–14; narrative,
    focus 44–5; social problems, presence
    51–4; staff meeting scenes 47; storyline
    13–14, 41
As Time Goes By (Niahua sishui)
    58–9
Attendant *(daying)* 21

baby, having (avoidance) 122
bailing (white-collar) 66
Baogang, Zhao 6
*Beautiful Daughter-in-Law (Xifu de
    meihao shidai)* 8
Beijing Television Arts Center 78–9
Beijing Youth (Beijing qingnian) 6
Bethune, Henry 45
big tigers 25–6
biopolitics 111
"bitter emotion," reading 7–8
blind masseurs 104–5; clinic 101–2;
    examination 98–9; hardships/challenges
    102–3
blogs, usage 9
"body biopolitics" 111
body, exposure 111
Boxiong, Guo 26
broken marriages, reasons 82–3
Burberry 71
Bureau of Civil Administration, divorce
    case 86
Buy Me the Sky (Xinran) 126

Caihou, Xu 26, 28
careers: choices 70–3; field, struggles/
    adventures 123–6; success 79–80, 122
Cartier 70
Central Military Commission 25
Central Political Commission 25
characters, personal/romantic
    relationships 59
childbearing, collectivization 116–17
China: audiences, propaganda institution
    manipulation/victimization 11–12;
    demographic dilemma, correction
    116; divorce rate, increase 80–1;
    employment, difficulty 100–1;
    gold-diggers 34; officialdom, factors
    (formation) 27; one-child policy,
    social repercussions 87–8, 116,
    126–9; political/workplace culture,
    historical drama (reflections) 20;
    social/political veracity, formation (TV
    viewing) 11; society, harmonization 40;
    socio-political reality 22–3
China Central Television Station (CCTV)
    34, 41; Channel One, drama (broadcast)
    100; discourse/narratives, challenge 111
Chinese Communist Party (CCP) 78;
    administration, optimism/support
    104; healthcare service provision 43;
    leadership, competency 25; medical care
    system malfunctioning 50; Propaganda
    Department, endorsement 48;
    propaganda, trend 47–8; TV goals 3–4
"Chinese Dream," prediction 50–1
Chinese females: elaboration 77; older
    generation, comparison 88
Chinese genes, quality (improvement) 52
Chinese haves/have-nots: fight, dramatic
    representation 108; social bonds 13–14;
    social relationship 40

138   *Index*

Chinese War of Resistance 45
Chinese white-collar workers,
  independent/impartial environment
  63–4
Chinese women: broken relationships/
  marriages, impact 84–5; coming-of-
  age/maturation experiences 83–4;
  Confucian-styled principles 81;
  emancipation 61–2; independence 83;
  subordination/subjugation 34–5
"Cinderella" character 92
citizens, competency/respect 97; image,
  configuration 104–5
"clean officials" *(qingguan)*, image 5
collective political body, members 72
Coming and Going (Lailaiwangwang) 79
commercialization, trend (acceleration)
  1–2
"commodity socialism" 45
compound *(hutong)* 92
concubines: hierarchical titles 21; married
  businessmen/government officials usage
  34; popularity, loss 31; representation
  68–9
"concubine" women, representation 68–9
"conformist" role 8–9
Confucian sage morality 108
"connections," usage 42
consciousness, employee crisis 62
consumer society, representation 70–1
consumption, impact 70–3
contemporary females, imperial
  concubines (contrast) 33–5
"corporeal right," character claim 109
"criminal knight": characters, creation 107;
  righteousness, representation 108
"criminal-like" demeanor, intimidation 107
*Crouching Tiger, Hidden Dragon
  (Wohucanglong)* 20–1
cruelty, survival tactic 30–3
cultural public sphere, TV drama
  (nurturing) 9–16
cultural storm, occurrence 12

Dame *(pin)*, concubine title 21
Dangdang Web 58–9
DB (fictitious business enterprise) 59,
  61–2, 68; career, advancement 69;
  employment 68
deceit, survival tactic 30–3
dependency, situation 83
dictatorial power, exaltation 133
disabilities: employment, finding
  (difficulty) 100–1; love experiences
  109–10; model 105; suffering 99; TV

examination 14–15; victimization/
  mistreatment 103
disabled people: family values 105–8; life,
  difficulty 99–103; love 105–8; love/
  sex, field of combat 109–12; traditional
  relationships 105–8
disabled subjectivity 107
disadvantaged groups 108
"disadvantaged groups," government
  identification 108
divorce 110; proceedings, dramatic
  enactment 86
divorced women: configuration 86–91;
  generations 81–6; impact 77; model 77
domestic sphere, conflicts 119–22
*Double Sided Adhesive Tape
  (Shuangmianjiao)* 40–1
Dove 70
dramas of bitter emotion *(kuqingxi)*,
  proliferation 98
dynasty dramas 23

economic autonomy 84
economic production/exchange, processes
  (influencing/structuring) 60
elderly-devouring young adults (NEET)
  105, 119
elite disabled cohort, hardships/
  challenges 102
emotional adaptability/values 126
Emperor: bloc, grandsons 27; favor,
  winning (TV drama) 22, 28–9; fever 23;
  power/dominance 24
*Emperor of the Han Dynasty, The
  (Hanwudadi)* 23
Empress *(fei)*, concubine title 21
Empress Dowage, clothes (wearing) 32
Empresses in the Palace (Zhenhuanzhuan)
  8, 20–3, 134–5; central plot, focus
  29; character building 22–3, 32; "cold
  palace" 30; concubines, popularity
  (loss) 31; de-politicizing path 24;
  ethics, salience 30; government
  policy/propaganda engagement 23–7;
  imperial harem, life/conflicts 13, 31;
  inner-factional/interfactional struggles
  30; internal fighting 29–30; life-and-
  death struggles 32; Netflix release 20–1;
  plot design, in-depth textual analysis
  22–3; retaliation, voyage 24–5; revenge
  29; sensation 12–13
"entertainment with indoctrination"
  (socialist realism paradigm) 78
ER (TV show) 54
erogenous body, revealing 111

Index 139

exemplary model doctors, usage 40
exemplary-type doctors, creation 43–8

factional struggles 27–30
fake romance 110
family: ancestral line, familial obligation
122; life, breakdown (destabilization)
79–80; values, decline 97
Feiyu, Bi 100–1
female culture, rejection 34–5
female image: new female image 64–70;
post-reform TV drama serials 79–81
Feng, Lei 45
filial liabilities, theme 119
filial piety 67; traditional virtue 119
foreign-invested enterprise, operations/
weaknesses 64
foreign-owned firm, employment
(impact) 68
Founding of a Republic (Jianguodaye) 26
4+2+1 family pattern 117

Gang of Four, crackdown 28
*Garrulous Zhang Damin's Happy Life
(Pinzui Zhang Damin de xingfu
shenghuo)* 7–8
gender discrimination, presence 61–2
gendered role cultivation 83–4
generational gap 118–19
Giorgio Armani 70
globalization, impact 60, 63, 71
Go Lala Go! (Du Lala shengzhiji) 7,
58; trans-media reading 58; TV/film
adaptations 58
"gold-diggers": characters 34, 68, 73;
social stigma 52
"good wife–wise mother" female,
promotion 88
government: accountability, absence 87–8;
malfunction, perspective 50; media
campaigns 53; policy, engagement 23–7
government propaganda: engagement
23–7; impact 3–6
Great Han Emperor Wu, The (Hanwudadi)
(TV serial) 4
guanxi (influence) 60–1
gugan (backbone) 66
guidance *(daoxiang)* 6

harmonious society, building 43, 97
haves/have-nots *see* Chinese haves/
have-nots
healthcare: providers/patients, conflicts
(moderation) 48–51; service 43
Hermes 71

Hibiscus Town (Furongzhen) 78
high school morality 106–7
history, "orthodox" interpretation 23
Holding Hands (Qianshou) 79–80
Honey Bee Man (Woai nanguimi) 15,
77; broken marriages, reasons 82–3;
characters, polarization 84; couple,
accounts (settling) 86; divorced women,
generations (representation) 81–6;
mismatched couples 91–2; opening
sequence 85–6; post-divorce life 15,
81; quickie marriage/divorce 82, 85–6;
transformations, plot explication 82;
unsuccessful marriage, catalysts 87;
virtuousness/devotion 85
household: burden, shouldering 105;
duties, participation (absence) 120;
extendedness 118
Hua, Yan 4
Huifang, Liu 79
huotong 92

IBM 70
"ideal woman image" construction 77
imperial concubines, contemporary
females (contrast) 33–5
Imperial Noble Empress *(huangguifei)*,
concubine title 21
imperial seraglio 22, 24–5
income gap, widening 44
incomplete childhood, compensation 123
intellectual disabilities, suffering 99
intellectual thinking, impact 3–6
internationalization 60
*In This Struggling Year (Wo zai zhe
zhandoude yinianli)* 58–9
"iron bowls": loss 123; stability 125

Jewel in the Palace (Dachangjin) 33
Jiaxin, Yao (murder case) 127
Jing, Chai 49–50
Jinglei, Xu 58–9, 70
jingying (elite) 66
Jinping, Xi 25–8, 43
Jintao, Hu 27–8, 43
job: opportunities, seeking 102–3;
resignation, dramatic representation 90
joint ventures, operation 64

Kangxi Dynasty (Kangxi wangchao) 23
Ke, Li 14, 58, 69; novel, appeal 70

Lee, Ang 20
"left-over women" 66, 80; government-led
derogatory portrayal 52; shelved

140   *Index*

women, comparison 69–70; term,
  Beijing Women's Federation coinage 51
*Legend of the Tianyun Mountain
  (Tianyunshan chuanqi)* 78
Legislative Affairs Committee 25
Lenovo Group Ltd. 70–1
Liangyu, Chen 27–8
life: acumen, absence 127; difficulty
  99–103
*Life in Two Cities (Shuangcheng
  shenghuo)* 8
Lipton 70
"little emperors/princesses," treatment 117
Liuliu 40
Living aptitude 126
Lixing, Huang 72
Lotto 70
Louis Vuitton 71
love: field of combat 109–12; seeking 112;
  stories, consideration 110–11
Luodan, Wang 72

"maid" characters, portrayal 98
mainstream/main melody ideology,
  incorporation 133–4
male equality, rejection 34–5
*Marching towards the Republic (Zouxiang
  gonghe)* 10
marital status, post-reform TV drama
  serials 79–81
market economy, competition 99–100
marriage: breakage 83; institution,
  destabilization 79–80; pre-marriage/
  post-marriage life, contrast 90–1;
  values, reexamination 90
marry-only-for-money social stigma 52
massage center, running 101
"mass incidents" (protests) 51–2;
  occurrence 129
"material girls" 68–9
May Fourth Movement 77–8
Mazda 70
medical disturbance phenomenon 49
medical disturbance phenomenon,
  controversy 49
mental disabilities, suffering 99
Meteor Garden (Liuxing Huayuan) 33
microblogs *(weibo)*, usage 9, 107
middle-age women, hysteria 88
middle-class aesthetics 14
middle class, emergence 46
middle-class flavor, manufacture 72
middle-class identity (configuration),
  consumption/career choice (impact)
  70–3

"mismatched" couples: design, political
  usefulness 92; production 15, 77
modernization, young people's
  perspective 126
modern roles *(jiaose)*, challenges 82–3
money, pursuit (unscrupulousness)
  52–3
Motorola Mobility 70–1
Mr. Six (Laopaoer) 108
mutual trust/understanding/support 106
*My Youthfulness (Wode Qingchun
  shuizuozhu)* 6

Narrow Dwelling (Woju) 10, 30–1
*Native of Beijing in New York, A
  (Beijingren zai niuyue)* (TV drama
  serial) 1
NEET 105, 119
neo-authoritarianism 23
neo-conservative schools, political
  views 4
neo-conservativism 23
neoliberal ethos, exhibition 105
neoliberalism, aspirational story 98
Netflix 20
new female image 64–70
New Left: intellectual school, political
  viewpoints 4, 43; political reforms
  44; response, exemplary-type doctors
  (creation) 43–8; schools 23
newspaper editorials (commentaries),
  propaganda officials (usage) 33
Noble Empress *(guifei)*, concubine
  title 21
Noble Lady *(guiren)*, concubine title 21
"Nobody Shall Sleep!" aria 106
Nokia 70
"nonconforming" readings, prompting 12
nouveau riche social echelons,
  emergence 46

"office ladies" (OL) 64–5
office politics 14
"official second generation" 59
one-child generations: domestic conflicts/
  predicaments 118–19; "little emperors,"
  labeling 117; self-centered/self-pleasing
  nature 125; viewing expectations 134
one-child policy 82; cessation 117;
  launching 116; "little emperors/
  princesses," treatment 117; side effects
  87; social repercussions 116–7, 126–9;
  whitewashing 118
only-child couples: burden 121;
  confinement 122

Index 141

only-child generations: life acumen/social proficiencies, absence 127; willful/ egocentric characters 125–6
Opening Up reform 44–5, 65, 83; antagonism, intensification 41–2; beneficiaries 117; impact 78, 125; initiation 1–2
"ordinary folk" dramas 7

"pampered" groups, selfishness/social skill deficiency 126
"paratroopers," positions (importance) 53
Parents of the Single Child (Dushengzinu de popomama) 15–16, 116; bargaining 120–1; career field, struggles/adventures 123–6; domestic sphere, conflicts 119–22; extra-extended household 118; family-based drama 15–16; household duties, participation (absence) 120; personal funds, battle 121; single-child family, story 118–19
peer pressure 123
"personal funds," battle 121
"pink drama" 80
Politburo Standing Committee 26
political reforms (New Left) 44
political/workplace culture, historical drama (reflections) 20
post-divorce life 15; presentation 89
post-reform TV drama serials 79–81
"practical-cum-romantic" love relationship 73
preferred femininity 15, 77
pre-globalization 63–4
pre-marriage/post-marriage life, contrast 90–1
princeling clique 27–8
"princelings" 27; faction, political strategy/ tactics 28
"problematic" characters, government identification 108
"problematic" women characters, creation 53
professional women, signifiers 66
Professor Tian and His Twenty-eight Maids (Tian jiaoshou jiade ershiba ge baomu) 5
propaganda: engagement 23–7; heroism, theme 47–8; impact 3–6; rhetoric, permeation 135–6
Propaganda Department (CCP) 48
propaganda-informed/inspired TV drama subgenres, audience interpretation 134–5
protests ("mass incidents") 51–2
public servants, TV drama (reflection) 97–8

Qinghong, Zeng 26–8
Qishan, Wang 25, 26
quasi-parental role, impact 89
Queen Empress *(huanghou)*, imperial concubine title 21
"quickie" marriage/divorce, experience 82, 85–6

"rat race," peer pressure 123
Red classics *(hongsejingdian)*, repackaging 5
relationships, third parties 79–80
Respondent *(changzai)* 21
revolutionary films, cultural/artistic creation 78
"rich men," characteristic 87
"rich second generation" 59
romance 110
romantic love, decline 97

SARS party line 47–8
screen, factional struggles 27–30
"second spring" 77; finding 88
"Seeing"/"Kanjian" (theme song) 108
See without Looking (Tuina) (TV drama) 97; adaptation 100; character, high school morality 106–7; disabilities, examination 14–15; encouragement, superficial attitude 104; forlorn/ lovestruck figure 110
self-assurance 84
self-centered utilitarian approach, exposure 120–1
self-determination 109
self-determining strong women, self-supporting 68
self-discipline, implementation 98
self-employed entrepreneurs, economic makeover 87
self-identity, absence 83
"self-imposed" political conformity 23–4
self-renovation 97
self-salvation, inspirational story 98
self-value, care 69–70
sensuality, exposure 111
Sex and the City 71
sex, field of combat 109–12
sex ratio imbalance 116, 128–9
sexual gratification, seeking 112
Shanghai faction 27–8
"shelved ladies" 66, 80; economic capability 67; left-over women, comparison 69–70
"shidu" family 116, 127; growth 127–8
"shidu" parents, loneliness 128

142 Index

Shuo, Wang 78–9
"sibling-less" adults, abilities/skills 117
single-child family: in-law relationships, complications/problems 40–1; story 118–19
single-child generations, defects 126–7
single-child parents 116; child, loss (difficulties) 128
SMART *see* specific, measurable, attainable, relevant, and time-based
smog problems, government solution (inability) 50
social changes, TV drama (mirroring) 6–9
social experiences, absence 123
socialism, failure (transformation) 98
socialist China, nascence 83
socialist moral coaching 83–4
social mores, decline 97
social problems, presence *(Angel Heart)* 51–4
social proficiencies, absence 127
social reality, TV drama (mirroring) 6–9
social skills: absence 118; deficiency 126
social stability, state ideology 97
social standing *(ren'ge)* 82–3
social status 84
social topics, TV drama (impact) 134
social welfare system, effectiveness 99
society-at-large, interaction 97
socio-economic signs, symbolic meanings/ cultural connotations (exploitation) 70
soft censorship 23
specific, measurable, attainable, relevant, and time-based (SMART) idea 61
stability, maintenance 43–4
State Administration for Radio, Film and Television (SARFT): criticism 4; intervention 10
state discourse, defending/upholding 86–91
status, disparateness (representation) 92
Story of Lala's Promotion, A (Du Lala shengzhiji) 14, 58; authority, challenge 63–4; backdrop, business/cultural landscape 49; characters, list 59–60; cultural product, examples 71–2; filial piety 67; motto, importance 62; narratives, consumer society (representation) 70–1; novel/ TV adaptation, dramatic plots 73; opening sequence 65–6; stress 62–3; trans-media reading 58; TV/film adaptations 58

"strong" citizens, exemplification 88–9
"strong" professional woman, conversion 89
"Strong woman" phenomenon 14, 64–70
"strong women": social phenomenon 58; struggle 83–4
Struggle (Fendou) 6
"substitute" readings, prompting 12
"subversive reading" 12
"sugar daddies" 68
survival, tactics 30–3
Swan Dive for Love *(Bei shang guang bu xiangxin yanlei)* 6

television, Chinese access 72
"3S ladies" 66
Touch of Sin (Tianzhuding) 107
trans-media reading 58
TV drama: "conformist" role 8–9; government propaganda, impact 3–6; intellectual thinking, impact 3–6; mirroring 6–9; nurturing 9–16; production, state power/market force (impact) 133; "seditious" reading 135–6; series, studies 31–2
TV drama subgenre 105–6; emergence 133
TV narratives, creation (cooperated efforts) 2
TV propaganda, guidance *(daoxiang)* 6

"ugly duckling" men/women *(fenghuangnan/fenghuangnu)* 72–3
Undercover (Qianfu) 8–9
Under the Heavy Dome (Qiongdingzhixia) 49–50
"unmatched" couples, stories 92
"unqualified/incompetent wives," remolding 15, 77
"unspoken rules" *(qianguize)* 9, 119, 123; permeation 124–5
"unsuitable" men, remarrying 91

vulnerable people 97

Web-based fan clubs, impact 135–6
weibo (microblog), usage 9, 107
Western company culture, Chinese employee immersion/assimilation 61
Western corporate culture, openness 63
Westernization, impact 71
"white-collar beauty" *(bailingliren)* 65
white-collar lifestyle 14

Women of Marriage Age Should Get Married (Danudangjia) 52
"women's tradition," absence 81
work: obligatory attainment 97; result, demonstration 124; values, reexamination 90
workplace: Chinese women, aspiration/struggle 58; focus 7; globalization 60–4; "unspoken rules" 119; Westernization 60–4
workplace culture: adaptation 118; complication 124–5; historical drama, reflections 20

Xiaogang, Feng 108
Xiaoping, Deng 1–2

Xilai, Bo 27–8
Xinran, Xue 126

Yandong, Liu 27
Yat-sen, Sun 10
Yearning (Kewang) (TV drama serial) 1, 78–9
Yinhe, Li 66–7
Yongkang, Zhou 27–8
Yongzheng Dynasty (Yongzheng wangchao) (TV drama serial) 4, 23
Youth Trilogy (Baogang) 6

Zemin, Jiang 26–8
Zhengsheng, Yu 27
Zhongnanhai (imperial harem) 34